# *More Praise from the Experts...*

"Lauren Haworth has done it again. First, her *PROC TABULATE by Example* book unlocked the mysteries of that SAS procedure for countless SAS software users. Her new book, *Output Delivery System: The Basics,* brings the power of ODS within the grasp of beginning to advanced SAS software users. Her ability to convey often complex technical details clearly and concisely is enhanced by effective examples and explanations of what ODS is doing and why it is doing it. This book belongs on the desk of every SAS software user."

**Andrew H. Karp**
**Sierra Information Services, Inc.**

"Lauren Haworth has created another 'must have' book. This time, Lauren sets her sights on the Output Delivery System. *Output Delivery System: The Basics* is a great introduction to ODS for SAS users. It is easy to read, loaded with examples, and profusely illustrated. This book is peppered with tips and ideas on how to use ODS. While the book is intended for SAS users who are new to ODS, many of the examples demonstrate how to resolve problems encountered by more advanced users. Lauren's style makes it easy to find exactly the right solution, with sample code and examples of the output. *Output Delivery System: The Basics* is a great reference on the fundamentals of ODS."

**S. David Riba**
**JADE Tech, Inc.**

"Lauren has a knack for starting at ground zero and walking you through all the steps necessary to get a job done. Someone completely unfamiliar with ODS could pick up this book and in a very short time not only understand what ODS is and how to use it, but understand why it does what it does. This important point is often neglected in technical writing."

**Pete Lund**
**Information Systems Manager**
**Northwest Crime and Social Research**

# Output Delivery System

## THE BASICS

Lauren E. Haworth

SAS Publishing

The correct bibliographic citation for this manual is as follows: Haworth, Lauren E. 2001. *Output Delivery System: The Basics*. Cary, NC: SAS Institute Inc.

**Output Delivery System: The Basics**

ISBN 1-58025-859-X

SAS Institute Inc., SAS Campus Drive, Cary, North Carolina 27513.

1st printing, April 2001
2nd printing, March 2004

SAS Publishing provides a complete selection of books and electronic products to help customers use SAS software to its fullest potential. For more information about our e-books, e-learning products, CDs, and hard-copy books, visit the SAS Publishing Web site at **support.sas.com/pubs** or call 1-800-727-3228.

# Table of Contents

# Acknowledgments

This book would not have been possible without a lot of support from a number of people.

At SAS Institute, Julie Platt and John West were invaluable in providing constant encouragement, and in handling all of the details that go into publishing a book. In addition, the efforts of Sandy McNeill, David Kelley, and Brian Schellenberger to keep me up to date with the rapidly growing features of the Output Delivery System are greatly appreciated.

Finally, I'd like to thank the SAS user community for all of their suggestions. In particular, the SAS-L contributors gave me a number of ideas about topics to address. Also, the many users I have met at regional conferences and at SUGI provided valuable feedback.

# *How to Use This Book*

## Where to Start

This book is aimed at all levels of users, but some parts may be more helpful than others, depending on your level of expertise. Here's a guide to what parts of the book will be the most help for you.

**Beginning users:** If you are new to SAS and have little or no experience with ODS, you should read "The Basics" in detail. After that, the examples in "Intermediate Topics" will be more understandable, and you can use them as needed.

**Intermediate users:** If you have already created simple ODS output, you can skim "The Basics" and move on to read "Intermediate Topics" in more detail.

**Advanced users:** If you are already comfortable with ODS output production, you will want to skim both "The Basics" and "Intermediate Topics." You may find some features you didn't know about. However, you will probably find more helpful techniques in the second book in this series, *Output Delivery System: Advanced Techniques*.

**All users:** Appendix 2, "Operating System Differences," is a must-read for anyone not using the Windows platform.

## How to Use the Examples

You don't have to read this book cover to cover to take advantage of the Output Delivery System (ODS) techniques it contains. The book is set up as a series of examples so that you can zoom in on the information that best meets your needs.

If you flip through the book, you will see that the description of each example and the SAS code are always on the left-hand page, and the corresponding example output is always on the facing right-hand page. Everything you need to understand each section is right in front of you so you don't have to turn any pages. When you need help creating a particular type of ODS output, follow these steps:

1.  Find the chapter that covers the general type of output you're interested in. For example, if you need help with HTML output, try Chapter 3, "HTML Output." Alternatively, if you need help with ODS output for PROC GLM, check the index to find pages with references to that procedure.

2.  Flip through the chapter or examples and look at the output until you find an example that looks roughly like the output you're trying to create.

3.  After reading the explanation, use the example code to start creating your own output. Substitute your variables and data sets for the variables and data sets in the example code. If the example uses different SAS procedures than you need, figure out which procedures you want to use, and substitute them for the procedures in the example code.

4. Do a test run of your code to see if you have the approximate result you were looking for. If you run into problems, reread the explanation.

5. Once the basic structure is correct, you can work on cleaning up and refining your output. Chapters 9–12 cover topics related to revising the appearance of your output.

## The Code in This Book

A great deal of code is presented in this book. Some of it is ordinary SAS procedures and DATA steps. In general, this code will not be explained. Consult SAS OnlineDoc or your printed manuals for more information. The focus of the explanation in this book will be on the ODS code.

In the code examples in this book, the ODS code is mixed in. To make it easier to spot the ODS code, all ODS statements are displayed in UPPERCASE. The rest of the code is in lowercase or mixed case. Do not be confused by this convention. ODS statements or options are equally correct whether they appear in uppercase, lowercase, or mixed case.

In general, all of the code in this book uses the default SAS options settings. However, two settings were changed from the default. The NOCENTER and NODATE options were both used in creating the output displayed for the examples. This was done to make the output easier to display in the book. It has little or no impact on the results themselves. If you want your output to match the output in the book, add the statement OPTIONS NODATE NOCENTER at the top of your code.

## Tips and Warnings

Throughout the text, you will see tips and warnings related to some of the examples. They have distinctive icons to set them off from the rest of the text. Be sure to read any warnings associated with the examples before you try the code in your own programs.

This is the symbol used to identify a warning. Warnings generally contain additional information about potential risks associated with the technique used in the example.

This is the symbol used to identify a tip. Tips generally contain additional information about the example, or explain an alternate technique that can be used to create the example table.

## New Features

ODS is a very new feature, and it has been changing rapidly since it was introduced in Version 7 of the SAS System. This book is based on Release 8.2 of SAS. While every effort has been made to include the latest information available at the time of printing, it is likely that new features will be made available in subsequent versions. Be sure to check out the Changes and Enhancements section of the "Guide to the Output Delivery System" in SAS OnlineDoc for each new release of SAS.

# Part

# 1

*Introduction*

# Chapter

# 1

## *Why Use ODS?*

---

If all you want are quick results displayed on screen or roughly printed out in a stack of output, you can put this book away right now.

However, if you're like the rest of us, you want more from your output. That's because most SAS output is shared with others.

You want your output to be appealing, to help you tell a story. You want your output to be impressive: it should look like you worked on it for hours, even if it only took you a few minutes. You also want your output to be easy to share with other software packages and other users, whether they are across the hall or across the globe.

This chapter shows how you can take some basic SAS output and transform it from simple line-printer output into a beautiful integrated Web page, a word-processor-friendly RTF file, high-resolution printed output, or a bookmarked PDF file.

This chapter will not show any ODS code, but rather it will just give you a taste of the types of output you can produce and what they look like. Subsequent chapters get into the details of the code.

## Limitations of Traditional SAS Output

Before you can appreciate the wonder of ODS, you need to see where we're starting from. The following example is a series of simple procedures that describe some sales data. It includes a PROC FREQ, a PROC UNIVARIATE, and a PROC PRINT for some outliers.

```
options formdlim=' ';
title "Frequencies";
proc freq data=sales;
    table ProductName Department;
run;

title "Univariate";
proc univariate data=sales;
    var ItemsSold;
run;

title "Outliers for Price";
proc print data=sales;
    where ItemPrice>13;
    var ItemPrice;
run;
```

The procedures have been run in SAS Release 6.12, producing Output 1.1. Because three different procedures are used here, the resulting output is a series of reports—first, a report with two frequency tables, then a report with univariate statistics, and finally a report with line-item details for the outliers. (Some of this output has been trimmed in order to fit the results on the page.)

By default, SAS puts each of these results on a separate page. To keep this output as short as possible, the FORMDLIM option has been used to remove the page breaks. However, even without the page breaks, the resulting output sprawls across a number of pages. In Output 1.1, only the frequency tables and the first part of the univariate results will fit on the first page.

If you only have time to quickly glance at the top page of this report, this output doesn't tell you much of a story. You can't see all of the results. For example, what if the outliers for ItemsSold and ItemPrice are the most important message in the report? This information is buried on the second page. You can't see the extreme values for ItemsSold and the outlier report for ItemPrice.

Also, this report is just plain ugly. Because this is SAS listing output, spaces are used to line up the columns of data and headings. This forces you to use a monospace font rather than a proportional font. Proportional fonts (like the Times New Roman used for the text you are reading right now) are much easier to read. But if you used a proportional font with SAS listing output, nothing would line up. To see what SAS listing output would look like with a proportional font, look at Output 1.2.

**Output 1.1**

```
                              Frequencies
                                Product

                                       Cumulative    Cumulative
     ProductName    Frequency    Percent   Frequency      Percent

     Kona                  83     16.60          83        16.60
     Colombian             88     17.60         171        34.20
     French Roast          74     14.80         245        49.00
     Italian Roast         85     17.00         330        66.00
     Guatemalan            98     19.60         428        85.60
     Sumatran              72     14.40         500       100.00


                               Department
                                       Cumulative    Cumulative
     Department     Frequency    Percent   Frequency      Percent

     Wholesale            134     26.80         134        26.80
     Internet             208     41.60         342        68.40
     Mail Order            87     17.40         429        85.80
     Retail                71     14.20         500       100.00


                               Univariate
              Variable:    ItemsSold   (Items Sold)


                                Moments

     N                      500    Sum Weights            500
     Mean               297.542    Sum Observations    148771
     Std Deviation   143.283945    Variance         20530.2888
     Skewness        0.03353578    Kurtosis         -1.1733197
     Uncorrected SS    54510235    Corrected SS     10244614.1
     Coeff Variation   48.155872   Std Error Mean   6.40785281


                        Basic Statistical Measures

          Location                    Variability

     Mean      297.5420    Std Deviation       143.28394
     Median    292.0000    Variance                20530
     Mode      200.0000    Range             498.00000
                           Interquartile Range  244.00000


     NOTE: The mode displayed is the smallest of 2 modes with a count of 5.


                        Tests for Location: Mu0=0


     Test           -Statistic-     -----p Value------

     Student's t    t  46.43396     Pr > |t|    <.0001
     Sign           M       250     Pr >= |M|   <.0001
     Signed Rank    S     62625     Pr >= |S|   <.0001
```

*(... remaining output trimmed in order to fit results on this page ...)*

## Difficulties with Importing Standard Listing Output into a Word Processor

When you're delivering a set of results, frequently you need to combine them with a text-based report that explains what is going on. Ideally, you'd like to combine the results and the text into a single document.

With SAS listing output, it's possible to import your results into a word processor and add explanations and annotations. However, it takes a bit of work to make the results look nice.

Output 1.2 shows what the output from the previous example looks like when it is opened in Word. Because the default font in Word was set to Arial, a proportional font, these results look terrible. Nothing lines up. In addition, the lines under the table headings have been converted to a bunch of strange characters. This is because these lines were originally rendered in the SAS Monospace font. The codes that generate the smooth lines in table headings work just great if you stick to this monospace font, but as soon as you switch fonts, you get nonsense characters.

To fix this output, the font can be changed to SAS Monospace. Now, if you look at Output 1.3, you can see that everything lines up properly. However, it's still not very attractive. Monospace fonts are not as easy on the eye as proportional fonts. Table 1.1 illustrates some common proportional and fixed (monospace) fonts, and shows the difference proportional spacing can make. Not only are proportional fonts more appealing, but they also save space. Notice how much longer the lines of fixed-width fonts have to be to display the same text.

**Table 1.1**

| Font | Sample text | Type |
|------|-------------|------|
| Arial | This is some sample text to show how the font looks. | Proportional |
| Times New Roman | This is some sample text to show how the font looks. | Proportional |
| Courier | This is some sample text to show how the font looks. | Fixed |
| SAS Monospace | This is some sample text to show how the font looks. | Fixed |

If you want to use a proportional font yet still keep your columns straight, you need to convert this output into Word tables. Then you can change to any font and everything will still line up.

Word is good at converting text to tables, but SAS listing output presents a challenge. The items are separated by spaces, and Word creates a new table column wherever spaces occur. This means that if you've got a space within a column, such as between the words "French" and "Roast" in the row labels of the PROC FREQ, Word will split this column into two columns.

While there's no doubt you can use a word processor to clean up your SAS listing output, it's a lot of work because it requires so much tweaking to get things to look right. Now that ODS has arrived, there's no need to go through all this. Turn the page to enter the world of ODS.

**Output 1.2 SAS Listing Output after Importing into Word**

**Output 1.3 Results of Changing to a Monospace Font**

## ODS Output: A Variety of Formats to Fit Your Needs

Output 1.4 is produced by the same SAS code as the previous example, but now ODS has directed the output to HTML. You are looking at how the output would appear if you were viewing it with a Web browser.

**Output 1.4**

For a color version of Output 1.4, see page 282 in Appendix 3.

Instead of sprawling from page to page, as the listing output did, this output is neatly packaged with a table of contents to take you directly to whatever you want to view. Instead of using ugly fixed-width fonts, the HTML output uses several good-looking fonts. Instead of being in black and white, the HTML output appears in shades of blue and gray.

All of this adds up to a packaged set of results that you wouldn't be embarrassed to share with your boss. And because this is HTML output, you can place it on your company intranet or Internet site. This way your boss can view the report even if he or she is out of the country.

But why stop with HTML output? With ODS you can create the same report in a number of formats sure to please every user. Output 1.5 shows the same results as in the previous examples, this time converted to RTF and imported into Word. The RTF version does not have the table of contents, because this feature is not currently supported for the RTF destination, but the rest of the output appears the same in HTML or RTF.

**Output 1.5**

| Product | | | | |
|---|---|---|---|---|
| ProductName | Frequency | Percent | Cumulative Frequency | Cumulative Percent |
| Kona | 83 | 16.60 | 83 | 16.60 |
| Colombian | 88 | 17.60 | 171 | 34.20 |
| French Roast | 74 | 14.80 | 245 | 49.00 |
| Italian Roast | 85 | 17.00 | 330 | 66.00 |
| Guatemalan | 98 | 19.60 | 428 | 85.60 |
| Sumatran | 72 | 14.40 | 500 | 100.00 |

| Department | | | | |
|---|---|---|---|---|
| Department | Frequency | Percent | Cumulative Frequency | Cumulative Percent |
| Wholesale | 134 | 26.80 | 134 | 26.80 |
| Internet | 208 | 41.60 | 342 | 68.40 |
| Mail Order | 87 | 17.40 | 429 | 85.80 |
| Retail | 71 | 14.20 | 500 | 100.00 |

Note the striking difference between this output and the ugly results we got when we imported SAS listing output into Word in the previous example (Outputs 1.2 and 1.3). The ODS output has been converted into Word tables and is ready to go, with no tweaking needed.

If you want to change the font used for this output, you can do so without losing the column alignments. Now that your output is in a word processor, it's easy to add explanatory text and annotations. For example, if you want to explain something about the mail order figure, you can use a Word callout box to add a note with an arrow pointing to the number it describes.

The RTF output is nice if you need to incorporate other information, or if you plan to send your output to others for further editing or annotation. However, if all you need is an attractive printout, you can use ODS to send high-resolution output directly to your printer. Output 1.6 shows the same results as earlier, but as they appear when printed using ODS PRINTER.

**Output 1.6**

| Product | | | | |
|---|---|---|---|---|
| ProductName | Frequency | Percent | Cumulative Frequency | Cumulative Percent |
| Kona | 83 | 16.60 | 83 | 16.60 |
| Colombian | 88 | 17.60 | 171 | 34.20 |
| French Roast | 74 | 14.80 | 245 | 49.00 |
| Italian Roast | 85 | 17.00 | 330 | 66.00 |
| Guatemalan | 98 | 19.60 | 428 | 85.60 |
| Sumatran | 72 | 14.40 | 500 | 100.00 |

| Department | | | | |
|---|---|---|---|---|
| Department | Frequency | Percent | Cumulative Frequency | Cumulative Percent |
| Wholesale | 134 | 26.80 | 134 | 26.80 |
| Internet | 208 | 41.60 | 342 | 68.40 |
| Mail Order | 87 | 17.40 | 429 | 85.80 |
| Retail | 71 | 14.20 | 500 | 100.00 |

This output looks even better than the Word output. In fact, if your goal is to create the most professional looking results from your output, printer output is the way to go. You get crisp table lines and fonts, and you can use color if you have a color printer.

ODS printer output also gives you the option of creating a PDF file so you can make this printable file available via the Internet. HTML output looks great and loads quickly for people with slow Internet connections, but printing capabilities are limited. If you expect visitors to your Web site to print out your results, PDF format is the best approach.

There's one more type of ODS output we haven't seen yet. The previous examples all showed ways of producing reports from your output. But what if you want to do further analysis? In the past, only some SAS procedures were able to produce output data sets that contained some of their results. Now, ODS allows you to create a data set from most procedures. The data set contains all of the results the procedure is capable of producing in printed output.

Though you can create data sets from any part of the output, in this example, the frequencies and the extreme observations from the univariate analysis were chosen. Output 1.7 shows what these data sets look like.

**Output 1.7**

```
Output data set: Frequencies
```

| Obs | Table | ProductName | Frequency | Percent | Cum Frequency | Cum Percent | Department |
|---|---|---|---|---|---|---|---|
| 1 | ProductName | Kona | 83 | 16.60 | 83 | 16.60 | |
| 2 | ProductName | Colombian | 88 | 17.60 | 171 | 34.20 | |
| 3 | ProductName | French Roast | 74 | 14.80 | 245 | 49.00 | |
| 4 | ProductName | Italian Roast | 85 | 17.00 | 330 | 66.00 | |
| 5 | ProductName | Guatemalan | 98 | 19.60 | 428 | 85.60 | |
| 6 | ProductName | Sumatran | 72 | 14.40 | 500 | 100.00 | |
| 7 | Department | | 134 | 26.80 | 134 | 26.80 | Wholesale |
| 8 | Department | | 208 | 41.60 | 342 | 68.40 | Internet |
| 9 | Department | | 87 | 17.40 | 429 | 85.80 | Mail Order |
| 10 | Department | | 71 | 14.20 | 500 | 100.00 | Retail |

```
Output data set: Extreme observations from Univariate
```

| Obs | VarName | Low | LowObs | High | High Obs |
|---|---|---|---|---|---|
| 1 | ItemsSold | 51 | 48 | 547 | 154 |
| 2 | ItemsSold | 52 | 264 | 547 | 392 |
| 3 | ItemsSold | 52 | 143 | 548 | 142 |
| 4 | ItemsSold | 52 | 58 | 549 | 66 |
| 5 | ItemsSold | 54 | 440 | 549 | 127 |

If you compare the data set from the frequency distributions to the output shown on the previous page, you can see that the output data set contains every number that was in the table. Unlike previous versions of SAS, Version 8 allows you to obtain a data set from virtually every result it can produce in printed output.

With these data sets, you can now run further analyses using procedures or the DATA step, or you can create summarized reports with selected results.

# Chapter

# 2

## ODS Basics

Because ODS is a brand-new tool, it comes with some new terminology. This chapter explains these new terms and goes over the basics of what ODS does.

You could skip this chapter and go straight on to creating ODS output in Chapters 3 6. However, knowing the basics of ODS and the terminology for its components will make the following chapters more understandable.

This chapter provides a brief overview of ODS terminology, followed by a simple syntax summary. You may want to bookmark the syntax summary to use as a reference later.

## Overview

So, what is the Output Delivery System? In previous versions of SAS, procedures and DATA steps produced output. With ODS, the procedures and DATA steps simply produce raw data, and ODS supplies the structure and format for the output. For example, if you run a simple PROC CORR to get the correlation coefficient for two variables, ODS can create the HTML output shown in Output 2.1.

The CORR procedure did not create the tables, the formatting, or even the labels for the rows and columns. It simply produced the raw data for the table cells. This raw data is shown in Figure 2.1. (This figure is a simplification. The data is actually stored as double-precision floating-point values.) The data includes the names of the two variables, the number of observations, the Pearson correlation coefficient, and the probability result.

ODS takes this information and combines it with several *table definitions* to produce the results that are displayed in Figure 2.2. The table definitions for each procedure are supplied by the procedure. PROC CORR uses two table definitions to control the structure of its output. First, there is a table definition that tells ODS how to display the variables information table at the top of the output. This definition specifies a table with a column for the variable names. It also specifies which labels to use for the table, row, and column headings.

A second table definition tells ODS how to display the correlation results. It specifies the column for each VAR variable and the row for each WITH variable. It also specifies that the table cell(s) will display the correlation coefficient and probability. If this PROC CORR had specified additional options, like a request for simple statistics, ODS would supply additional table definitions to structure the other types of output.

However, applying these table definitions is not all that ODS does. If ODS stopped here, your output would look much like the basic listing output displayed in Figure 2.2. Table definitions control the basic structure of the output and some aspects of its formatting. When you create HTML, RTF, or printer output, you also need a style definition.

The *style definitions* specify the background color, table borders, and color scheme, as well as the fonts, sizes, and color of the text and numbers. In this case, the style definition for HTML calls for a gray background and a table with standard HTML borders. Within the table, the style definition calls for a darker gray background for the row and column headings. The text and numbers are formatted in the Arial font, with various colors and font sizes for the headings and table values.

Finally, ODS allows you to specify *output destinations*, which determine where and how the results are stored. These destinations include HTML, as in this example, and also RTF, PostScript and PCL printer files, PDF files, and output data sets. New output destinations are being added all the time. XML, CSV, LaTeX, troff, and WML are currently under development.

These table definitions, style definitions, and output destinations allow ODS to take simple procedure results — two variable names and two statistics generated by PROC CORR — and create the HTML output shown in Output 2.1.

So ODS is an interface between your simple results and the varied, complex output you want to create.

**Output 2.1**

## The CORR Procedure

| 1 With Variables: | ItemPrice |
|---|---|
| 1 Variables: | ItemsSold |

| Pearson Correlation Coefficients, N = 500<br>Prob > \|r\| under H0: Rho=0 | |
|---|---|
| | **ItemsSold** |
| ItemPrice<br>Item Price | 0.04976<br>0.2667 |

**Figure 2.1**

| ItemPrice | ItemsSold | 500 | 0.04976 | 0.2667 |
|---|---|---|---|---|

**Figure 2.2**

| 1 With Variables: | ItemPrice |
|---|---|
| 1 Variables: | ItemsSold |

| Pearson Correlation Coefficients, N = 500 | |
|---|---|
| Prob > \|r\| under HO: Rho=0 | |
| | ItemsSold |
| ItemPrice | 0.04976 |
| Item Price | 0.2667 |

## Table Definitions and Style Definitions

As explained in the previous example, table definitions are used by ODS to control how procedure and DATA step results are displayed. They define the structure and basic layout for your results. What makes ODS so powerful is that it enables you to modify these table definitions to change the structure or content of your output.

For example, the PROC CORR from the previous example creates two output objects: a table with the variable names, and a table with the number of observations, correlation coefficient, and probability. However, you're not limited to this output. ODS allows you to specify which tables you'd like to create.

PROC CORR has some built-in control over output. In this example, the NOSIMPLE option has already been used to get rid of one unwanted output table, the display of simple summary statistics. However, with only two variables, the table of variable names is also unwanted. The output is perfectly clear with just the correlation matrix. But the table of variable names cannot be removed from within PROC CORR.

Instead, you can use ODS to get rid of the table of variable names. Output 2.2 shows the result. Now only the correlation matrix itself is displayed. Chapter 8, "Limiting ODS Output," covers how to select and exclude output objects to create customized results for each output destination.

In addition to allowing you to specify which output objects you want, ODS allows you to modify the way they are displayed. If you want to share these results with a nonprogrammer, the label "The CORR Procedure" may not be very helpful. You can use ODS to remove this label. You can also change or remove the table borders. Output 2.3 shows the resulting output after the procedure label and table borders have been removed. These techniques are covered in Chapter 11, "Modifying Output Structure."

Finally, ODS allows you to change the appearance of procedure output. This is done by modifying the style definition. Style definitions control colors for backgrounds and fonts, typeface selection, and other aesthetic aspects of ODS output.

Going back to the PROC CORR example, the style definition can be modified to use a different font. Output 2.4 shows what the output looks like if all of the fonts are changed to "Comic Sans MS." Though this output looks rather silly, it does illustrate the power of style definitions. Techniques for modifying style definitions are covered in Chapter 9, "Style Definitions."

**Output 2.2**

**The CORR Procedure**

| Pearson Correlation Coefficients, N = 500 Prob > \|r\| under H0: Rho=0 | |
| --- | --- |
| | **ItemsSold** |
| **ItemPrice** Item Price | 0.04976 0.2667 |

**Output 2.3**

| Pearson Correlation Coefficients, N = 500 Prob > \|r\| under H0: Rho=0 | |
| --- | --- |
| | **ItemsSold** |
| **ItemPrice** Item Price | 0.04976 0.2667 |

**Output 2.4**

| Pearson Correlation Coefficients, N = 500 Prob > \|r\| under H0: Rho=0 | |
| --- | --- |
| | **ItemsSold** |
| **ItemPrice** Item Price | 0.04976 0.2667 |

## Output Objects and Output Destinations

Once the table definitions are applied, each SAS procedure can then produce output objects. In the PROC CORR example, two output objects were created: the list of variables and the correlation matrix. You can then send these output objects to one or more output destinations.

The default output destination is traditional SAS listing output. Listing output has been revised somewhat for Version 8 in order to standardize output appearance across procedures, but it's basically the same output you are used to from Version 6.

On the facing page, Output 2.6 through Output 2.9 show a simple result that has been routed to a number of destinations, creating a number of pieces of ODS output. The PROC CORR step was run only once, producing the raw data that is combined with the table definition to create the basic output object. Then the style definitions interact with the output objects to create the output for each destination.

This is a simple example with just a single output object. By default most procedures produce a number of output objects.

Output 2.5 shows the listing destination. Here the table definition has been applied to configure the output, but the style definition does not apply.

Output 2.6 shows the HTML destination. Here many aspects of the style definition apply, so we get colors and an assortment of typefaces and font sizes.

Output 2.7 shows the RTF destination. This output looks very similar to the HTML output. There are just minor differences in how the style definitions are implemented to create RTF output.

Output 2.8 shows the printer destination. This output looks very similar to the RTF and HTML output. It will vary somewhat, depending on your printer settings.

Finally, Output 2.9 shows the output destination. Here only the table definition comes into play. The table definition determines the structure of the raw data. Style definitions are not used, since the output will be a data set.

So one procedure that produces one result can be diverted to five different output destinations, creating five unique pieces of ODS output.

Other possible output destinations include LaTeX, XML, CSV, troff, and WML. At the time of writing, these destinations are not yet available or are only experimental. Expect more destinations to be offered in the future.

To help you keep track of all of these output objects, SAS provides a new window, the Results window. If you turn the page to Output 2.10, you can see a view of the Results window for the output shown in these examples. This window displays each of the output objects you have created, along with an icon to indicate the output destinations to which it has been sent.

**Output 2.5 Listing Output**

```
Pearson Correlation Coefficients, N = 500
         Prob > |r| under H0: Rho=0


                        Items
                        Sold

Item Price            0.04976
                       0.2667
```

**Output 2.6 HTML Output**

| Pearson Correlation Coefficients, N = 500 Prob > \|r\| under H0: Rho=0 | |
| --- | --- |
| | **ItemsSold** |
| **Item Price** | 0.04976 0.2667 |

**Output 2.7 RTF Output**

| Pearson Correlation Coefficients, N = 500 Prob > \|r\| under H0: Rho=0 | |
| --- | --- |
| | ItemsSold |
| **Item Price** | 0.04976 0.2667 |

**Output 2.8 Printer Output**

| Pearson Correlation Coefficients, N = 500 Prob > \|r\| under H0: Rho=0 | |
| --- | --- |
| | **ItemsSold** |
| **ItemPrice** Item Price | 0.04976 0.2667 |

**Output 2.9 Output Data Set**

| RowName | Label | Items Sold | PItems Sold |
| --- | --- | --- | --- |
| ItemPrice | Item Price | 0.04976 | 0.2667 |

**Output 2.10**

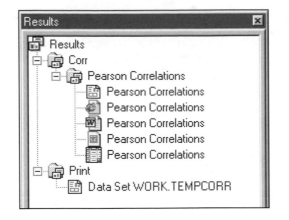

## ODS Syntax

The following is a quick reference to ODS syntax. This is a simplified listing, as each item will be covered in detail in a subsequent chapter. This page is for reference only.

```
ODS HTML BODY|FILE=file-specification <(NO_BOTTOM_MATTER
                                          NO_TOP_MATTER URL= TITLE=)>
        <CONTENTS=file-specification (URL=)>
        <PAGE=file-specification (URL=)>
        <FRAME=file-specification (URL=)>
        <ANCHOR= AUTHOR= BASE= GFOOTNOTE GPATH= GTITLE= HEADTEXT=
         KEYWORDS= METATEXT= NEWFILE= PATH= RECORD_SEPARATOR=
         STYLE= STYLESHEET TRANTAB= STARTPAGE=>;
ODS HTML CLOSE;


ODS RTF FILE=file-specification <STYLE= SUBJECT= TITLE= STARTPAGE=>;
ODS RTF CLOSE;


ODS PRINTER|PS|PCL|PDF <COLOR= FILE= FONTSCALE= PRINTER= SAS STYLE=
                        UNIFORM PDFMARK PDFNOTE>;
ODS PRINTER CLOSE;


ODS OUTPUT output-object-specification<(MATCH_ALL PERSIST=PROC|RUN)>
        <=SAS-data-set>;
ODS OUTPUT CLOSE;


ODS LISTING <DATAPANEL=DATA|PAGE FILE=>;
ODS LISTING CLOSE;


ODS _ALL_ CLOSE;


ODS <ODS-destination¹ > SELECT selection(s)<(PERSIST)>|ALL|NONE;
ODS <ODS-destination¹> EXCLUDE exclusion(s)<(PERSIST)>|ALL|NONE;
ODS OUTPUT CLEAR;


ODS <ODS-destination> SHOW;

ODS TRACE ON </ LABEL LISTING>;
ODS TRACE OFF;

ODS PATH <libname.>item-store <(READ|UPDATE|WRITE)>;

ODS VERIFY <ON|OFF|ERROR>;

ODS NORESULTS|RESULTS;

ODS NOPTITLE|PTITLE;

ODS PROCLABEL 'text';
```

In addition to the ODS statements, PROC TEMPLATE is used to modify the table and style definitions used by ODS. The syntax for this procedure is lengthy and complex, and is covered in Chapters 9–12.

---

[1] ODS SELECT and ODS EXCLUDE work for all destinations except OUTPUT.

# Part
# 2

*The Basics*

# Chapter

# 3

*HTML Output*

In the Version 6 release of SAS software, standard output was limited to listing files. When the Internet boom hit, a series of macros were created to help users deliver their output to the Web.

However, these early SAS HTML tools were simple. Their output was just standard listing output with a few HTML tags so that it could be interpreted by Web browsers.

With Version 8, SAS can generate fully fledged HTML output. It uses enhanced fonts, colors, and table designs that make the most of your results. It also organizes your output with an HTML table of contents and table of pages, and it can incorporate your output into an existing Web site.

HTML has gone from a barely supported feature to state of the art. In Version 8, you might find that HTML becomes your preferred output format, even if you're not creating output for the Web, just because it has so many features.

This chapter explains how to generate HTML output and provides a basic description of the HTML that is generated. It then goes on to show a few of the enhancements that you can add to take your results to the next level. Finally, it shows how to export your HTML results to a word processor or spreadsheet or other package for further customizing.

## Generating Your First HTML File

Creating an HTML file from your SAS results is quite simple. You need just three things: a file to send the results to, an instruction to ODS to open the file and start generating HTML, and an instruction to ODS to stop generating HTML and close the file.

So the first thing you need to do is specify a file for your output. You can specify the file directly when you call ODS to create the HTML output, or you can create a filename reference ahead of time and use that in the ODS call. If you choose to create a filename reference, the syntax is something like this (depending on your operating environment):

```
filename myfile 'myhtmlfile.html';
```

The HTML filename needs to end in ".htm" or ".html" in order for a browser to be able to interpret your file. Most operating systems now support ".html" as the naming convention. This example is for the Windows operating system. The file naming conventions vary slightly by operating system, and you may need to make adjustments for your system (see Appendix 2, "Operating System Differences," for more information). Once you've created the filename, you can then issue your call to ODS to request HTML output. The syntax is

```
ODS HTML BODY=myfile;
```

If you did not choose to create a filename reference, the syntax would change to

```
ODS HTML BODY='myhtmlfile.html';
```

This is all it takes to turn on ODS HTML output. The output from every procedure or DATA step following this statement will be directed to the HTML file you specified. This is in addition to the standard listing output, which will be directed to the output window as always.

Once you have run the procedures that you want to send to the HTML file, you need to turn the HTML destination off so that the file will be finished and closed. Then you can view your HTML file with the SAS Results Viewer or your favorite browser. The syntax to end HTML generation is

```
ODS HTML CLOSE;
```

That's the last of the three pieces you need to create HTML output. Viewed together, they look like this:

```
filename myfile 'myhtmlfile.html';
ODS HTML BODY=myfile;
proc means data=billings;
   class WorkDate;
   var Hours BillableAmt;
run;
ODS HTML CLOSE;
```

In this example, the output from PROC MEANS will be stored in the file referenced by myfile. The HTML output, viewed through a browser or the SAS Results Viewer, is shown in Output 3.1.

**Output 3.1**

## The MEANS Procedure

| Quarter | Variable | Label | N | Mean | Std Dev | Minimum | Maximum |
|---|---|---|---|---|---|---|---|
| 1999-1 | Hours | Hours Worked | 57 | 6.11 | 2.93 | 1.00 | 11.00 |
| | BillableAmt | Amount Billable | 57 | 338.92 | 145.94 | 80.43 | 583.43 |
| 1999-2 | Hours | Hours Worked | 63 | 6.27 | 2.90 | 1.00 | 11.00 |
| | BillableAmt | Amount Billable | 63 | 348.42 | 145.11 | 79.44 | 591.44 |
| 1999-3 | Hours | Hours Worked | 60 | 6.47 | 2.84 | 1.50 | 11.00 |
| | BillableAmt | Amount Billable | 60 | 357.60 | 142.19 | 106.45 | 589.45 |
| 1999-4 | Hours | Hours Worked | 63 | 5.86 | 2.67 | 1.00 | 11.00 |
| | BillableAmt | Amount Billable | 63 | 326.03 | 133.07 | 76.46 | 585.46 |
| 2000-1 | Hours | Hours Worked | 58 | 5.91 | 2.76 | 1.00 | 10.50 |
| | BillableAmt | Amount Billable | 58 | 330.02 | 137.53 | 87.46 | 565.47 |
| 2000-2 | Hours | Hours Worked | 58 | 6.05 | 2.74 | 1.00 | 10.50 |
| | BillableAmt | Amount Billable | 58 | 337.04 | 137.42 | 80.47 | 565.47 |
| 2000-3 | Hours | Hours Worked | 62 | 5.89 | 2.82 | 1.00 | 11.00 |
| | BillableAmt | Amount Billable | 62 | 328.48 | 140.31 | 82.49 | 586.49 |
| 2000-4 | Hours | Hours Worked | 63 | 5.87 | 2.85 | 1.00 | 11.00 |
| | BillableAmt | Amount Billable | 63 | 327.21 | 142.46 | 80.49 | 581.49 |
| 2001-1 | Hours | Hours Worked | 16 | 6.25 | 3.16 | 1.50 | 11.00 |
| | BillableAmt | Amount Billable | 16 | 345.44 | 157.01 | 109.50 | 578.50 |

## Exploring the Body File: The Basics of HTML

When ODS creates HTML output, it takes the SAS listing results and converts them to an HTML file that can be understood by Web browsers like Internet Explorer and Netscape.

The SAS listing results are just text and numbers separated by spaces and line breaks. In order for them to be displayed in a browser like Internet Explorer or Netscape, they need to be coded with HTML *tags*. These tags control things like the page layout in the browser window and the fonts and colors used for the text and numbers.

To illustrate this process, we'll look at a simple bit of ODS HTML output. The following code creates an HTML file called "procmeans.html" that contains a table with summary statistics for a single variable. The resulting HTML output is shown in Output 3.2.

```
ODS HTML BODY='procmeans.html';
proc means data=billings nonobs maxdec=2 mean min max;
   var BillableAmt;
run;
ODS HTML CLOSE;
```

To see how ODS has created this Web page, look at Output 3.3, which shows what the HTML code looks like. Only the essential HTML code is discussed and displayed. ODS generates more HTML than is actually shown in Output 3.3. However, for the purpose of understanding the basic structure of the HTML output, this will suffice.

What makes this an HTML file are the <HTML> and </HTML> tags at the beginning and end of the file. The <HEAD> and </HEAD> tags coupled with the <TITLE> and </TITLE> tags enclose the text ("SAS Output") that will be displayed in the browser title bar. Everything between <BODY> and </BODY> will be displayed in the main window of the browser.

Browsers are not very good at lining up text unless you are using fixed-width (monospace) fonts, so to align the output on the screen, all of the results are organized into tables with rows and columns. The <TABLE> and </TABLE> tags mark the beginning and end of each table. This output has two tables, one for the procedure title "The MEANS Procedure" and one for the actual results.

Within each table, <TR> and </TR> mark the beginning and end of each row. Finally, within each row, <TD> and </TD> mark the beginning and end of each table cell. The first table, with the procedure title, has only one row and one table cell. The second table has three rows. The first row contains the table header and has only one cell. The second row contains the column headings and has three cells. The third row contains the numeric results and also has three cells.

The example HTML file also includes a pair of <FONT ... > and </FONT> tags which ask for a specific typeface, size, and color for the text. The actual results displayed in Output 3.2 were generated from an HTML file with dozens of font tags. This allows different typefaces, sizes, and colors to be used for each part of the output. The actual HTML file also uses a number of attributes on the table tags to control the use of row and column rules and background colors.

Although this example is an oversimplification, it does provide a basic idea of how HTML files work and how they are used to display your SAS output.

**Output 3.2**

**Output 3.3**

```
<HTML>
<HEAD>
   <TITLE>SAS Output</TITLE>
</HEAD>
<BODY>
<FONT FACE="Arial" SIZE="3" COLOR="#002288">
   <TABLE>
      <TR><TD>The MEANS Procedure</TD></TR>
   </TABLE>
   <TABLE>
      <TR><TD COLSPAN=3>Analysis Variable : BillableAmt Amount Billable</TD></TR>
      <TR><TD>Mean</TD><TD>Minimum</TD><TD>Maximum</TD></TR>
      <TR><TD>336.92</TD><TD>76.46</TD><TD>591.44</TD></TR>
   </TABLE>
</FONT>
</BODY>
</HTML>
```

 If you don't like the generic "SAS Output" title that appears in the browser title bar, you can change the text using the TITLE= option on your ODS HTML statement:

```
ODS HTML BODY='procmeans.html' (TITLE='My Title');
```

## Exploring the Body File: Graphics

Most ODS HTML output is created as in the previous example. The results are organized into tables with rows and columns of headings and statistics.

However, graphics procedures are different. They produce an image, rather than text results surrounded by HTML tags. Graphics output will be covered in detail in Chapter 14, "Graphics Output," but this simple example will give you a basic understanding of graphical HTML output.

The ODS statements you use to create HTML graphics output are nearly identical to those used to create tabular output. You still need the three basics: an ODS HTML statement to open the HTML output destination, a body filename to specify where to send the output, and an ODS HTML CLOSE statement to close the HTML output destination.

For graphics procedures, you need three extra things. First, you need to specify the GIF or JPEG device driver. The GIF format is easily interpreted by Web browsers and is relatively compact so that it can be quickly downloaded from the Internet. Second, you need a GPATH option on your ODS HTML statement. The option setting tells ODS where to put the GIF once it is created. Generally, you will want to point the GPATH to the same location as your body file. Third, you should add a URL=NONE option. This keeps the graphics path from being included in the HTML output, thus allowing you to move the resulting HTML and GIF output to your Web server.

```
GOPTIONS DEVICE=GIF;
ODS HTML BODY='c:\temp\mygraph.html' GPATH='c:\temp\' (URL=NONE);
proc gchart data=Billings;
   vbar3d Quarter /
      name="billqtr"
      sumvar=BillableAmt type=mean;
run; quit;
ODS HTML CLOSE;
```

Submitting this code generates Output 3.4. This HTML page contains a single image with the chart and all of the associated text. The HTML code generated by ODS is shown in Output 3.5. Again, for the purposes of illustration, this code has been greatly simplified.

The <HEAD>, <TITLE>, and <BODY> tags are the same as the previous example. Instead of <TABLE> tags, this output is organized by the <CENTER> and </CENTER> tags, which align the output in the center of the browser window. The output itself, instead of being text results and labels, is an image.

Images are displayed in browsers by using the <IMG> tag. Unlike the other tags in this example and the previous examples, this tag is not one of a pair. There is no </IMG> tag. In addition, this tag uses parameters. The first parameter is the name of the GIF file: "billqtr.gif" (the name comes from the NAME= option on the VBAR3D statement). The second parameter specifies that no border be displayed around the graphic image.

This HTML output was generated using the default settings for the graph. Chapter 14, "Graphics Output," discusses how to create more complex output and how to modify the option settings.

**Output 3.4**

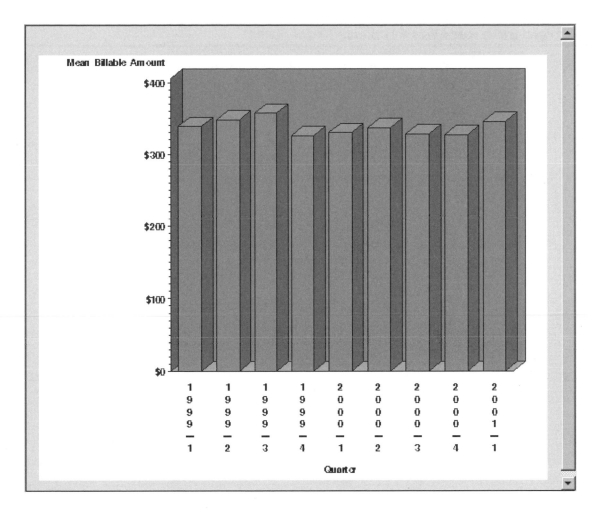

**Output 3.5**

```
<HTML>
  <HEAD>
    <TITLE>SAS Output</TITLE>
  </HEAD>
  <BODY>
    <CENTER>
      <IMG SRC="billqtr.gif" border="0">
    </CENTER>
  </BODY>
</HTML>
```

## Combining the Results of Several Procedures

The previous two examples showed how to send output from a single procedure to an HTML file. However, ODS also allows you to send a number of results from a series of procedures to the same HTML file. This allows you to build a combined report from a number of procedures and data sets and place it all on a single Web page.

In this example, the output from three procedures is combined into a single HTML file. Two PROC MEANS steps and a PROC PRINT step are placed between two ODS HTML statements.

```
title 'Quarterly Report';
ODS HTML BODY='QReport.html';
title2 'Revenue by Customer';
proc means data=Billings nonobs mean sum;
    class CustomerName;
    var BillableAmt;
run;
title2 'Revenue by Division';
proc means data=Billings nonobs mean sum;
    class Division;
    var BillableAmt;
run;
title2 'Top Performers';
proc print data=Totals noobs;
    where BillableAmt>10000;
    var EmployeeName BillableAmt;
run;
ODS HTML CLOSE;
```

Because all output between the ODS HTML and ODS HTML CLOSE statements is routed to the HTML destination, the output from all three procedures goes to the file specified in the BODY= option.

The resulting file is shown in Output 3.6. In this screen view, you can see the result from the first procedure and the top of the results of the second procedure. To see more, you would have to scroll down in the browser window.

SAS builds this HTML file by appending the results of each procedure to the end of the HTML file. If you run a large number of procedures, you'll end up with an extremely long file that requires a lot of scrolling to see all the results. (The NEWFILE= option can help with this. See "Breaking Output into Separate Files" on page 38.) Unlike traditional listing output, HTML output does not contain page breaks. A horizontal bar is added between each type of output, but if you print this page, it will print continuously. That is because *HTML does not have any code or tag to mark a page break*. HTML is a very simple coding scheme that allows text and images to be viewed on the Web, but it's not a great printing tool.

If you need to deliver printable output via the Web, see the examples on PDF output in Chapter 5, "Printer Output."

**Output 3.6**

## *Quarterly Report*
## *Revenue by Customer*

### *The MEANS Procedure*

| Analysis Variable : BillableAmt Amount Billable | | |
|---|---:|---:|
| Customer | Mean | Sum |
| IPO.com | 365.5745833 | 8773.79 |
| Bricks and Mortar, Inc. | 362.1439130 | 8329.31 |
| Virtual Co. | 309.8741935 | 9606.10 |
| Sweat Shops Athletic | 334.4563333 | 10033.69 |
| Smith & Smith | 295.8818182 | 9764.10 |

## *Quarterly Report*
## *Revenue by Division*

### *The MEANS Procedure*

| Analysis Variable : BillableAmt Amount Billable | | |
|---|---:|---:|
| Division | Mean | Sum |
| Applications | 310.3919048 | 6518.23 |
| Analysis | 288.3442857 | 6055.23 |
| Reporting | 334.8728571 | 7032.33 |
| Systems | 325.7992308 | 8470.78 |
| Documentation | 335.9058333 | 8061.74 |
| QA | 370.3100000 | 10368.68 |

## Generating a Table of Contents

The previous example showed how the results of several procedures could be combined into a single HTML output file. This makes a nice summary report, but it does require the reader to scroll through several pages of output. To make this report even better, you can use ODS to generate a table of contents that allows you to click on an item of interest and jump right to that item.

The code involved is quite simple. When you request a single HTML file for your output, you use a BODY= option. To get a table of contents, you add a CONTENTS= option. You should also add a FRAME= option. The CONTENTS= option creates the table of contents, but in order for a Web browser to display both the table of contents and the body file on the same screen, you need a frame file.

```
title 'Quarterly Report';
ODS HTML BODY='body.html'
         CONTENTS='contents.html'
         FRAME='frame.html';
title2 'Revenue by Customer';
proc means data=Billings nonobs mean sum;
    class CustomerName;
    var BillableAmt;
run;
title2 'Revenue by Division';
proc means data=Billings nonobs mean sum;
    class Division;
    var BillableAmt;
run;
title2 'Top Performers';
proc print data=Totals noobs;
    where BillableAmt>10000;
    var EmployeeName BillableAmt;
run;
ODS HTML CLOSE;
```

In this example, the body file is called "body.html," the contents file is called "contents.html," and the frame file is called "frame.html." To view the results, you open the frame file. As you can see in Output 3.7, the frame file contains the body and contents file. The contents file is displayed in the left frame, and the body file is contained in the right frame.

If you were to click on the label for the PROC PRINT procedure, the browser would take you directly to that output, with no scrolling required.

In this example, the HTML output files were named to match their function. The contents file is named "contents.html," the body file "body.html," and the frame file "frame.html." This is handy because it helps you remember what each file does, but it is not required. You can call the files anything you want ("x.html," "y.html," and "z.html," for example) and SAS will still build the proper structure and crosslinks.

**Output 3.7**

## *Quarterly Report*
## *Revenue by Customer*

**The MEANS Procedure**

| Analysis Variable : BillableAmt Amount Billable | | |
|---|---|---|
| **Customer** | **Mean** | **Sum** |
| IPO.com | 365.5745833 | 8773.79 |
| Bricks and Mortar, Inc. | 362.1439130 | 8329.31 |
| Virtual Co. | 309.8741935 | 9606.10 |
| Sweat Shops Athletic | 334.4563333 | 10033.69 |
| Smith & Smith | 295.8818182 | 9764.10 |

As you look at this output, you may be thinking that it would be nice if the table of contents displayed the title instead of the procedure label, "The Means Procedure." In fact, you can do that. See the example for the PROCLABEL option later in this chapter.

## Exploring the Frame Files

In the previous example, ODS was used to generate a table of contents to organize the results. To set up this output, three files were created.

The first file is the body file, which contains the actual results. The second file is the contents file. This contains the procedure names and links to each procedure's output. The HTML code for this file is shown in Output 3.8. This code has been greatly simplified. The actual file contains several complex scripts that allow you to expand or collapse the table of contents items in the browser. Nevertheless, the important part of the code is shown here.

This file is composed of a series of titles: "The MEANS Procedure," "The PRINT Procedure," etc. Each title is followed by a subtitle that further explains the output: "Summary Statistics," "Data Set WORK.TOTALS." The subtitles are links to that part of the output in the body file. Notice the <A HREF= TARGET=> and </A> tags. The <A> and </A> mark the beginning and end of a hyperlink. The text between them is the text that is displayed in the table of contents. The HREF= attribute specifies the location to link to (in this case, various locations in the body file). Finally, the TARGET= attribute tells the browser to continue to display the body file in the main frame of the window. These links and references will be further explained in an example later in this chapter.

The third file involved in displaying the output with a table of contents is the frame file. This tells the browser how to display the body file and contents file. The code for the frame file is shown in Output 3.9. This file is very simple. Instead of having a body section (note that there are no <BODY> tags), this file has <FRAMESET> and </FRAMESET> tags. These tags have a number of parameters, but the important one is the COLS= option. This tells the browser how many columns the page will have and how big they will be. In this case, there will be two columns. The first one will take up 23% of the page width, and the second one will occupy the remainder of the page.

Inside the <FRAMESET> tags are two sets of <FRAME> and </FRAME> tags. These specify which files will be displayed in the two columns on the screen. They indicate that the left frame will be used to display the file "contents.html" and the right frame will be used to display the file "body.html."

Together, these three files make up a frame Web page. SAS and ODS set up all of these files for you automatically, but it's useful to know how they work.

If you are incorporating your SAS output into an existing Web site, be careful about how you set up your pages. If your Web site is already set up with frames, and you add a link to your SAS output, which has its own frames, you could end up with ugly and confusing output. This frames-within-frames problem is illustrated in Output 3.10. To solve this problem, code the hyperlink on your existing Web page to open up your ODS output in a new window. You do this by adding the code TARGET="_blank_" to your hyperlink. (Edit your existing Web page, not the ODS-generated page.)

For additional information about how the table of contents page works, see "Exploring Links and Anchors" on page 44.

**Output 3.8**

```
<HTML>
   <HEAD>
      <TITLE>SAS Output Table of Contents</TITLE>
   </HEAD>
   <BODY>
   Table of Contents<br>
   The Means Procedure<br>
      <A HREF="body.html#IDX" TARGET="body">Summary statistics</a><br>
   The Means Procedure<br>
      <A HREF="body.html#IDX1" TARGET="body">Summary statistics</a><br>
   The Print Procedure<br>
      <A HREF="body.html#IDX2" TARGET="body">Data Set WORK.TOTALS</a><br>
   </BODY>
</HTML>
```

**Output 3.9**

```
<HTML>
   <HEAD>
      <TITLE>SAS Output Frame</TITLE>
   </HEAD>
   <FRAMESET FRAMEBORDER=yes FRAMESPACING=1 COLS="23%,*">
      <FRAME SRC="contents.html" NAME="contents" SCROLLING=auto>
      <FRAME SRC="body.html" NAME="body" SCROLLING=auto>
   </FRAMESET>
</HTML>
```

**Output 3.10**

## Breaking Output into Separate Files

All of the examples thus far have shown the results in a single body file. To view each of the results, you have to scroll down the page or click on the appropriate table of contents link. To print one of the results, you have to print the whole page. If your output is lengthy, or your users may need to access it via a slow dial-up connection, you may want to break your output into smaller files.

The ODS HTML statement supports an option that creates a separate body file for each procedure. Alternatively, you can put the results from a few procedures in one body file and the results from the next few procedures in another. The code below shows how to take our sample program from the previous examples and output it to three body files, one for each procedure.

```
ODS HTML BODY='body1.html' NEWFILE=PROC
        CONTENTS='contents.html'
        FRAME='main.html';
title2 'Revenue by Customer';
proc means data=Billings nonobs mean sum;
    class CustomerName;
    var BillableAmt;
run;
title2 'Revenue by Division';
proc means data=Billings nonobs mean sum;
    class Division;
    var BillableAmt;
run;
title2 'Top Performers';
proc print data=Totals noobs;
    where BillableAmt>10000;
    var EmployeeName BillableAmt;
run;
ODS HTML CLOSE;
```

In this code, there are just two changes. First, the name of the body file is changed to "body1.html." The second change is the addition of the NEWFILE=PROC option, which calls for a new HTML file for each procedure. The first file will be named "body1.html," the next file will be named "body2.html," and so on. The contents file will include links to the multiple files. The results are shown in Output 3.11. You can also start a new file for each page (NEWFILE=PAGE) or for each output table (NEWFILE=OUTPUT).

This looks just like the previous output, but now if you print the screen, you'll only get the output from a single procedure. In addition, if you scroll down in this output, you cannot get to the next procedure. You have to use the table of contents to get to the next procedure.

ODS also supports the creation of a table of pages, as an alternative to a table of contents (or you can have both a table of contents and a table of pages). To add a table of pages, add PAGE='fileref' to your ODS HTML statement. Output 3.12 shows how this example would look with a table of pages instead of a table of contents.

**Output 3.11**

## Quarterly Report
## Revenue by Customer

*The MEANS Procedure*

| Analysis Variable : BillableAmt Amount Billable | | |
|---|---|---|
| **Customer** | **Mean** | **Sum** |
| IPO.com | 365.5745833 | 8773.79 |
| Bricks and Mortar, Inc. | 362.1439130 | 8329.31 |
| Virtual Co. | 309.8741935 | 9606.10 |
| Sweat Shops Athletic | 334.4563333 | 10033.69 |
| Smith & Smith | 295.8818182 | 9764.10 |

**Output 3.12**

## Quarterly Report
## Revenue by Customer

*The MEANS Procedure*

| Analysis Variable : BillableAmt Amount Billable | | |
|---|---|---|
| **Customer** | **Mean** | **Sum** |
| IPO.com | 365.5745833 | 8773.79 |
| Bricks and Mortar, Inc. | 362.1439130 | 8329.31 |
| Virtual Co. | 309.8741935 | 9606.10 |
| Sweat Shops Athletic | 334.4563333 | 10033.69 |
| Smith & Smith | 295.8818182 | 9764.10 |

## Changing Procedure Labels in the Table of Contents

In the previous examples, you may have noticed that every time a table of contents was generated for a PROC MEANS step, the heading in the table of contents was displayed as "The MEANS Procedure," and the subheading was always "Summary Statistics." This could get very confusing if your SAS program generates 50 PROC MEANS results. You wouldn't be able to tell them apart in the table of contents. To help with this, ODS provides a statement to specify a custom procedure label.

The ODS PROCLABEL statement is shown in the following code. In this example, the TITLE2 statement calls for the output to be headed by the title "Hours Billed by Customer." The ODS PROCLABEL statement asks for the same thing, except that it applies to the table of contents and the Results window.

```
ODS HTML BODY='body.html'
         CONTENTS='contents.html'
         FRAME='main.html';
ODS PROCLABEL 'Hours Billed by Customer';
title2 'Hours Billed by Customer';
proc means data=Billings nonobs mean sum;
    class CustomerName;
    var Hours;
run;
ODS HTML CLOSE;
```

The results are shown in Output 3.13. Notice the revised procedure label in the table of contents. It now reads "Hours Billed by Customer." The subheading "Summary Statistics" remains the same.

You can also use this technique to get rid of the procedure labels in the table of contents. This can save space on your Web page, though you may lose some clarity. To remove the procedure labels, assign a blank label to the procedure, as in the following example:

```
ODS HTML BODY='body.html'
         CONTENTS='contents.html'
         FRAME='main.html';
ODS PROCLABEL ' ';
title2 'Hours Billed by Customer';
proc means data=Billings nonobs mean sum;
    class CustomerName;
    var Hours;
run;
ODS HTML CLOSE;
```

The output is shown in Output 3.14. Now the label has gone away. Unfortunately, a number and a blank line are still left in place. See the example in Chapter 11, "Modifying Output Structure," for how to use the TEMPLATE procedure to get rid of the number and line.

**Output 3.13**

| Table of Contents | Quarterly Report Hours Billed by Customer |
|---|---|
| 1. Hours Billed by Customer<br><br>·Summary statistics | The MEANS Procedure |

**Quarterly Report**
**Hours Billed by Customer**

**The MEANS Procedure**

| Analysis Variable : Hours Hours Worked | | |
|---|---|---|
| **Customer** | **Mean** | **Sum** |
| IPO.com | 6.4 | 598.5 |
| Bricks and Mortar, Inc. | 6.5 | 575.0 |
| Virtual Co. | 5.7 | 569.5 |
| Sweat Shops Athletic | 6.1 | 658.0 |
| Smith & Smith | 5.7 | 628.0 |

**Output 3.14**

Table of Contents

1. ·Summary statistics

**Quarterly Report**
**Hours Billed by Customer**

**The MEANS Procedure**

| Analysis Variable : Hours Hours Worked | | |
|---|---|---|
| **Customer** | **Mean** | **Sum** |
| IPO.com | 6.4 | 598.5 |
| Bricks and Mortar, Inc. | 6.5 | 575.0 |
| Virtual Co. | 5.7 | 569.5 |
| Sweat Shops Athletic | 6.1 | 658.0 |
| Smith & Smith | 5.7 | 628.0 |

## Changing Multiple Procedure Labels

The previous example shows a table of contents for a single procedure. But chances are, if you need to use ODS PROCLABEL to clean up your labels, it's because you have a bunch of procedures and a long table of contents.

In this example, there are two PROC MEANS and a PROC PRINT. An ODS PROCLABEL statement is used before the first PROC MEANS to change the label from "The MEANS Procedure" to "Hours Billed." A second ODS PROCLABEL statement is used to modify the label for the PROC PRINT.

```
ODS HTML BODY='body.html'
        CONTENTS='contents.html'
        FRAME='main.html';
title2 'Hours Billed by Customer';
ODS PROCLABEL 'Hours Billed';
proc means data=Billings nonobs mean sum;
   class CustomerName;
    var Hours;
run;
title2 'Hours Billed by Division';
proc means data=Billings nonobs mean sum;
    class Division;
    var Hours;
run;
title3 'Overtime Hours';
ODS PROCLABEL 'Overtime';
proc print data=Billings noobs;
    where Hours>8;
    var Hours Division WorkDate;
run;
ODS HTML CLOSE;
```

The output from this procedure is shown in Output 3.15. Notice how the label in the table of contents for the first PROC MEANS is changed to "Hours Billed." However, the second PROC MEANS is still labeled "The MEANS Procedure." Unlike most ODS statements, ODS PROCLABEL applies only to the next procedure. Even though the second procedure is a PROC MEANS just like the first one, ODS does not retain the PROCLABEL value.

To change the label for the second PROC MEANS, another ODS PROCLABEL statement is required.

**Output 3.15**

*Quarterly Report*
*Hours Billed by Customer*

*The MEANS Procedure*

| Analysis Variable : Hours Hours Worked | | |
| --- | --- | --- |
| Customer | Mean | Sum |
| IPO.com | 6.4 | 598.5 |
| Bricks and Mortar, Inc. | 6.5 | 575.0 |
| Virtual Co. | 5.7 | 569.5 |
| Sweat Shops Athletic | 6.1 | 658.0 |
| Smith & Smith | 5.7 | 628.0 |

## Exploring Links and Anchors

You don't have to understand HTML code to generate output with a table of contents or a table of pages. However, if you understand the basics of how the code works, this makes it easier to customize your output. The table of contents file has to communicate via the browser with the main body file. When you click on an item in the table of contents, the browser needs to know where to go in the body file. This is done using links and references. "Exploring the Frame Files" on page 36 showed how the table of contents and body pages are set up within a frame page. This example will show how the links between the two pages work.

The following code produces a simple Web page with a table of contents that you can use to explore how this works. The resulting output is shown in Output 3.16. In this screen view, you have just clicked the "Extreme Observations" label, so that portion of the output is displayed in the right frame.

```
ODS HTML BODY='body.html'
        CONTENTS='contents.html'
        FRAME='main.html';
proc univariate data=Billings plots;
    var Hours;
run;
ODS HTML CLOSE;
```

How did the browser know what to do when you clicked the "Extreme Observations" label? The answer is hyperlinks and anchors. When SAS builds the table of contents file, it uses HTML anchor tags <A> and </A> and embeds links to the body page using the HREF= parameter. If you look at Output 3.17, you will see a series of anchor tags in the HTML code for the table of contents. Each anchor tag contains an HREF= that points to a location in the body file.

Looking more closely at the anchor tag for the "Extreme Observations" label in the table of contents, you can see that it points to the HREF "body.html#IDX4." Also notice the TARGET= parameter. This tells the browser where to display the linked information (in this case, in the frame called "body"). What's the "#IDX4" about? This is how the browser knows to jump to the part of the body file that contains the extreme observations. SAS has seeded the body file with a numbered series of anchors, one before each table in the file. The table of contents file uses these numbered anchor names to enable the links to go to the right part of the file.

Output 3.18 shows a portion of the body file to show how this works. In this case, the HTML for the output itself has been deleted so you can see the anchor tags. SAS has inserted a pair of anchor tags before each output object in the results. Looking at the anchor tag that comes right before the extreme observations results, you can see that it is named "IDX4." So if the table of contents links to "body.html#IDX4," the browser knows to display the body file and to scroll down to the anchor named "IDX4." (By the way, the " " between the anchor tags just creates a single nonbreaking space. Anchor tags have to be wrapped around something, but you don't want an extra bit of text displayed in the browser, so SAS uses a blank space.)

To learn more about HTML, visit your local library, which will likely have a number of books on the subject. In addition, searching the Internet for "HTML tutorials" should turn up a number of sites that offer online or downloadable tutorials.

**Output 3.16**

| Table of Contents | Extreme Observations | | | |
|---|---|---|---|---|
| | Lowest | | Highest | |
| 1. The Univariate Procedure | Value | Obs | Value | Obs |
| ·Hours | 1 | 475 | 11 | 284 |
| ·Moments | 1 | 469 | 11 | 353 |
| ·Basic Measures of Location and Variability | 1 | 466 | 11 | 400 |
| ·Tests For Location | 1 | 426 | 11 | 423 |
| ·Quantiles | 1 | 334 | 11 | 445 |
| ·Extreme Observations | | | | |
| ·Plots | Stem Leaf | | | |

**Output 3.17**

```
<HTML>
<HEAD>
<TITLE>SAS Output Table of Contents</TITLE>
</HEAD>
<BODY>
Table of Contents<HR size=3>
The Univariate Procedure<br>Hours<br>
<A HREF="body_links.html#IDX" TARGET="body">Moments</a><br>
<A HREF="body_links.html#IDX1" TARGET="body">Basic Measures of Location and Vari-
ability</a>
<A HREF="body_links.html#IDX2" TARGET="body">Tests For Location</a>
<A HREF="body_links.html#IDX3" TARGET="body">Quantiles</a>
<A HREF="body_links.html#IDX4" TARGET="body">Extreme Observations</a>
<A HREF="body_links.html#IDX5" TARGET="body">Plots</a><br>
</BODY>
</HTML>
```

**Output 3.18**

```
(heading tags and body tag go here)
<A NAME="IDX"> </A>
(code for displaying moments goes here)
<A NAME="IDX1"> </A>
(code for displaying basic measures goes here)
<A NAME="IDX2"> </A>
(code for displaying tests for location goes here)
<A NAME="IDX3"> </A>
(code for displaying quantiles goes here)
<A NAME="IDX4"> </A>
(code for displaying extreme observations goes here)
<A NAME="IDX5"> </A>
(code for displaying plots and ending body and html tags go here)
```

## Using Links and Anchors to Link Your Results to Your Web Site

By default, SAS creates anchor tag names starting with IDX and then adds a number after each subsequent tag. This is nice because the structure and crosslinks are set up with no effort required by the programmer. In addition, this behavior is predictable, so you can take advantage of it to integrate your output into a Web site.

For example, let's say you want to add the PROC UNIVARIATE output from the previous example to a Web site that contains other information about billing policies and hours. Figure 3.1 shows this Web page. Our company, the fictitious Computer Consulting Corporation, has this page already set up. It has links to other files for policies and forms.

One way to add our PROC UNIVARIATE output from the previous example would be to link to the frame file. Then we'd have to show the whole page, with a table of contents and a body. It would be better to just add a couple of links to our existing page, pointing only to the relevant parts of the report. For example, we could have a Web page such as the one in Figure 3.2, which has a new section titled "Reports," and links to two parts of the SAS results.

This is very easy to do. First, you need to run the SAS code to generate a body file. Even if you don't specify a table of contents, SAS will put anchor tags using the "IDX" naming convention in your output.

```
ODS HTML BODY='body.html';
proc univariate data=Billings plots;
    var Hours;
run;
ODS HTML CLOSE;
```

Then, after creating the HTML file, all you have to do is upload it to your Web site and add two new links to the HTML code for your existing Web page. To add a hyperlink to the descriptive statistics at the top of the univariate output, add the following HTML code to your file:

```
<a href="http://www.compconscorp.com/billing/body.html#idx">
Descriptive statistics</a>
```

This code assumes that you've uploaded the "body.html" file you created to your Web site, and placed it in the directory "billing." This code will be displayed in the Web browser as the text "Descriptive statistics," and when you click on it, your SAS output will be displayed, showing the Moments section at the top of the output.

To add the hyperlink to the extreme observations, the code is similar:

```
<a href="http://www.compconscorp.com/billing/body.html#idx4">
Extremes</a>
```

In this case, we knew that the anchors were called "IDX" and "IDX4" because we'd been looking at the HTML code, but you can figure out the anchor names without looking at the HTML. Just count the output objects. For example, if you want to link to the third object, the anchor will be "IDX2." In this case, we wanted the first and fifth objects, so the anchors were "IDX" and "IDX4."

**Figure 3.1**

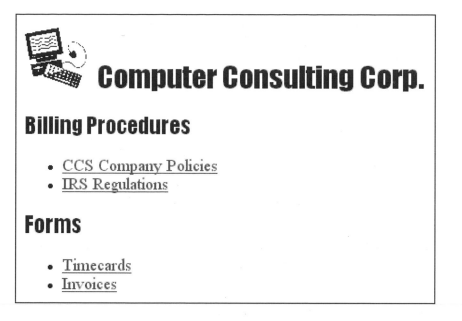

**Figure 3.2**

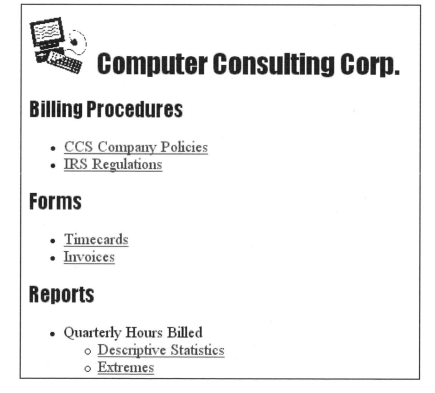

## Adding HTML Code to Customize Your Output

The previous examples in this chapter have introduced the basics of HTML tags. You may find yourself asking: why bother learning HTML tags when SAS can create them for you? The reason is that you can use your knowledge of HTML tags to add tags to your code to enhance your output. Moreover, you don't have to edit the HTML file to do so. You can use SAS to insert the extra tags when the HTML output is created.

As an example, we'll modify the simple output shown in Output 3.19. Notice how both the title and footnote are shown in the same font size. Also, notice how all of the column headings are the same size and color. It would be nice for the title to be large and the footnote small and unobtrusive. It would also be nice to do something to the column heading for overtime hours to call attention to this important data.

The following code inserts HTML tags into the title, footnote, and label statements to change the font appearance in each location. SAS will take these tags and pass them along to the output file, where they can be interpreted by a browser.

Unfortunately, SAS will also pass the tags along to the other output destinations, where they will appear in your title and footnote. This technique works only with the HTML destination, so you will want to close any other open destinations when using this technique. See Chapter 10, "Modifying Output Fonts," for discussion of how to use the TEMPLATE procedure to modify these fonts and colors for all destinations by changing the style definition.

Three pairs of tags have been added. First, the <H1> and </H1> tags are used to assign the title to heading style 1. This style requests the largest heading available from the browser. The second pair of tags <FONT SIZE=2> and </FONT> specify a much smaller font for the text in the footnote. Finally, the third pair of tags <I> and </I> specify italics for the hours column heading.

```
ODS HTML BODY='overtime2.html';
title '<H1>Employees Billing Overtime</H1>';
footnote '<FONT SIZE=2>Overtime defined as >10 hours</FONT>';
proc print data=Billings noobs label;
   where Hours>8;
   label Hours='<I>Overtime Hours</I>';
   var WorkDate JobType Hours;
run;
ODS HTML CLOSE;
```

The results are shown in Output 3.20. This is just a simple example. There are dozens of HTML tags you could use to tweak the appearance of your output.

Another way to add HTML formatting to your titles and footnotes is to use the new LINK=, FONT=, COLOR=, HEIGHT=, BOLD, ITALIC, and JUST= options available for the TITLE and FOOTNOTE statements. ODS will build the HTML code for you when you use these options. However, there are some limitations. You cannot use the built-in heading styles like <H1>, and the LINK= option turns the entire title or footnote into a hyperlink. Custom HTML tags give you total control.

**Output 3.19**

## Jobs Billing Overtime

| Date Work Completed | Job Type | Overtime Hours |
|---|---|---|
| 01/02/2001 | Consulting | 8.5 |
| 01/05/2001 | Consulting | 11.0 |
| 01/06/2001 | In-house | 10.0 |
| 01/12/2001 | Consulting | 10.0 |
| 01/14/2001 | Consulting | 9.5 |
| 01/19/2001 | Consulting | 9.5 |

*Overtime defined as >10 hours*

**Output 3.20**

## Employees Billing Overtime

| Date Work Completed | Job Type | Overtime Hours |
|---|---|---|
| 01/02/2001 | Consulting | 8.5 |
| 01/05/2001 | Consulting | 11.0 |
| 01/06/2001 | In-house | 10.0 |
| 01/12/2001 | Consulting | 10.0 |
| 01/14/2001 | Consulting | 9.5 |
| 01/19/2001 | Consulting | 9.5 |

*Overtime defined as >10 hours*

## Importing Your HTML Output into a Spreadsheet

Because the Internet has become so pervasive in our lives, HTML is becoming a widely accepted file format. This means that if you create HTML output from your SAS program, you can probably read it in to any other software you care to use. For example, you can take your HTML output and import it into a spreadsheet program. Because ODS HTML output is largely composed of tables, with rows and columns, a spreadsheet can easily interpret the results and format them properly.

The code below creates an HTML file with a quarterly report on hours. By creating it in HTML, it can be displayed on the corporate intranet for managers to review. Alternatively, it can be e-mailed to appropriate managers, who can easily view it in a browser. However, by importing it into a spreadsheet, you can also perform further manipulations and calculations.

```
ODS HTML BODY='avghours.html';
title 'Average Hours Billed';
proc report data=Billings nowd;
   column Month JobType Hours;
   define Month / group order=internal;
   define JobType / group;
   define Hours / analysis mean format=10.1;
run;
ODS HTML CLOSE;
```

To import the file into a spreadsheet, simply open the spreadsheet program, and open the HTML file "avghours.html" directly. Then save the file as a spreadsheet. Output 3.21 shows what you get if you open the file in Microsoft Excel and then save it as "avghours.xls." You get a spreadsheet that looks almost exactly like the HTML version.

You can now easily edit this Excel spreadsheet. The HTML table has been converted to Excel rows and columns, which means you can use Excel to do further computations. You can also add your results to an existing spreadsheet. This is helpful if you're combining results from a number of sources. You can import your HTML results into a spreadsheet by cutting and pasting from the browser window to the spreadsheet.

Using this technique, your spreadsheet will end up looking something like Output 3.22. The table itself retains the colors and styles of the HTML version, but the rest of the document is unaffected. However, the table row and column widths are not adjusted properly to fit your SAS output. If you use this technique, you will find that you have to adjust column widths. In Excel, you can do this easily by selecting the entire worksheet and then selecting Format/Column/Auto-fit from the menu bar.

However, with Excel, you may find that it is less work to simply import the entire file so that the columns are correct. If you need to add your SAS output to an existing spreadsheet file, the cut-and-paste technique will probably work better for you.

Another way to move your SAS output to Excel is to use the new CSV output destination. This was an experimental destination as of Release 8.2. The syntax is "ODS CSV FILE='myfile.csv';" (followed by "ODS CSV CLOSE;").

**Output 3.21**

| | A | B | C | D |
|---|---|---|---|---|
| 1 | | | | |
| 2 | *Average Hours Billed* | | | |
| 3 | | | | |
| 4 | **Month** | **Job Type** | **Hours Worked** | |
| 5 | January | Consulting | 6.6 | |
| 6 | | Contract | 6.1 | |
| 7 | | In-house | 5.5 | |
| 8 | February | Consulting | 7.8 | |
| 9 | | Contract | 4.8 | |
| 10 | | In-house | 6 | |
| 11 | March | Consulting | 5.5 | |
| 12 | | Contract | 6.8 | |
| 13 | | In-house | 4.9 | |

avghours

Ready                                         NUM

**Output 3.22**

| | A | B | C | D | E | F | G | H |
|---|---|---|---|---|---|---|---|---|
| 1 | Average Hours Billed | | | | | | | |
| 2 | | | | | | | | |
| 3 | Month | Job Type | Hours Worked | | | | | |
| 4 | January | Consulting | 6.6 | | | | | |
| 5 | | Contract | 6.1 | | | | | |
| 6 | | In-house | 5.5 | | | | | |
| 7 | February | Consulting | 7.8 | | | | | |
| 8 | | Contract | 4.8 | | | | | |

Sheet1 / Sheet2 / Sheet3

TIP

This example uses the default HTML output to create a spreadsheet. You may find that you get better results by switching to the Minimal style definition. For more information on switching style definitions, see Chapter 9, "Style Definitions."

## Importing Your HTML Output into a Slide Show

There are dozens of applications that can import HTML files. We'll go over just one more. However, you should take the time to explore the tools you normally use to present results to see which ones can use HTML files.

This example will show how to add your SAS results to a PowerPoint slide show. This is a great way to present your results at a meeting. Instead of passing out a report, you can show the results in full color on screen.

The code below creates an HTML file with a complicated regression analysis. You could send out these results via e-mail, or create RTF output to annotate in a word processor and hand it out as a summary report. However, it's also helpful to be able to explain complex results using a series of slides.

```
ODS HTML BODY='logistic.html';
title 'Logistic Regression Analysis: Overtime Hours';
proc logistic data=Billings;
   class JobType Division;
    model Overtime=JobType Division;
run;
ODS HTML CLOSE;
```

To import the file into a slide show, you could simply open PowerPoint and open the HTML file "logistic.html" directly. Then you can save the file as a PowerPoint presentation. As you can see in Output 3.23, you get a single slide with lots of tiny tables from the HTML output.

At this point, you need to cut and paste each table to its own slide, and then resize the tables so that they can be read. Once you've resized the tables, you'll find that you also need to resize all of the fonts. This ends up being a lot of work.

A better approach for moving HTML results to PowerPoint is to cut and paste directly from the browser window. To do this, first open PowerPoint and create a new slide show. You can select a theme and slide design if you like. Then open the "logistic.html" in a browser, select each table in the output one at a time, and copy and paste it into its own slide.

Using this technique, your presentation will look something like Output 3.24. In this example, a theme was chosen to add graphics and coordinating fonts. A title was typed into the heading of the slide. The HTML table was then pasted onto the slide. Finally, a space was created to add an explanation below the table. The table itself retains the colors and styles of the HTML version, but the rest of the document is controlled by PowerPoint.

To bring in the rest of the results, simply insert a new slide after the first one and copy and paste the next table from the browser. This ends up being more work than creating a word processor document or spreadsheet from your results, but the product is spectacular.

Another option for creating a slide show is to create RTF output and then import it into PowerPoint. See the next chapter for details.

**Output 3.23**

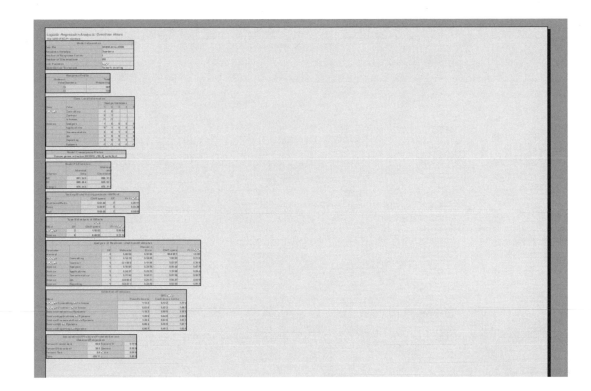

**Output 3.24**

# Logistic Regression Results

| Model Information | |
|---|---|
| Data Set | WORK.BILLINGS |
| Response Variable | Overtime |
| Number of Response Levels | 2 |
| Number of Observations | 500 |
| Link Function | Logit |
| Optimization Technique | Fisher's scoring |

Explanation of the model and data can be added here.

# Chapter 4

## RTF Output

---

HTML files via the Web are one common way to share your results with other users. After all, almost everyone you need to reach has a Web browser. However, there's another piece of software your users have in common: the word processor.

Whether they use WordPerfect, Word, or some other tool, virtually all word processors can import rich text format (RTF) files. Now ODS can create RTF output.

This output has all of the colors and formatting you've just seen in the previous chapter. Moreover, in some ways, RTF output is even better. Word processors give you even more control of the structure and appearance of tables than HTML, and ODS takes full advantage.

This is a very short chapter, as the syntax for ODS RTF output is very simple. Look for additional features to be rolled out in new releases.

## Creating Your First RTF File

The best thing about creating RTF output is that you only have to learn one new piece of syntax: just change the keyword HTML to RTF in your ODS statement. It only takes a single simple command to begin creating an RTF file:

```
ODS RTF FILE='myfile.rtf';
```

Just as with the ODS HTML statement, you can list a literal filename, or use a fileref to refer to a previously defined filename.

Next, you insert your procedure or DATA step to create some output. Finally, you close the RTF file with the following:

```
ODS RTF CLOSE;
```

To show how this works, we'll create a simple report using PROC MEANS. The code looks like this:

```
ODS RTF FILE='payroll.rtf';
title 'Payroll Report';
proc means data=hr nonobs maxdec=0 mean sum;
   class Department;
   var AnnualSalary;
run;
ODS RTF CLOSE;
```

The resulting RTF file can be opened using your favorite word processor. Output 4.1 shows what the file looks like if you open it with Microsoft Word. The RTF output looks similar to the HTML output, but more refined. The table borders are hidden, and only the table header is shaded. This is the default style definition for RTF output. Chapter 9, "Style Definitions," will cover how to change the style definition of your output.

Once the output is opened in a word processor, you can manipulate the output just like any other document. You can change the typeface or font size, use different colors or borders for the table, apply heading formats to the titles, or add explanatory text. In Word, you can also use the Table AutoFormat tool to create elaborate table designs.

How is all this accomplished? The RTF file contains not just the information in your results, but also a variety of complex formatting information. Output 4.2 shows a bit of the RTF file for this example, to give you a taste of how the files look. Unlike the HTML files in the previous chapter, this file is not easily understood (except by word processors). For that reason, we will not go into the details of RTF files.

**Output 4.1**

**Payroll Report**

| Analysis Variable : AnnualSalary Annual Salary | | |
| --- | --- | --- |
| **Department** | **Mean** | **Sum** |
| Administration | 42053 | 2943719 |
| Marketing | 44055 | 3171981 |
| R&D | 44141 | 2295319 |
| Manufacturing | 42384 | 8603897 |

**Output 4.2**

```
{\rtf1\ansi\ansicpg1252\uc1\deff0\deflang1033\deflangfe1033
{\fonttbl
{\f1\froman\fprq2\fcharset0 Times;}
}{\colortbl;\red0\green0\blue0;\red0\green0\blue255;\red0\green255\blue255;\red0\green
255\blue0;\red255\green0\blue255;\red255\green0\blue0;\red255\green255\blue0;\red255\
green255\blue255;
\red0\green0\blue128;\red0\green128\blue128;\red0\green128\blue0;\red128\green0\blue128;
\red128\green0\blue0;\red128\green128\blue0;\red128\green128\blue128;\red192\green192\
blue192;
}{\stylesheet{\widctlpar\adjustright\fs20\cgrid\snext0 Normal;}{\*\cs10\additive Default
Paragraph Font;}
}{\info{\title V8 SAS System Output}{\author SAS Version 8}{\operator SAS Version
8}{\version1}{\creatim\yr2000\mo6\dy27\hr7\min23\sec37}}
\widowctrl\ftnbj\aenddoc\formshade\viewkind1\viewscale75\pgbrdrhead\pgbrdrfoot\fet0\paperw115
19\paperh15023\margl360\margr360\margt360\margb360
\sectd\linex0\endnhere\headery720\footery720\marglsxn360\margrsxn360\margtsxn360\margbsxn360
```

*(... remaining RTF code trimmed to save space ...)*

## Importing Your RTF File into a Word Processor

There's not much to importing your file into a word processor. If you're on a Windows platform, you can just double-click on the file and it should open up in your default word processor. Alternatively, you can open the word processor first, and then open the RTF file from there.

If you are using Microsoft Word, select **File** and then **Open** from the menu bar. This will bring up a dialog box where you can specify RTF format and the name of your file. The dialog box is shown below, and the resulting Word document is shown on the previous page in Output 4.1.

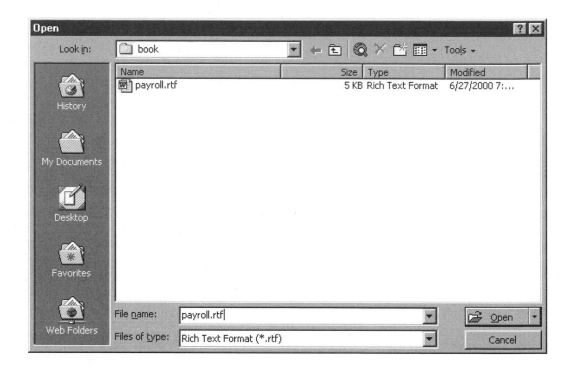

If you are using WordPerfect or StarOffice, the process is the same. You select **File** and then **Open**, choose RTF as your file type, and then type the name of the file. Output 4.3 shows how the RTF file looks in WordPerfect. Output 4.4 shows the same file in StarOffice.

ODS RTF output is designed to be compatible with Word 97 and later versions (though some features may work better in Word 2000). You can import RTF output into an earlier word processor, but results may vary somewhat. If you're on a non-Windows platform, you may need to adjust some option settings when you create the RTF file, and you may need to copy the file over to another computer in order to use your word processor. See Appendix 2, "Operating System Differences," for information on other operating systems.

**Output 4.3   RTF Output Imported into WordPerfect**

**Output 4.4   RTF Output Imported into StarOffice**

## Working with Headers and Footers in Microsoft Word

The previous samples of output from Microsoft Word show the document in print preview mode. This was done so that you could see how the titles would appear in a printed Word document. However, this is not what you see when you first open an ODS RTF file in Word.

When you first open an RTF document, you will see it in normal view or page layout view (depending on your default settings). In this view, you may be surprised by how faint the titles and footnotes look. Instead of the bold fonts you were expecting, you see pale gray fonts.

The RTF file from our previous examples is shown in Output 4.5, where you can see that the titles are barely visible. This is because Word takes your titles and footnotes and turns them into page headings and footers, which are displayed in a grayed out font in on the screen. To see them properly, you have to do a print preview, or switch to headers and footers view, as shown in Output 4.6.

Because ODS creates RTF files that specify your titles and footnotes as headers and footers, they will get converted to page headings and page footers in most word processors and may not look correct on screen. But rest assured, your document will print correctly.

If you would prefer that the titles and footnotes not be put in the header and footer, you can use the BODYTITLE option to force them into the body of the document. The syntax is

```
ODS RTF FILE='filename' BODYTITLE;
```

Output 4.7 shows the resulting RTF file. The only difference between the results shown in Output 4.7 and the previous version shown in Output 4.5 is that now the heading is part of the main document and can be edited without switching to a different view.

**Output 4.5   RTF Output with Title in Header**

**Output 4.6**

**Output 4.7   RTF Output with Title in Body**

## Handling Page Breaks in RTF Output

In order for ODS to figure out how to fit your SAS output onto a word processor page, ODS assumes that you will be using a standard page size of 8½ by 11 inches. Then, ODS uses this page width to determine how much information will fit in each *row* of your table. This ensures that your tables will not be too wide for the page. If a table will not fit the page width, ODS will break up the table and wrap the output. For example, the following code produces the output shown in Output 4.8.

```
ODS RTF FILE='SalaryWide.rtf';
title 'Salary Report';
proc freq data=hr;
   format AnnualSalary salft.;
   tables Department*AnnualSalary / norow nocol nopct;
run;
ODS RTF CLOSE;
```

Notice how this frequency table is broken into smaller tables so that it will fit in the page width. The first two tables are shown. Actually, it took four smaller tables to hold all of the salary ranges. ODS makes sure that your output will fit on a standard page width. However, ODS does not worry about the *length* of your output when creating RTF files. ODS hands off this responsibility to your word processor. If a table is too long to fit on the page, it is up to your word processor to break the table and to repeat the column headers on the next page.

The following code illustrates how this works. The FREQ procedure produces a tall table that will not fit on a single page. Output 4.9 shows how Microsoft Word has handled the table, breaking it into two parts and repeating the headers.

```
ODS RTF FILE='SalaryTall.rtf';
title 'Salary Report';
proc freq data=hr;
   tables AnnualSalary / nopct nocum;
run;
ODS RTF CLOSE;
```

Why does ODS handle output width and height problems differently? The answer is that solving the height problem is much more problematic. If ODS used the standard page height, but you added a header or edited your text to insert a note in your Word document, your output would no longer fit on the page and would break awkwardly.

By turning over responsibility for handling page breaks to the word processor, ODS assures that headers and footers will be taken into account when the decision is made about where to break the long tables in your output.

However, because ODS does not worry about page breaks in RTF output, this means that procedures that produce page totals might not put them at the bottom of the physical page. Also, the TABULATE procedure will not place a "Continued" label at the bottom of a page when the table is split onto two pages.

**Output 4.8**      *Salary Report*

| Table of Department by AnnualSalary | | | | | |
|---|---|---|---|---|---|
| **Department(Department)** | **AnnualSalary(Annual Salary)** | | | | |
| **Frequency** | **<$35,000** | **$35,000-$39,999** | **$40,000-$44,999** | **$45,000-$49,999** | **$50,000-$54,999** |
| Administration | 41 | 7 | 3 | 4 | 1 |
| Marketing | 45 | 3 | 3 | 1 | 3 |
| R&D | 31 | 5 | 1 | 3 | 2 |
| Manufacturing | 122 | 14 | 8 | 5 | 9 |
| Total | 239 | 29 | 15 | 13 | 15 |

| Table of Department by AnnualSalary | | | | | |
|---|---|---|---|---|---|
| **Department(Department)** | **AnnualSalary(Annual Salary)** | | | | |
| **Frequency** | **$55,000-$59,999** | **$60,000-$64,999** | **$65,000-$69,999** | **$70,000-$74,999** | **$75,000-$79,999** |
| Administration | 2 | 4 | 1 | 1 | 1 |
| Marketing | 0 | 1 | 3 | 2 | 1 |
| R&D | 0 | 1 | 1 | 3 | 0 |
| Manufacturing | 10 | 3 | 11 | 1 | 3 |
| Total | 12 | 9 | 16 | 7 | 5 |

**Output 4.9**                               *Salary Report*

| | |
|---|---|
| $45,000 | 4 |
| $45,500 | 2 |
| $46,000 | 2 |
| $47,000 | 1 |
| $47,500 | 1 |
| $48,000 | 1 |
| $49,500 | 2 |

| Annual Salary | |
|---|---|
| **AnnualSalary** | **Frequency** |
| $50,000 | 2 |
| $50,500 | 1 |
| $51,000 | 2 |
| $51,500 | 1 |
| $52,000 | 2 |

The bottom of the first page          The top of the second page

## Importing RTF Output into a Slide Show

The previous chapter showed how to import HTML output into a PowerPoint slide show. You can also use RTF output in this way. You may want to experiment with both to see which works better for you.

There are two ways you can get RTF output into PowerPoint. The first way is to open PowerPoint, and then open your RTF file directly. However, if you try this, you will discover that PowerPoint is not very good at reading RTF files. It will pull in your information, but it creates a slide for each title and a slide for each row in the table. You have to do a lot of editing if you use this approach.

The second, and better, way to import your RTF results into PowerPoint is to first open the RTF file in a word processor. Then select all of the output you want on the first slide, and copy and paste it onto a blank slide in PowerPoint. This way your output is recognized as a table by Power-Point.

Output 4.10 shows what RTF output looks like when it is first pasted into PowerPoint. The table structure is intact, but the table is too small for the slide, and it's not centered. To fix this, you need to drag the table to the center of the slide. Make sure you select the entire table when you move it. If you are not careful, you may select only the text in one of the table cells.

Once you have the table where you want it, and while it's still selected, you can resize it to fit your slide. In this example, the table is small and narrow, and needs to be resized so that it is larger and wider.

Depending on which word processor and which version of PowerPoint you are using, this may re-size the entire table, or it may resize just the table grid but not the text inside. You might find that you need to increase the font size to fit the table.

To fix the fonts, keep the entire table selected, and then use the toolbar button  to increase the font size. This will increase all of the fonts proportionately.

After you've centered and resized the table, as in Output 4.11, your results should look just like they did in your word processor. If you want, you can take the reformatting further, by using a design template to change the background or by applying a new slide layout.

Make sure you use a blank slide for pasting in your RTF output. Otherwise PowerPoint will add text boxes for the title and contents of the slide, which will get in your way as you reformat your SAS output. Once you have the SAS output set up the way you want, it's easy to add a text box for a title or explanatory text.

**Output 4.10**

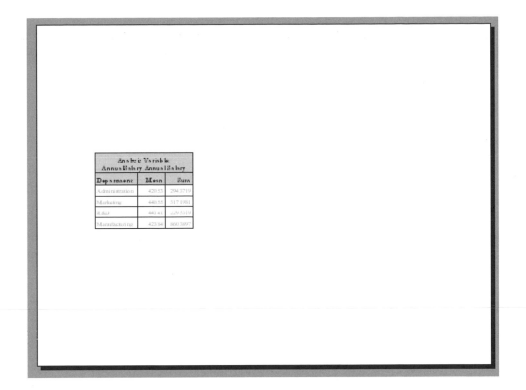

**Output 4.11**

# Payroll Status Report

| Analysis Variable: AnnualSalary Annual Salary | | |
|---|---|---|
| **Department** | **Mean** | **Sum** |
| Administration | 42053 | 2943719 |
| Marketing | 44055 | 3171981 |
| R&D | 44141 | 2295319 |
| Manufacturing | 42384 | 8603897 |

# *Printer Output*

The previous two chapters focused on ODS output formats that can be displayed and edited electronically. If we all worked in the so-called paperless office of the future, we wouldn't need any other output formats.

However, in the real world, most of us still deliver a large percentage of our results on old-fashioned paper. If you have no need to manipulate your output before it is delivered, the fastest way to get your SAS results to your customers is to send the output directly to a printer.

ODS printer output allows you to create attractive black and white or color output. This output has many of the features of HTML output but with proper page breaks. The tables and fonts look just as good as the RTF output, but you don't need to open up a word processor to view the output. You can print it automatically, or create a PostScript, PCL, or PDF file to print later.

However, there are some issues to keep in mind with ODS printer output. While PostScript and PCL are standard file formats, printer definitions and commands vary widely across operating systems. If you're not in a Windows environment, you may have to invest a little time to learn how best to handle ODS printer output on your system. This chapter covers some of the operating system differences. Appendix 2, "Operating System Differences," goes into further detail.

## Sending ODS Output to Your Printer

Creating ODS printer output is even easier than creating RTF output. If you want to send your output directly to your default printer from Windows, all you need is the following code:

```
ODS PRINTER;
title 'Monthly Complaint Summary';
proc freq data=complaints;
    tables location*outcome / norow nocol nopct;
run;
ODS PRINTER CLOSE;
```

The first ODS statement starts routing output to your SAS default printer. The second ODS statement ends the file and submits the print job. If you forget the second ODS statement, your file will not print until you end your SAS session.

The standard listing output for this code is shown in Output 5.1. It's a basic crosstab of two variables. The listing output is adequate, but it has some problems. For example, notice how the column labels for several of the categories are broken into two lines in an ugly fashion. Contrast the listing output with the printer output shown in Output 5.2. It has exactly the same information, but it's much more inviting. In addition, notice that the column widths have been adjusted so that none of the words break. ODS is quite an improvement.

In terms of readability, printer output is probably your best option among the ODS destinations. Though the appearance of your output will vary somewhat depending on your printer, you can be assured that it will fit on the page (unlike RTF and HTML, which are prone to awkward page breaks).

However, printer output has some drawbacks. First, you can't edit your results. Unless you're creating PDF output (see the example later in this chapter), you will not be able to change the printed page or the print file. Second, if you are not in a Windows environment, sending output directly to a printer isn't quite as easy as in this example. Information on other operating systems is covered briefly in this chapter and in more detail in Appendix 2, "Operating System Differences."

Actually, the statement that ODS PRINTER sends output to your default printer is not strictly true. ODS first checks your option settings. On Windows, ODS checks the SYSPRINT= option to see if a printer is specified. On other systems, ODS checks the PRINTERPATH= option. Only if these options are not set does SAS use your default printer.

If you use a network printer, you need to be careful about submitting ODS PRINTER commands like this. If you make a mistake in your code, you could inadvertently send hundreds of pages to the printer. See the examples later in this chapter on creating an output file instead.

**Output 5.1**

```
Monthly Complaint Summary

The FREQ Procedure

Table of Location by Complaint

Location(Store Location)      Complaint(Complaint Category)
```

| Frequency | Damaged | Not Delivered | Wrong Product | Not Satisfied | Salesperson | Price | Total |
|---|---|---|---|---|---|---|---|
| New York | 28 | 31 | 33 | 37 | 34 | 33 | 196 |
| Boston | 48 | 44 | 51 | 49 | 43 | 45 | 280 |
| Washington, D.C. | 10 | 19 | 25 | 26 | 8 | 18 | 106 |
| Total | 86 | 94 | 109 | 112 | 85 | 96 | 582 |

**Output 5.2**   *Monthly Complaint Summary*

| Frequency | Table of Location by Complaint | | | | | | |
|---|---|---|---|---|---|---|---|
| | | Complaint(Complaint Category) | | | | | |
| | Location(Store Location) | Damaged | Not Delivered | Wrong Product | Not Satisfied | Salesperson | Price | Total |
| | New York | 28 | 31 | 33 | 37 | 34 | 33 | 196 |
| | Boston | 48 | 44 | 51 | 49 | 43 | 45 | 280 |
| | Washington, D.C. | 10 | 19 | 25 | 26 | 8 | 18 | 106 |
| | Total | 86 | 94 | 109 | 112 | 85 | 96 | 582 |

## Selecting a Printer

The previous example showed how to send output to your default printer. You could send your output to a different printer by closing SAS, changing the default printer, and launching SAS again. However, there is an easier way to switch printers: the PRINTER= option.

This option is used on the first ODS PRINTER statement:

**ODS PRINTER PRINTER=*printername*;**

The value you fill in for "printername" is the name assigned to the printer you want to use. This can be a local printer or a network printer, or it could even be a file on disk.

You can find out the names of all your available printers by selecting **File** and then **Print** from within SAS. This will open up the print dialog box, which has a list of all the available printer names in a pull-down menu at the top. An example is shown in Output 5.3. In this example, if you wanted to send output to the highlighted printer, the syntax would be

**ODS PRINTER PRINTER="Lexmark 3200 Series ColorFine";**

You can take advantage of the PRINTER= option to send your printer output to more than one printer within the same job. For example, if you have a summary report you want to send to a high-quality color printer, and a long detailed report you want to send to a line printer, you can use two PRINTER= statements.

```
title 'Complaint Resolution Summary';
ODS PRINTER PRINTER="FancyColorPrinter;"
proc freq data=Complaints;
   tables Outcome / nocum;
run;
ODS PRINTER CLOSE;

title 'Complaint Resolution Detail';
ODS PRINTER PRINTER="LinePrinter";
proc print data=Complaints noobs label;
   var complaint outcome;
run;
ODS PRINTER CLOSE;
```

In this example, the output is sent to two printers. One is called "FancyColorPrinter" and the other is called "LinePrinter." Once you learn the names of your printers, it's easy to send your output exactly where you want.

**Output 5.3**

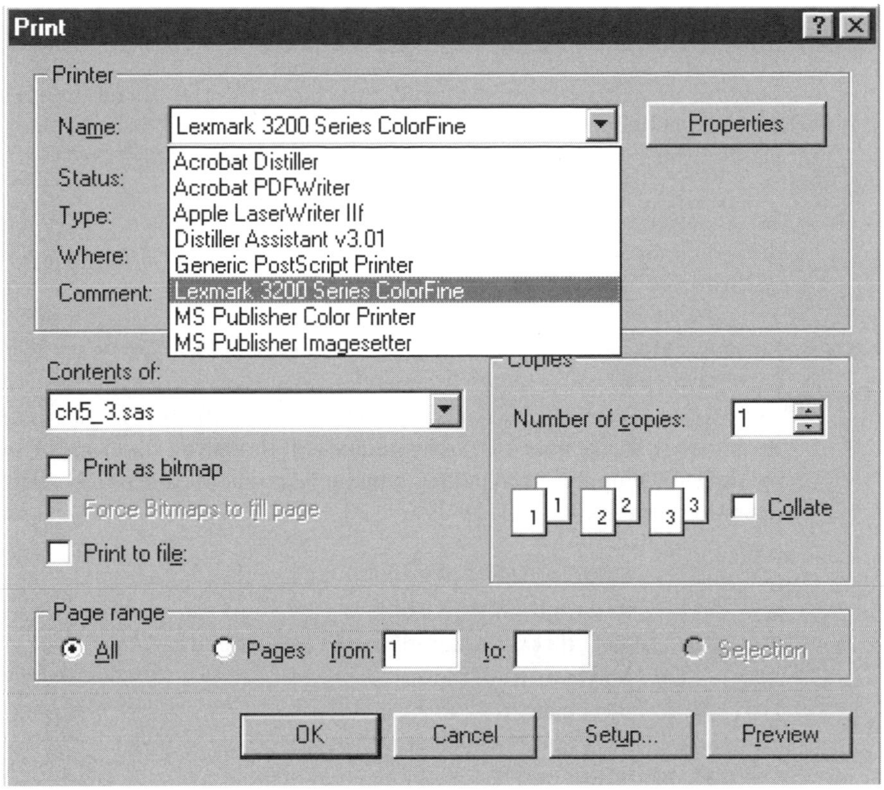
Print
Printer
Name:
Lexmark 3200 Series ColorFine
Properties
Status:
Type:
Where:
Comment:
Acrobat Distiller
Acrobat PDFWriter
Apple LaserWriter IIf
Distiller Assistant v3.01
Generic PostScript Printer
Lexmark 3200 Series ColorFine
MS Publisher Color Printer
MS Publisher Imagesetter
Contents of:
ch5_3.sas
Print as bitmap
Force Bitmaps to fill page
Print to file:
Copies
Number of copies:
1
Collate
Page range
All
Pages
from:
1
to:
Selection
OK
Cancel
Setup...
Preview

## Creating a File from Your ODS Printer Output

Sending output straight to your printer can be handy, but then the information is lost. If you want the same output again, you have to rerun the SAS program that created it. In addition, you may not have a printer available at the time you run your code.

To create a more permanent version of your output, you can ask ODS to create a file that you can then print at your convenience. The syntax for this is to add one of the following options to your ODS PRINTER statement.

> **FILE=fileref**    or    **FILE=file-specification**

Either option tells ODS to send your output to a specific file instead of the default printer. The following code shows how this works. It creates a PostScript file from a simple PROC PRINT. This example is set up for the Windows environment. The file naming convention will vary by operating system.

```
ODS PRINTER FILE='DamagedCD.ps';
title 'Damaged CDs Report';
proc print data=DamagedCDs label noobs;
   id location;
   var outcome;
run;
ODS PRINTER CLOSE;
```

If you print the file "DamagedCD.ps," you will get the output shown in Output 5.4. The technique for printing this file varies by operating system. See Appendix 2, "Operating System Differences," for information about your system.

This example covered how to create PostScript files. You also have the option of creating Printer Control Language (.pcl) files, if that is what your printer requires. Unless you have a very old printer, it is unlikely that it will have any difficulty with PostScript files, but check your owner's manual if you have problems printing. To get a PCL file, use an ODS PCL statement instead of ODS PRINTER. ODS currently supports PCL1 through PCL5. See SAS OnlineDoc for details on this option.

If you have problems printing the resulting PostScript file, see the example on the following page that uses the POSTSCRIPT option.

Don't forget to issue the ODS PRINTER CLOSE command. If you forget this command, your PostScript or PCL file will remain open and you will be unable to send it to a printer.

**Output 5.4**

## *Damaged CDs  Report*

| Store Location | Outcome of Complaint |
|---|---|
| New York | Apology |
| New  York | Apology |
| New York | Refund |
| New York | Apology |
| Boston | Refund |
| Boston | Unresolved |
| Boston | Refund |
| Boston | Refund |
| Boston | Apology |
| Boston | Apology |
| Boston | Refund |
| Boston | Apology |
| Boston | Apology |
| Boston | Unresolved |
| Washington, D.C. | Refund |
| Washington, D.C. | Apology |

## Using the SAS Printer Drivers

In Windows, when you send output to your default printer or specify another printer to use, ODS uses the driver for that printer to generate your output. This means that your output will vary slightly depending on which printer you select.

On all other operating systems, ODS uses SAS-supplied printer drivers to generate output. If you'd like your SAS output to be generated the same way on all operating systems, you can add the SAS option to your ODS PRINTER statement when running SAS on Windows. This statement has no effect on other operating systems.

```
ODS PRINTER SAS;
```

If you don't want to use the SAS printer drivers, you can choose the opposite option setting: HOST. The default option setting of SAS or HOST is set when you first install SAS, and the setting is based on your operating system. Unless you are having problems with printer output, you probably do not want to change this setting. In Windows, it is safe to use either setting. On other systems, the HOST setting may cause ODS PRINTER to fail because no host drivers can be found.

Even if you do successfully change the setting, you are unlikely to see any noticeable difference. Output 5.5 and Output 5.6 show the results of using the HOST and SAS options. Except for minor margin differences, they are identical.

## Using the SAS PostScript Driver

If you're printing to PostScript printers, you have the option of using a generic PostScript driver supplied by SAS. This will create a standard PostScript file that you can print on any PostScript printer. This avoids the problem of creating a file based on your default printer at the time, and then having trouble printing it to a different make or model of PostScript printer.

To request this driver, request the POSTSCRIPT printer in your ODS PRINTER statement. Better yet, you can use the shorthand option PS or just ODS PS (dropping the PRINTER). The three following statements are equivalent.

```
ODS PRINTER SAS PRINTER=POSTSCRIPT;
ODS PRINTER PS;
ODS PS;
```

Like the SAS and HOST options, the PS option is not likely to make much of a difference. Output 5.7 shows the effect of adding the PS option to the run that produced Output 5.5. Again, there is no noticeable difference. Generally, you would only use this option if you plan to print your file on multiple printers, or if you intend to view or distill your file using a third-party software product like Adobe Acrobat or GhostScript.

```
ODS PS FILE='MySharedFile.ps';
```

On the other hand, if you're printing directly to a single printer from Windows, you'll probably get the best results by using the driver for that specific printer. In this case, you should not use the SAS or POSTSCRIPT option.

**Output 5.5  HOST Option**

## *Delivery  Failures*

| Store Location | | |
|---|---|---|
| **Location** | **Frequency** | **Percent** |
| **New York** | 31 | 32.98 |
| **Boston** | 44 | 46.81 |
| **Washington, D.C.** | 19 | 20.21 |

**Output 5.6  SAS Option**

## *Delivery Failures*

| Store Location | | |
|---|---|---|
| **Location** | **Frequency** | **Percent** |
| **New York** | 31 | 32.98 |
| **Boston** | 44 | 46.81 |
| **Washington, D.C.** | 19 | 20.21 |

**Output 5.7  POSTSCRIPT Option**

## *Delivery Failures*

| Store Location | | |
|---|---|---|
| **Location** | **Frequency** | **Percent** |
| **New York** | 31 | 32.98 |
| **Boston** | 44 | 46.81 |
| **Washington, D.C.** | 19 | 20.21 |

TIP

The PS option may be useful if you're having trouble getting your ODS printer output to print or display correctly. Sometimes your Windows printer driver may cause problems with ODS printer output. Using the generic SAS PostScript driver is one possible solution. (Checking online for an updated driver for your printer is another.)

## Printing in Color

In the chapters on HTML and RTF output, you learned that you can use ODS to generate attractive color output. You can do the same with ODS printer output. However, if you're printing to a black and white laser printer, this isn't very useful.

You use two option settings to create ODS printer output that is tailored to your printer and to the style of output you would like. You can have simple black and white "book style" output with black text, black table borders, and no shading. Alternatively, you can have output that uses color for the text, table borders, and shading. Yet another choice is to create grayscale output that looks somewhat like the full-color output but will print on a black and white printer.

By default, SAS tries to generate color output. An example of this is shown in the color version of Output 5.8 on page 282 in Appendix 3. If the printer you select is not a color printer, then you get grayscale output that imitates color. An example of this is shown in Output 5.9.

The reason you get this grayscale output is the default setting of two options. First, the system option COLORPRINTING is turned on by default. Second, the COLOR= option on the ODS PRINTER statement defaults to YES. If you don't like the output shown in Output 5.8 and Output 5.9, then you need to change one or both of these options. If you just want to turn off color printing for a particular set of results, you can use the COLOR=NO option on the ODS PRINTER statement, as follows:

```
ODS PRINTER COLOR=NO STYLE=DEFAULT;
```

Alternatively, the option can be specified as

```
ODS PRINTER NOCOLOR STYLE=DEFAULT;
```

The STYLE= option is explained in Chapter 9, "Style Definitions." It is used here to specify a style definition that uses colors to better illustrate this example. This creates the printed output shown in Output 5.10.

If you never want color output, you should turn off the system COLORPRINTING option by issuing the following command:

```
OPTIONS NOCOLORPRINTING;
```

This way you don't have to remember to add the NOCOLOR option every time you use ODS PRINTER. With this option in place, your output will look like Output 5.10 if you have specified COLOR=NO, and like Output 5.9 if you have not.

When you first try the color printing options, you may have trouble getting anything but grayscale output. That is because the default ODS style definition for printer output uses shades of gray as its colors. To see the full effect of color output, you need to switch to a different style definition. The examples on this page use the Default style definition (instead of Printer). See Chapter 9, "Style Definitions," for more information on style definitions.

**Output 5.8  COLOR=YES sent to color printer**

*Delivery Failures*

*The FREQ Procedure*

| Store Location | | |
| --- | --- | --- |
| Location | Frequency | Percent |
| New York | 31 | 32.98 |
| Boston | 44 | 46.81 |
| Washington, D.C. | 19 | 20.21 |

For a color version of Output 5.8, see page 282 in Appendix 3.

**Output 5.9  COLOR=YES sent to black and white printer**

*Delivery Failures*

*The FREQ Procedure*

| Store Location | | |
| --- | --- | --- |
| Location | Frequency | Percent |
| New York | 31 | 32.98 |
| Boston | 44 | 46.81 |
| Washington, D.C. | 19 | 20.21 |

**Output 5.10  COLOR=NO (regardless of printer type)**

*Delivery Failures*

*The FREQ Procedure*

| Store Location | | |
| --- | --- | --- |
| Location | Frequency | Percent |
| New York | 31 | 32.98 |
| Boston | 44 | 46.81 |
| Washington, D.C. | 19 | 20.21 |

## Creating a PDF File

With ODS printer output, your results are either a printout or a file. If you're sharing your results at a meeting in your office, a printout may be fine. However, to share your results electronically, you need a different option. Attaching a PostScript file to an e-mail might work if you are sure the person you are sending it to has a PostScript printer and knows the appropriate command to print the file. However, this isn't very convenient for the person on the other end.

A better solution is to create PDF output. PDF is a proprietary format created by Adobe that allows other users to see your printed output exactly as you see it, even if they don't have the same printer. They don't have to print it unless they want a copy. Once users have downloaded the free Adobe Acrobat Reader, they can review your results on screen.

Creating PDF files not only allows you to create very attractive output using the features of ODS PRINTER, but it also allows you to send it electronically. This is a perfect solution when you have information you expect others will want to print. ODS HTML output is easily shared electronically, but it is difficult to print because it doesn't have proper page breaks. Creating PDF output is very simple. Just use ODS PDF instead of ODS PRINTER, as follows. You will also want to use a FILE= option to name the resulting file.

```
ODS PDF FILE='myfile.pdf';
```

The following code routes the results of PROC REPORT to a file called ComplaintReport.pdf.

```
ODS PDF FILE='ComplaintReport.pdf';
proc report data=Complaints nowd;
    column Product Complaint Location NumComplaints;
    define Product / group order=formatted;
    define Complaint / group order=formatted;
    define Location / group order=formatted;
    define NumComplaints / analysis sum;
    break after Product / page summarize;
run;
ODS PDF CLOSE;
```

The results are shown in Output 5.11, displayed using Acrobat Reader software. The first page is shown. Notice how the page has a proper page break at the end of the first table. If this output were created using ODS HTML, the next table would start on page 1 and continue on the next page. If page breaks are important, then PDF is the electronic document format you should use.

The Acrobat Reader software is available for a number of platforms (Windows, Macintosh, UNIX) and can be downloaded free of charge at www.adobe.com.

**Output 5.11**

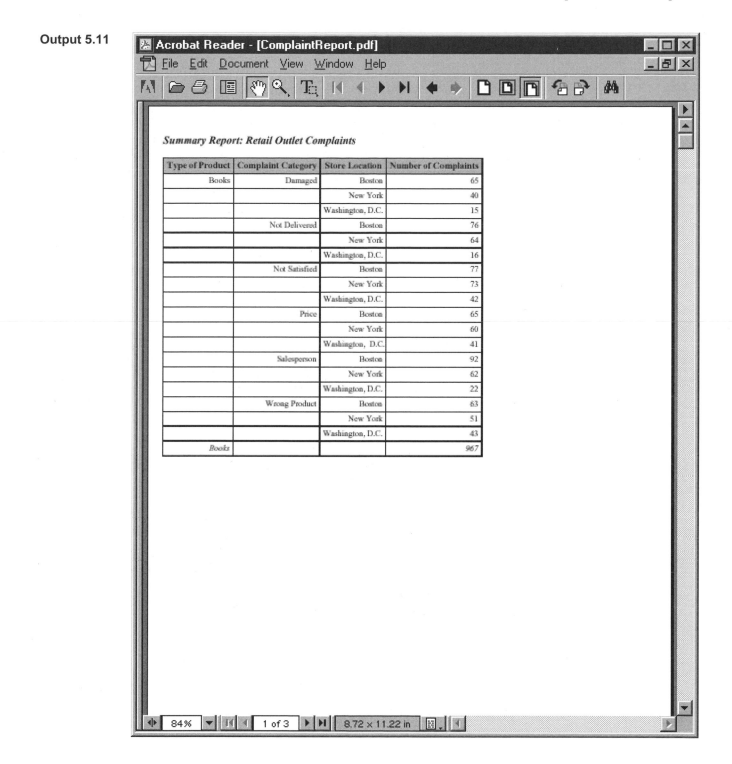

## Creating Bookmarks in Your PDF File

With ODS HTML output, you can generate a table of contents to help you find the results you want in a lengthy report. With ODS PDF output, you also get a table of contents.

The PDF format supports the creation of bookmarks, which are displayed by Acrobat Reader in a window to the left of the main PDF file. By clicking on a bookmark, you can jump directly to the correct output page. The PDF bookmarks created by ODS are basically the same as the headings and subheadings created in an ODS HTML table of contents.

To illustrate this feature in action, look at the following code. It produces a three-page output file with a number of different tables.

```
title 'Analysis of Consumer Complaints';
ODS PDF FILE='ComplaintAnalysis.pdf';
proc rsreg data=Complaints;
   model NumComplaints=Product Location;
run;
ODS PDF CLOSE;
```

The resulting PDF file is shown in Output 5.12. Notice the window on the left with the bookmark tab. It displays a tree view of the output file structure. It has a top-level link to the Coding results and the Anova results. Below Anova, there are links to the various components of the Anova output. If you click on one of the links, the page with that section or table will be displayed in the window on the right.

If the bookmarks do not appear when you open the PDF, you may need to bring them up by selecting **Show Bookmarks** from the Windows pull-down menu (or press F5).

As with HTML output, if you use the ODS PROCLABEL statement to assign a new label to the procedure, that label will be displayed in the bookmarks. For example, the same text used in the TITLE statement of our example could also be used to generate a procedure label, as follows:

```
title 'Analysis of Consumer Complaints';
ODS PROCLABEL 'Analysis of Consumer Complaints';
ODS PDF FILE='ComplaintAnalysis.pdf';
proc rsreg data=Complaints;
   model NumComplaints=Product Location;
run;
ODS PDF CLOSE;
```

Output 5.13 shows the new results. Notice how the top label has changed from "Rsreg" to "Analysis of Consumer Complaints."

TIP

If you don't want to have this table of contents in your PDF file, you can turn it off by adding the NOTOC option to your ODS PDF statement.

**Output 5.12**

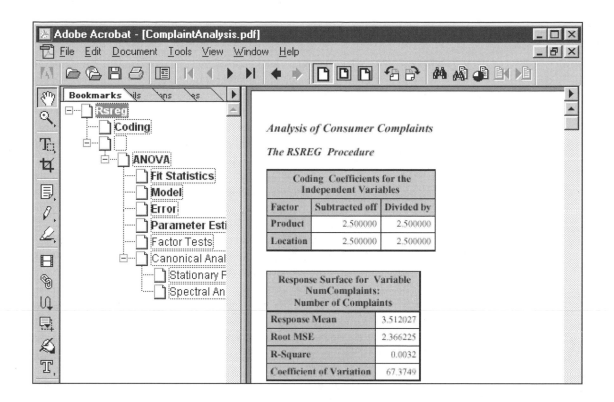

**Output 5.13**

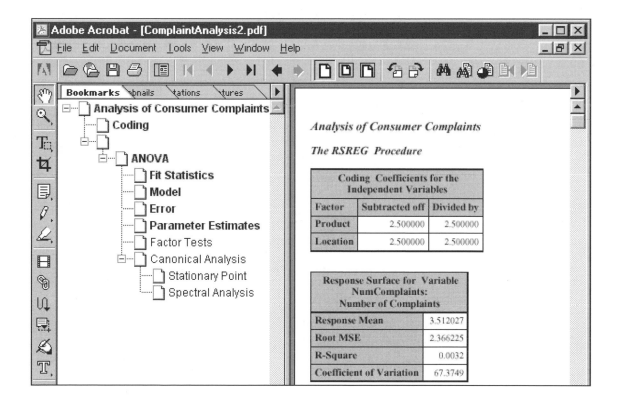

## Converting a File to PDF with Acrobat

Generally, using the ODS PDF statement will produce perfect PDF output from your SAS results. However, you don't have much control over the conversion process. There are a number of decisions that go into creating a PDF file. You can let SAS make them for you, or, if you want to invest in another piece of software, you can take control of the conversion yourself.

To create PDF files outside of SAS, you need to purchase software that distills PostScript files. Distilling is the term used to describe converting a file from PostScript to PDF. The most common distiller on the market is Adobe Acrobat. Unlike the free Acrobat Reader, Adobe Acrobat is a commercial product that you must purchase.

If you install Adobe Acrobat, you will find that you have two new printer definitions available on your system: Acrobat PDFWriter and Acrobat Distiller. These can both be configured with various options. To change the default options on Acrobat PDFWriter, select **Printers** from the Control Panel and then modify the properties of Acrobat PDFWriter.

However, if you want full control over the conversion process, it is recommended that you use Acrobat Distiller. To change the default options for Acrobat Distiller, open the Acrobat Distiller software and select one of the three optimization settings (Press, Print, or Screen). Figure 5.1 shows the main Distiller window.

Then select **Job Options** from the Settings menu. This gives you access to dozens of conversion options. These options affect things such as how graphic images are processed and compressed (useful if you don't like the looks of your graphics output) and whether the PDF file is optimized for printing or screen display. Output 5.14 shows the Job Options menu.

To send ODS output to Acrobat PDFWriter or Acrobat Distiller, use ODS PRINTER and the PRINTER= option, as follows. Do not use ODS PDF, as this will invoke the built-in PDF driver from ODS instead of invoking the Acrobat driver you just customized.

```
ODS PRINTER PRINTER="Acrobat PDFWriter";
ODS PRINTER PRINTER="Acrobat Distiller";
```

The preceding code works if you are using a system where Acrobat is installed. However, if Acrobat is not available for the operating system you are running, then getting customized PDF output is a two-step process.

First, you need to create a PostScript file from ODS. Use the ODS PS statement and specify an output file with FILE=, as follows:

```
ODS PS FILE="MyMainframeOutput.ps";
```

Then take that file to a computer where Adobe Acrobat is installed and distill it there. In Windows, if you open a file with the ".ps" extension, Acrobat Distiller will automatically launch and will create the PDF for you.

**Figure 5.1**

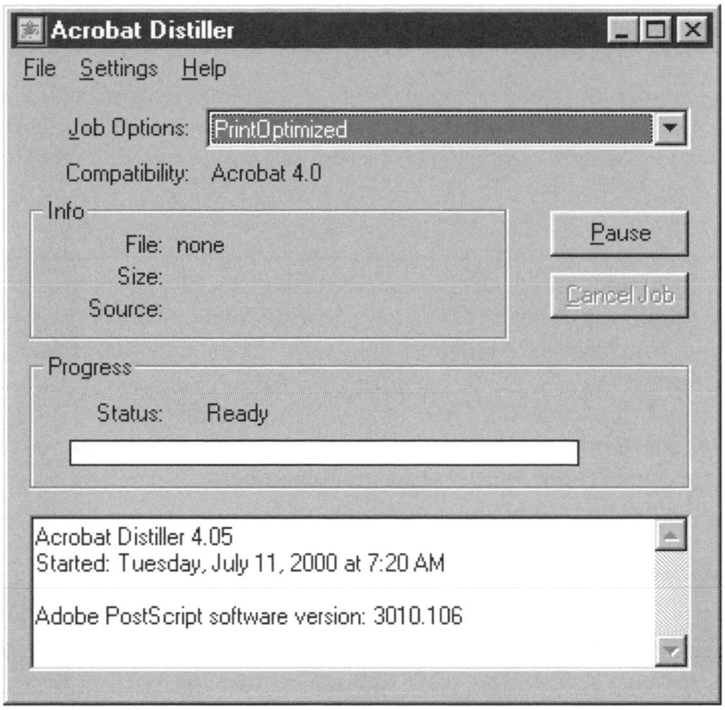

**Output 5.14**

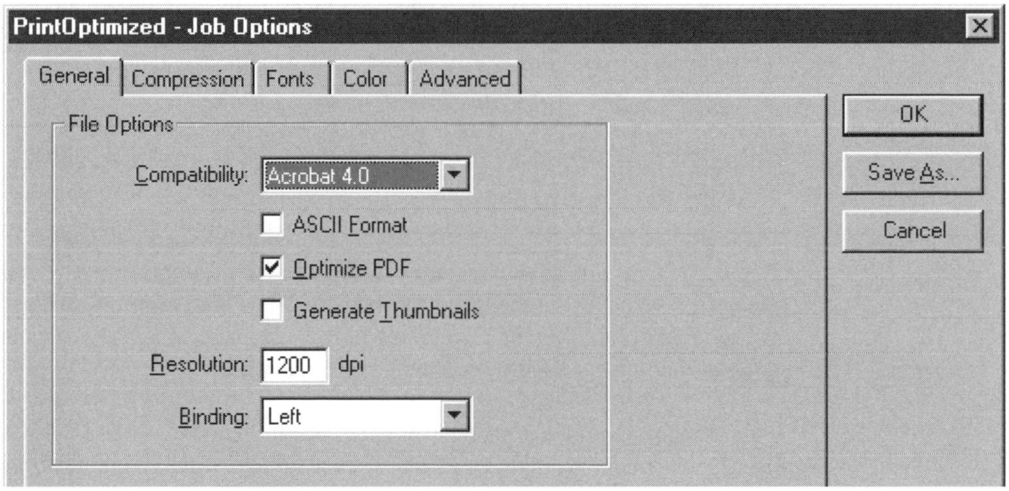

Adobe Acrobat is not the only product that can be used to create PDF files. There are several other freeware, shareware, and commercial products (GhostScript, for one) that also produce PDF output. Acrobat is the most widely used.

If you want to include bookmarks in a PDF file you create by printing to PDFWriter or Distiller or by distilling a PostScript file, you need to add the PDFMARK option to your ODS PRINTER statement.

## Creating Consistent Printed Pages

If your output runs to more than one page, you may want to think about using the ODS UNIFORM option. This option calls for ODS to use the same column widths across all pages of your output. If you're creating a long report, this option creates a more consistent look for all of the pages.

However, this improvement comes at a price. To figure out the best column width to use, the ODS UNIFORM option forces ODS to read the entire table before creating the first page of output. This requires additional memory. If you have an extremely long set of results or have limited memory available, you may want to skip this option. To see the difference this option makes, look at the following example.

```
ODS PRINTER;
proc print data=Uniforms noobs label;
    var UniformType Color Sales;
run;
ODS PRINTER CLOSE;
```

Part of the output for this code is shown in Output 5.15. It shows the tops of pages 1 and 5. Notice how the column heading for type of uniform on page 5 is much wider than the column heading on page 1. If this doesn't bother you, then don't worry about the UNIFORM option. However, if you would like consistent output, turn on the UNIFORM option. The syntax for the UNIFORM option is simple; just add the option to your first ODS PRINTER statement, as follows:

```
ODS PRINTER UNIFORM;
proc print data=Uniforms noobs label;
    var UniformType Color Sales;
run;
ODS PRINTER CLOSE;
```

The new printout is shown in Output 5.16. The only change is that now the column heading is wide on both page 1 and page 5. Because the UNIFORM option was turned on, ODS reviewed the entire table before picking a column width. Since page 5 required a wider column heading, ODS applied that wider column heading to page 1 as well.

This example points out another thing to keep in mind about the UNIFORM option. In addition to using more memory, it also uses more space on the printed page. ODS applies this option by using the widest column size across all pages. This may mean that your output requires extra pages.

If you have an extremely long table, but still want the column widths to be consistent, you could look into editing the table definition to force the width you want. This is an advanced technique that will be covered in the second book of this series.

**Output 5.15**

### *Uniform Sales Summary*

| Type of Uniform | Color | Units Sold |
|---|---|---|
| Maid | White | 181 |
| Maid | Red | 372 |
| Maid | Red | 415 |
| Maid | White | 138 |
| Maid | Green | 91 |

Page 1

### *Uniform Sales Summary*

| Type of Uniform | Color | Units Sold |
|---|---|---|
| Extremely Pretentious Doorman | Red | 323 |
| Extremely Pretentious Doorman | White | 201 |
| Extremely Pretentious Doorman | White | 173 |
| Extremely Pretentious Doorman | Green | 45 |
| Extremely Pretentious Doorman | Green | 56 |

Page 5

**Output 5.16**

### *Uniform Sales Summary*

| Type of Uniform | Color | Units Sold |
|---|---|---|
| Maid | White | 181 |
| Maid | Red | 372 |
| Maid | Red | 415 |
| Maid | White | 138 |
| Maid | Green | 91 |

Page 1

### *Uniform Sales Summary*

| Type of Uniform | Color | Units Sold |
|---|---|---|
| Extremely Pretentious Doorman | Red | 323 |
| Extremely Pretentious Doorman | White | 201 |
| Extremely Pretentious Doorman | White | 173 |
| Extremely Pretentious Doorman | Green | 45 |
| Extremely Pretentious Doorman | Green | 56 |

Page 5

## SAS System Options That Affect ODS PRINTER

This chapter has already shown you the impact of one system option that affects ODS PRINTER output, the COLORPRINTING option. However, you should know about a few more system options. Most system options have some impact on your output. Here are the ones specifically for ODS PRINTER. Be aware that because many of the options are printer and operating system dependent, they may not work for you.

| Option | Effect on ODS | Recommendation |
|---|---|---|
| PRINTERPATH= | Specifies a printer and file for all jobs routed to the ODS printer destination. | Use PRINTER= and FILE= on the ODS PRINTER statement instead. |
| ORIENTATION= | Set to LANDSCAPE or PORTRAIT. | Default is PORTRAIT. Change to LANDSCAPE if your output requires it. Output 5.17 and Output 5.18 illustrate the same table produced both ways. |
| COLORPRINTING | Turn on (default) to enable color printing. Otherwise, all output is grayscale or black and white. | Leave this on unless you do not have a color printer and never intend to produce color. Even if you do not have a color printer, you may want to leave this on so you can create color PDFs. |
| DUPLEX, BINDING= | Controls whether output is single or double sided. If double sided, the binding option controls whether it is printed assuming that the binding is along the long edge or short edge. | If your printer can handle double-sided output, this is a paper saver. |
| LEFTMARGIN=, RIGHTMARGIN=, TOPMARGIN=, BOTTOMMARGIN= | Specifies the margin size in inches. These are printer margins: ODS assumes your printer is physically incapable of printing outside this margin. | If your output is crowded too close to the edge of the page, use these options to specify a minimum margin. These are different from the margin options you have in some style definitions. |
| COPIES= | Controls the number of copies to print (default is 1). | This is a dangerous option to change. If you forget to switch it back, you'll waste a lot of paper. |
| COLLATE | Generates collated output (if COPIES>1). | This option does not work on most printers. |
| PAPERSOURCE=, PAPERDEST=, PAPERTYPE= | Specifies the paper tray, output bin, and paper type for printer to use. | These options do not work on most printers. They are worth a try if selecting a particular tray, output bin, or paper type is important to you. |

Note: In Windows, the default settings for most of these options are based on the current settings of your default printer. So if you adjust the settings on your default printer, you should not need to change these options. However, if you want to vary these settings within a single SAS session, you'll need to use the SAS system options.

**Output 5.17**

*Simple Statistics on Complaints Count*

*The MEANS Procedure*

| | | | | Analysis Variable : NumComplaints Number of Complaints | | | | | | | | |
|---|---|---|---|---|---|---|---|---|---|---|---|---|
| N | N Miss | Mean | Std Dev | Minimum | 5th Pctl | 10th Pctl | 25th Pctl | Median | 75th Pctl | 90th Pctl | 95th Pctl |
| 582 | 0 | 3.5120275 | 2.3598097 | 0 | 0 | 0 | 1.0000000 | 4.0000000 | 6.0000000 | 7.0000000 | 7.0000000 |

| Analysis Variable : Num Complain ts Number of Complain ts |
|---|
| Maximum |
| 7.0000000 |

**Output 5.18**

*Simple Statistics on Complaints Count*

*The MEANS Procedure*

| | | | | Analysis Variable : NumComplaints Number of Complaints | | | | | | | | |
|---|---|---|---|---|---|---|---|---|---|---|---|---|
| N | N Miss | Mean | Std Dev | Minimum | 5th Pctl | 10th Pctl | 25th Pctl | Median | 75th Pctl | 90th Pctl | 95th Pctl | Maximum |
| 582 | 0 | 3.5120275 | 2.3598097 | 0 | 0 | 0 | 1.0000000 | 4.0000000 | 6.0000000 | 7.0000000 | 7.0000000 | 7.0000000 |

# Part 3

## Intermediate Topics

Chapter

# 6

*Exploring ODS Output*

The previous chapters displayed the output generated by a variety of ODS statements and options. The results you see in your Web browser, in your word processor, on your printer, or in the Results window are built from one or more output objects, which are the basic building blocks of ODS output.

This chapter explores these output objects in detail, as well as a number of procedure results that show how output objects are combined to produce ODS output.

Though it might be tempting to skip this chapter and get on to learning about how to modify your results, this chapter has some important background information that you may need to understand the chapters to come.

For example, knowing how to identify output objects becomes helpful when you get to the next chapter, which shows how to select and exclude output objects from your results.

## The TRACE Statement

A single SAS procedure can produce a single ODS output object, or it can produce dozens. In order to be able to customize your results, you need to be able to identify these output objects. ODS provides a statement that generates a description of each output object: the TRACE statement. The syntax for this statement is

```
ODS TRACE ON;
   *procedures and/or DATA steps go here;
ODS TRACE OFF;
```

This TRACE statement is used twice, the first time to turn output tracing on, and the second time to turn it off again. What happens in between is that ODS sends information about each output object to the log.

To see this statement in action, look at the following code:

```
ODS TRACE ON;
proc freq data=sales;
   tables Department / chisq;
run;
ODS TRACE OFF;
```

Here we've asked for a single procedure with a single variable. We haven't specified any ODS destinations, so we get the default listing output shown in Output 6.1. It looks like one piece of output. However, if you look at the log file, shown in Output 6.2, you can see that there are actually two output objects. Each one is described in a section of the log titled "Output Added."

The first output object is the frequency table itself. The ODS TRACE information in the log tells you that this part of the output is named "OneWayFreqs." It has a label of "One-Way Frequencies." You can think of the name and label just like variable names and labels. The only difference is that in this case the name and label refer to an output object. This information is important, because if you want to select or exclude part of your ODS output, you have to know how to identify it.

The ODS TRACE information also supplies the name of the table definition (template) that has been applied to this output object. The formatting of the frequency table is controlled by the table definition called "Base.Freq.OneWayFreqs." Notice how this table definition is named. It starts with "Base," because this is a base SAS procedure. The next segment of the name is the procedure name, "Freq." This is followed by the name of the output object, "OneWayFreqs." This naming convention helps keep all of the table definitions organized, making it easier to figure out which one you need to modify to affect each procedure. However, if you can't sort out the name of the table definition you need, you can always run a TRACE to find the name.

The final piece of information is the path. This is a specific road map to this output object. Every one-way frequency table will have the same name, label, and table definition. The path tells you how to identify this individual one-way frequency table. Notice how the pathname includes the variable name.

The second set of TRACE information shows the name, label, template, and path for the chi-square statistics. Notice how the naming conventions follow a similar pattern.

**Output 6.1**

|                     |           | Department |                         |                       |
|---------------------|-----------|------------|-------------------------|-----------------------|
| Department          | Frequency | Percent    | Cumulative Frequency    | Cumulative Percent    |
| Wholesale           | 134       | 26.80      | 134                     | 26.80                 |
| Internet            | 208       | 41.60      | 342                     | 68.40                 |
| Mail Order          | 87        | 17.40      | 429                     | 85.80                 |
| Retail              | 71        | 14.20      | 500                     | 100.00                |

| Chi-Square Test for Equal Proportions | |
|------------------------|-----------|
| Chi-Square             | 90.6400   |
| DF                     | 3         |
| Pr > ChiSq             | <.0001    |

Sample Size = 500

**Output 6.2**

```
10    ods trace on;
11    proc freq data=sales;
12        tables Department / chisq;
13    run;

Output Added:
- - - - - - - - - - - -
Name:       OneWayFreqs
Label:      One-Way Frequencies
Template:   Base.Freq.OneWayFreqs
Path:       Freq.Department.OneWayFreqs
- - - - - - - - - - - -

Output Added:
- - - - - - - - - - - -
Name:       OneWayChiSq
Label:      One-Way Chi-Square Test
Template:   Base.Freq.StatFactoid
Path:       Freq.Department.OneWayChiSq
- - - - - - - - - - - -
NOTE: There were 500 observations read from the data set WORK.SALES.
NOTE: PROCEDURE FREQ used:
      real time            0.60 seconds

14    ods trace off;
```

TIP

If you want, you can simply turn TRACE on and leave it on for the duration of your SAS session. Then all of your ODS output would be documented in the log. In practice, you'll find that you may need to run TRACE from time to time as you get to know each procedure and its output, but you may not want it on all of the time. Your log file would get quite large and hard to read if every procedure were traced every time it was run.

## Identifying Output Objects in Your Listing

To get to know ODS output, you will find it helpful to turn ODS TRACE on at least the first time you run each procedure. After a while, you'll get to know the common procedures, and you may not need to trace your output every time.

The best way to run TRACE for a new procedure is to turn on the LISTING option. This tells TRACE to display its information in your listing output, instead of in the log. The syntax is as follows:

```
ODS TRACE ON / LISTING;
proc reg data=sales;
   model itemprice=itemssold department;
run;
ODS TRACE OFF;
```

You get the results shown in Output 6.3. Preceding each piece of the PROC REG output is a set of tracing information that names the output object, its table definitions, and its path. This makes it easy to see which names go to what parts of the output.

Of course, it also makes your results a bit hard to read, so you'll want to rerun the procedure later with TRACE set to OFF.

In this example, the procedure creates three output objects. The first object is called ANOVA, and it includes the analysis of variance results. The second output object is called FitStatistics. It contains a number of statistics that measure the fit of the model. The third output object is called ParameterEstimates. It contains the parameter estimates for each term in the model.

Every time you run a PROC REG with the same option settings and type of model, you will get these three output objects.

Not only are the output object names consistent across runs of the same procedure, they're also consistent across similar results from different procedures. If you run another model that generates analysis of variance results, you will get an output object named ANOVA. Similarly, you'll get your fit statistics in an output object named FitStatistics.

For example, if you run a PROC GLM with the same model as the PROC REG above, you get five output objects: NObs, OverallANOVA, FitStatistics, ModelANOVA, and ParameterEstimates. The NObs object is different from PROC REG, which does not report an N. In addition, PROC GLM has two analysis of variance objects, so one is called OverallANOVA and the other ModelANOVA. However, the FitStatistics and ParameterEstimates objects are named just like the PROC REG.

ODS is modular. The output from each procedure is built from a common set of building blocks, the named output objects. Of course, some procedures generate highly specialized output objects, so some output object names are used in only one procedure.

**Output 6.3**

```
The REG Procedure
Model: MODEL1
Dependent Variable: ItemPrice Item Price

Output Added:
-------------
Name:        ANOVA
Label:       Analysis of Variance
Template:    Stat.REG.ANOVA
Path:        Reg.MODEL1.Fit.ItemPrice.ANOVA
-------------
```

Analysis of Variance

| Source | DF | Sum of Squares | Mean Square | F Value | Pr > F |
|---|---|---|---|---|---|
| Model | 2 | 668.30262 | 334.15131 | 117.85 | <.0001 |
| Error | 497 | 1409.25014 | 2.83551 | | |
| Corrected Total | 499 | 2077.55277 | | | |

```
Output Added:
-------------
Name:        FitStatistics
Label:       Fit Statistics
Template:    Stat.REG.FitStatistics
Path:        Reg.MODEL1.Fit.ItemPrice.FitStatistics
-------------
```

| Root MSE | 1.68390 | R-Square | 0.3217 |
|---|---|---|---|
| Dependent Mean | 9.43716 | Adj R-Sq | 0.3189 |
| Coeff Var | 17.84327 | | |

```
Output Added:
-------------
Name:        ParameterEstimates
Label:       Parameter Estimates
Template:    Stat.REG.ParameterEstimates
Path:        Reg.MODEL1.Fit.ItemPrice.ParameterEstimates
-------------
```

```
The REG Procedure
Model: MODEL1
Dependent Variable: ItemPrice Item Price
```

Parameter Estimates

| Variable | Label | DF | Parameter Estimate | Standard Error | t Value | Pr > \|t\| |
|---|---|---|---|---|---|---|
| Intercept | Intercept | 1 | 10.98083 | 0.20818 | 52.75 | <.0001 |
| ItemsSold | Items Sold | 1 | 0.00075405 | 0.00052611 | 1.43 | 0.1524 |
| Department | Department | 1 | -0.57441 | 0.03756 | -15.29 | <.0001 |

## Identifying Output Objects by Path

The previous example showed how to find the names associated with each output object. When all of your output objects have unique names, this is the simplest way to identify each object.

However, sometimes an output object name is not unique. In the simple example that follows, two frequency tables are created, and they both have the same output object name: OneWayFreqs.

```
ODS TRACE ON / LISTING;
proc freq data=sales;
   tables EmployeeName;
run;
proc freq data=sales;
   tables ProductName;
run;
ODS TRACE OFF;
```

Output 6.4 shows the traced results of these two procedures. Notice how the name, label, and template[1] are the same for both procedures. Only the path is different. If you wanted to modify the format or structure of only one of the two tables, you'd have to identify it by its path.

Freq.EmployeeName.OneWayFreqs uniquely identifies the first table, and Freq.ProductName.OneWayFreqs uniquely identifies the second table. Actually, you can abbreviate these paths. You only have to use enough of the path, starting from the end and moving left, to get to the unique part. Therefore, EmployeeName.OneWayFreqs and ProductName.OneWayFreqs are adequate.

So why aren't all of the identifiers unique? Why do the two tables have the same name and label? The reason is that sometimes it's useful to be able to identify them as a group.

For example, if you want to change the table definition to display fewer decimal places for the percentages, you probably want to change both tables. The output would look odd if only one table was modified. By changing the table definition for OneWayFreqs, you can affect both tables at the same time.

On the other hand, if you were running tables with chi-square statistics, and wanted to add or remove statistics for one of the tables but not the other, you'd want to be able to address the chi-square statistics output object for that one table. The best way to do that is by using the path.

There are more ways to identify a unique output object. See Chapter 8, "Limiting ODS Output," for an explanation of how to identify output objects by sequence number and by label path.

---

[1]   Terminology can get confusing here. Templates and table definitions are the same thing. When the ODS TRACE statement identifies a "template" in its output, it is referring to the table definition that controls how the output is displayed. See Chapter 2, "ODS Basics," for an explanation of ODS terminology.

**Output 6.4**

---

```
The FREQ Procedure

Output Added:
-------------
Name:        OneWayFreqs
Label:       One-Way Frequencies
Template:    Base.Freq.OneWayFreqs
Path:        Freq.EmployeeName.OneWayFreqs
-------------
```

### Employee

| Employee<br>Name | Frequency | Percent | Cumulative<br>Frequency | Cumulative<br>Percent |
|---|---|---|---|---|
| Smith | 88 | 17.60 | 88 | 17.60 |
| Knight | 103 | 20.60 | 191 | 38.20 |
| Haworth | 107 | 21.40 | 298 | 59.60 |
| Jones | 98 | 19.60 | 396 | 79.20 |
| Platt | 104 | 20.80 | 500 | 100.00 |

```
The FREQ Procedure

Output Added:
-------------
Name:        OneWayFreqs
Label:       One-Way Frequencies
Template:    Base.Freq.OneWayFreqs
Path:        Freq.ProductName.OneWayFreqs
-------------
```

### Product

| ProductName | Frequency | Percent | Cumulative<br>Frequency | Cumulative<br>Percent |
|---|---|---|---|---|
| Kona | 83 | 16.60 | 83 | 16.60 |
| Colombian | 88 | 17.60 | 171 | 34.20 |
| French Roast | 74 | 14.80 | 245 | 49.00 |
| Italian Roast | 85 | 17.00 | 330 | 66.00 |
| Guatemalan | 98 | 19.60 | 428 | 85.60 |
| Sumatran | 72 | 14.40 | 500 | 100.00 |

## Viewing the Results

If you run SAS interactively, then in addition to using the TRACE statement, you can also view your output objects in the Results window. The Results window is a tree view of the output created during your current SAS session.

The top level of the tree is a SAS procedure or DATA step. Beneath the procedure are items for each of the output objects that the procedure creates. If you click on a procedure or an output object label in the Results window, it brings up the Output window and jumps to the part of your output that shows the ODS listing output created from that output object (assuming you have ODS LISTING turned on so that there is output in the Output window).

To illustrate this, look at the following example.

```
ODS TRACE ON;
proc univariate data=sales;
    var ItemPrice;
run;
ODS TRACE OFF;
```

The Results window is shown below in Output 6.5. The log file with the TRACE information is shown in Output 6.6.

In the Results window, the tree has an item for the Univariate procedure and then items below that for each of the output objects. Notice how the names of the items in the tree—Moments, Basic Measures of Location and Variability, etc.—match up with the labels shown in the TRACE output.

You can use a label to identify an output object in place of the name or path of the object. Because the labels are used in the Results window, sometimes this is a handy way to identify output objects. You don't even need to run a TRACE, because the labels are right there in the Results window.

**Output 6.5**

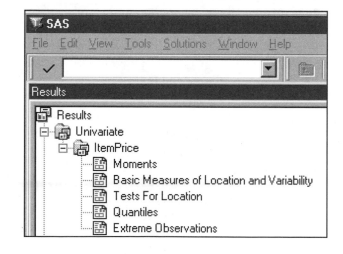

**Output 6.6**

```
13   ODS TRACE ON;
14   proc univariate data=sales;
15      var ItemPrice;
16   run;


Output Added:
-------------

Name:       Moments
Label:      Moments
Template:   base.univariate.Moments
Path:       Univariate.ItemPrice.Moments
-------------

Output Added:
-------------

Name:       BasicMeasures
Label:      Basic Measures of Location and Variability
Template:   base.univariate.Measures
Path:       Univariate.ItemPrice.BasicMeasures
-------------

Output Added:
-------------

Name:       TestsForLocation
Label:      Tests For Location
Template:   base.univariate.Location
Path:       Univariate.ItemPrice.TestsForLocation
-------------

Output Added:
-------------

Name:       Quantiles
Label:      Quantiles
Template:   base.univariate.Quantiles
Path:       Univariate.ItemPrice.Quantiles
-------------

Output Added:
-------------

Name:       ExtremeObs
Label:      Extreme Observations
Template:   base.univariate.ExtObs
Path:       Univariate.ItemPrice.ExtremeObs
-------------
NOTE: There were 500 observations read from the data set WORK.SALES.
NOTE: PROCEDURE UNIVARIATE used:
      real time            0.26 seconds


17   ODS TRACE OFF;
```

## TRACE Examples: Other Procedures

While the previous examples have emphasized the similarities in ODS output objects across procedures, there are some procedures that are unique. For example, PROC CHART uses monospace fonts to produce low-resolution graphics.

```
ODS TRACE ON;
proc chart data=sales;
    vbar ProductName;
run;
ODS TRACE OFF;
```

As you can see in Output 6.7, this procedure step produces a single output object called VBAR, which is actually a graph. For this procedure, the output objects are named for the chart type, and each chart is an output object.

Another interesting procedure is PROC CONTENTS, which produces a number of output objects that are unique to this procedure. The three output objects created by this code are described in Output 6.8.

```
ODS TRACE ON;
proc contents data=sales;
run;
ODS TRACE OFF;
```

Some procedures produce ODS output only in certain conditions. Generally, PROC FORMAT is used to create and store formats. However, it can produce output. In the following example, the FMTLIB option is used to generate a listing of the formats stored in the format library called LIBRARY. It produces an output object that is unique to this procedure, the Format object (see Output 6.9).

```
ODS TRACE ON;
proc format library=library fmtlib;
run;
ODS TRACE OFF;
```

Finally, some procedures don't produce ODS output at all. In this next example, we'll look at PROC PRINTTO. Though it does produce output, it does not produce listing output, so it does not invoke ODS. In the following example, the PROC MEANS generates ODS output, but the PROC PRINTTO does not, as shown in Output 6.10.

```
ODS TRACE ON;
proc printto print=printf new; run;
proc means data=sales;
    var ItemsSold;
run;
proc printto; run;
ODS TRACE OFF;
```

**Output 6.7**

```
Output Added:
------------
Name:       VBAR
Label:      VBAR of ProductName
Data Name:  BatchOutput
Path:       Chart.VBAR
------------
```

**Output 6.8**

```
Output Added:
------------
Name:       Attributes
Label:      Attributes
Template:   Base.Contents.Attributes
Path:       Contents.data set.Attributes
------------
```

```
Output Added:
------------
Name:       EngineHost
Label:      Engine/Host Information
Template:   Base.Contents.EngineHost
Path:       Contents.data set.EngineHost
------------
```

```
Output Added:
------------
Name:       VariablesAlpha
Label:      Variables
Template:   Base.Contents.Variables
Path:       Contents.data set.VariablesAlpha
------------
```

**Output 6.9**

```
Output Added:
------------
Name:       FORMAT
Label:      FMTLIB Listing
Data Name:  BatchOutput
Path:       Format.FORMAT
------------
```

**Output 6.10**

```
Output Added:
------------
Name:       Summary
Label:      Summary statistics
Template:   base.summary
Path:       Means.Summary
------------
```

# Output Data Sets

In earlier versions of SAS software, some procedures produced output data sets, and others did not. For example, you could get an output data set from PROC MEANS or PROC FREQ, but not from PROC TABULATE.

In addition, some procedures that could produce output data sets did not always include the variables you wanted. For example, the PROC FREQ output data set did not include cumulative frequencies.

With Version 8, you can still produce output data sets from these procedures the old way, but now you can also use ODS to create complete output data sets from almost every SAS procedure. These output data sets contain virtually every bit of information that you see in the listing results.

This chapter provides a number of examples from different procedures to give you an overview of output data sets.

## Creating a Single Output Data Set

The first thing you need to know about ODS output data sets is that you can create a lot of them. A single procedure frequently generates multiple output data sets.

Before learning the complexities of handling these multiple output data sets, we're going to start out simple. This first example will look at creating just one output data set.

To request an output data set, use the following ODS statement:

```
ODS OUTPUT output-object<=data-set-name>;
```

If you just issue "ODS OUTPUT;" by itself, there is no default output data set produced. Specifying an output object is not optional.

In this example, we are going to create an output data set with the results from a PROC MEANS. The code to do this is

```
ODS OUTPUT "Summary Statistics"=Stats;
proc means data=Traffic;
    var MPH;
run;
ODS OUTPUT CLOSE;
```

The output object we want is labeled "Summary Statistics," and it will be routed to the output data set called Stats. To identify this object, you can run an ODS TRACE. Another option is to run the procedure once and then look at the label in the Results window.

When you run a PROC MEANS, the Results window displays a folder labeled "Means." If you drill down to the next level, you will see the label "Summary Statistics," shown in Output 7.1. These labels, at the most detailed level of the Results window, are the output object labels that you need for ODS OUTPUT.

When the ODS OUTPUT code above is submitted, the PROC MEANS results are displayed in the Output window, and a data set called Stats is generated. You can then print the data set to see what it looks like. To illustrate this example, RTF output was generated from the PROC MEANS and is displayed in Output 7.2. Then a PROC PRINT was run on the output data set, and the resulting RTF output is displayed in Output 7.3. By comparing the procedure output and the output data set, you can see how the two relate.

Each of the results from the MEANS procedure is included in the output data set. Each of the output variables has a name that indicates the original variable and the statistic it contains.

As you begin using ODS output data sets, you will find it helps to explore the data in order to learn the relationships between the procedure output and the output data set structures.

**Output 7.1  The Results Window**

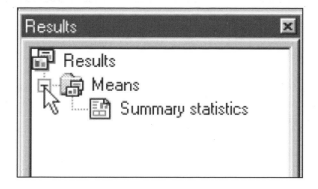

**Output 7.2  Output from the MEANS Procedure**

| Analysis Variable : MPH Average Speed | | | | |
|---|---|---|---|---|
| N | Mean | Std Dev | Minimum | Maximum |
| 189 | 27.8756614 | 18.0832631 | 0 | 65.0000000 |

**Output 7.3  Output Data Set from the MEANS Procedure**

| Obs | MPH_N | MPH_Mean | MPH_StdDev | MPH_Min | MPH_Max |
|---|---|---|---|---|---|
| 1 | 189 | 27.875661376 | 18.083263104 | 0 | 65 |

There is one risk to selecting output objects by their labels instead of their names. If your code will be run by users in regions with different languages, the label will not be the same in their version of SAS. Output object names are the same no matter which language version of SAS is used.

## Comparing ODS Output Data Sets to Printed Output

To further explore the relationship between procedure results and output data sets, let's look at a more complex procedure. The previous example generated only one output data set. This time we'll look at a procedure that creates two.

Output 7.4 shows the results of a PROC CORR. If you look carefully at this RTF output, you can see that there are two tables of results. The first table describes the two variables, and the second table displays the correlation coefficients.

These are two separate output objects. To see this, you can look at the Results window displayed in Output 7.5. It shows two items under the "Corr" folder. One object is labeled "Variables Information" and the other is labeled "Pearson Correlations."

The output object we are going to use for this example is the one that contains the main results, the correlation coefficients. The code to request an output data set for this object is

```
ODS OUTPUT "Pearson Correlations"=PearsonCorr;
proc corr data=Traffic nosimple;
   var TimeOfDay;
   with MPH;
run;
ODS OUTPUT CLOSE;
```

When this code is submitted, the correlation results are displayed in the Output window, and a data set called PearsonCorr is generated. This data set has been printed in Output 7.6. Each of the pieces of information in the correlation matrix is included in the output data set. However, the format is different. The correlation matrix has a crosstab format, but the output data set has just one record. The two results have been included as two variables: TimeOfDay is the correlation coefficient, and PTimeOfDay is the *p*-value.

If you wanted to create a data set from the other output object, the table of variable information, the code would be modified as follows:

```
ODS OUTPUT "Variables Information"=VarInfo;
proc corr data=Traffic nosimple;
   var TimeOfDay;
   with MPH;
run;
ODS OUTPUT CLOSE;
```

When this code is submitted, the correlation results are displayed in the Output window, and a data set called VarInfo is generated. This data set has been printed in Output 7.7. Each of the pieces of information in the variable information table is included in the output data set. This time the format is the same in both the printed results and the output data set. Both have two rows of information. ODS has created one record for each variable in the variables table.

**Output 7.4**

| 1 With Variables: | MPH |
|---|---|
| 1    Variables: | TimeOfDay |

| Pearson Correlation Coefficients, N = 189 Prob > \|r\| under H0: Rho=0 | |
|---|---|
| | **TimeOfDay** |
| **MPH** **Average Speed** | -0.03555 0.6272 |

**Output 7.5**

| Results | ✕ |
|---|---|
| 🗗 **Results** | |
| ⊟ 🗐 Corr | |
|    ⊞ 🗐 Variables Information | |
|    ⊞ 🗐 Pearson Correlations | |

**Output 7.6**

| Obs | Variable | Label | TimeOfDay | PTimeOfDay |
|---|---|---|---|---|
| 1 | MPH | Average Speed | -0.03555 | 0.6272 |

**Output 7.7**

| Obs | NVars | Variables | VarNames |
|---|---|---|---|
| 1 | 1 | With Variables: | MPH |
| 2 | 1 | Variables: | TimeOfDay |

Some procedures supply additional variables in their output data sets that are not part of the printed output. These variables are not generally useful for printing but might be useful for subsequent processing in the DATA step. Watch for these extra variables.

## Creating Multiple Output Data Sets from a Single Procedure

In the previous example, we used two procedures to create two output data sets. However, if you want two output data sets from the same procedure, you don't have to run the procedure twice. You can just request two different output data sets from the same procedure.

For example, if you run a PROC FREQ and generate not just a frequency distribution but also a series of chi-square statistics, you can create output data sets for both results with just one PROC FREQ.

Output 7.8 shows the two output objects that are created: "Cross-Tabular Freq Table" and "Chi-Square Tests." The code below uses two ODS OUTPUT statements before the procedure code to request two data sets, and a single ODS OUTPUT CLOSE statement to end data set creation.

```
ODS OUTPUT "Cross-Tabular Freq Table"=FreqTable;
ODS OUTPUT "Chi-Square Tests"=FreqChiSq;
proc freq data=Traffic;
   tables highway*event / chisq norow nocol nopct;
run;
ODS OUTPUT CLOSE;
```

A slightly simpler way to write this is to put both data set requests in a single ODS OUTPUT statement. The code below is equivalent to the code above.

```
ODS OUTPUT "Cross-Tabular Freq Table"=FreqTable
           "Chi-Square Tests"=FreqChiSq;
proc freq data=Traffic;
   tables highway*event / chisq norow nocol nopct;
run;
ODS OUTPUT CLOSE;
```

The resulting data sets are shown in Output 7.9 and Output 7.10. Notice that the structures of the two data sets are very different. The first data set has detailed data on observation counts for the two variables, so it has one record for each combination of the two variables. The second data set has summary statistics and has one record for each statistic.

This is why ODS OUTPUT produces multiple data sets. If you tried to create a single data set from all of the different types of output objects produced by a procedure, you'd end up with very confusing results.

Sometimes what you get in your output data set is not what you expected. For example, you might think that the output data set for PROC FREQ would have the same shape as the table: rows for the row variable ("Highway") and columns for the column variable ("Event"). Instead, PROC FREQ output data sets have a row for every combination of row and column variable, plus rows at the end for the totals. This is a common format for ODS output data sets when the procedure creates crosstabular results. So before you assume that "what you see is what you get," take the time to print and review your ODS data sets.

**Output 7.8**

**Output 7.9**

| Obs | Table | Highway | Event | _TYPE_ | _TABLE_ | Frequency | Missing |
|---|---|---|---|---|---|---|---|
| 1 | Highway_by_Event | 80 | Disabled | 11 | 1 | 17 | . |
| 2 | Highway_by_Event | 80 | Minor | 11 | 1 | 20 | . |
| 3 | Highway_by_Event | 80 | Injury | 11 | 1 | 22 | . |
| 4 | Highway_by_Event | 80 | Fatal | 11 | 1 | 18 | . |
| 5 | Highway_by_Event | 80 | . | 10 | 1 | 77 | . |
| 6 | Highway_by_Event | 101 | Disabled | 11 | 1 | 21 | . |
| 7 | Highway_by_Event | 101 | Minor | 11 | 1 | 16 | . |
| 8 | Highway_by_Event | 101 | Injury | 11 | 1 | 14 | . |
| 9 | Highway_by_Event | 101 | Fatal | 11 | 1 | 18 | . |
| 10 | Highway_by_Event | 101 | . | 10 | 1 | 69 | . |
| 11 | Highway_by_Event | 280 | Disabled | 11 | 1 | 6 | . |
| 12 | Highway_by_Event | 280 | Minor | 11 | 1 | 7 | . |
| 13 | Highway_by_Event | 280 | Injury | 11 | 1 | 12 | . |
| 14 | Highway_by_Event | 280 | Fatal | 11 | 1 | 18 | . |
| 15 | Highway_by_Event | 280 | . | 10 | 1 | 43 | . |
| 16 | Highway_by_Event | . | Disabled | 01 | 1 | 44 | . |
| 17 | Highway_by_Event | . | Minor | 01 | 1 | 43 | . |
| 18 | Highway_by_Event | . | Injury | 01 | 1 | 48 | . |
| 19 | Highway_by_Event | . | Fatal | 01 | 1 | 54 | . |
| 20 | Highway_by_Event | . | . | 00 | 1 | 189 | 0 |

**Output 7.10**

| Obs | Table | Statistic | DF | Value | Prob |
|---|---|---|---|---|---|
| 1 | Highway_by_Event | Chi-Square | 6 | 8.9756 | 0.1750 |
| 2 | Highway_by_Event | Likelihood Ratio Chi-Square | 6 | 8.9395 | 0.1770 |
| 3 | Highway_by_Event | Mantel-Haenszel Chi-Square | 1 | 2.2730 | 0.1316 |
| 4 | Highway_by_Event | Phi Coefficient | _ | 0.2179 | _ |
| 5 | Highway_by_Event | Contingency Coefficient | _ | 0.2129 | _ |
| 6 | Highway_by_Event | Cramer's V | _ | 0.1541 | _ |

## Creating Output Data Sets from Procedures with Complex Output

In the next example, we explore how a single procedure creates 15 output objects! It's not a complicated procedure—just a simple PROC UNIVARIATE with a CLASS variable. The output structure is shown in Output 7.11.

The reason we get so many output objects is the CLASS variable "Highway." Without a CLASS variable, this procedure produces five output objects: "Moments," "Basic Measures of Location and Variability," "Tests for Location," "Quantiles," and "Extreme Observations."

If you want just one of the output objects, you can request an output data set that contains that object for each of the three values of the CLASS variable:

```
ODS OUTPUT "Moments"=UnivMPH;
proc univariate data=Traffic;
   class Highway;
   var MPH;
run;
ODS OUTPUT CLOSE;
```

This code creates a single data set called UnivMPH that contains the results for all three highways. A printout of this data set is shown in Output 7.12. This single data set contains three output objects. This works because all three objects have the same label: "Moments."

To identify each of the three output objects, you can look at the value of the variable Highway. Notice how the first group of results in the output data set is for Highway 80, which is the first of the three class groups, and the first output object. You can see that each of the results in the Moments data set is shown for Highway 80, and then they repeat for the next two class groups.

Be careful when combining data sets from different output objects. Just because they look similar and come from the same procedure does not mean that their formats are identical. You may have a variable that is shorter in one data set than in another, which will cause it to be truncated when you combine the data sets.

**Output 7.11**

Results

- Results
  - Univariate
    - MPH
      - Highway = 80
        - Moments
        - Basic Measures of Location and Variability
        - Tests For Location
        - Quantiles
        - Extreme Observations
      - Highway = 101
      - Highway = 280

**Output 7.12**

| VarName | Highway | Label1 | cValue1 | nValue1 | Label2 | cValue2 | nValue2 |
|---|---|---|---|---|---|---|---|
| MPH | 80 | N | 95 | 95.000000 | Sum Weights | 95 | 95.000000 |
| MPH | 80 | Mean | 29.4052632 | 29.405263 | Sum Observations | 2793.5 | 2793.500000 |
| MPH | 80 | Std Deviation | 18.5435506 | 18.543551 | Variance | 343.86327 | 343.863270 |
| MPH | 80 | Skewness | 0.38263239 | 0.382632 | Kurtosis | -0.969807 | -0.969807 |
| MPH | 80 | Uncorrected SS | 114466.75 | 114467 | Corrected SS | 32323.1474 | 32323 |
| MPH | 80 | Coeff Variation | 63.0620122 | 63.062012 | Std Error Mean | 1.90252815 | 1.902528 |
| MPH | 101 | N | 57 | 57.000000 | Sum Weights | 57 | 57.000000 |
| MPH | 101 | Mean | 27.4649123 | 27.464912 | Sum Observations | 1565.5 | 1565.500000 |
| MPH | 101 | Std Deviation | 18.6784013 | 18.678401 | Variance | 348.882675 | 348.882675 |
| MPH | 101 | Skewness | 0.32224301 | 0.322243 | Kurtosis | -0.9451599 | -0.945160 |
| MPH | 101 | Uncorrected SS | 62533.75 | 62534 | Corrected SS | 19537.4298 | 19537 |
| MPH | 101 | Coeff Variation | 68.0082322 | 68.008232 | Std Error Mean | 2.47401469 | 2.474015 |
| MPH | 280 | N | 37 | 37.000000 | Sum Weights | 37 | 37.000000 |
| MPH | 280 | Mean | 29.9189189 | 29.918919 | Sum Observations | 1107 | 1107.000000 |
| MPH | 280 | Std Deviation | 18.1966547 | 18.196655 | Variance | 331.118243 | 331.118243 |
| MPH | 280 | Skewness | 0.32404229 | 0.324042 | Kurtosis | -0.9614173 | -0.961417 |
| MPH | 280 | Uncorrected SS | 45040.5 | 45041 | Corrected SS | 11920.2568 | 11920 |
| MPH | 280 | Coeff Variation | 60.8198938 | 60.819894 | Std Error Mean | 2.99151161 | 2.991512 |

## Creating Output Data Sets from Multiple Procedures

Not only does ODS allow you to combine output objects from a single procedure into a common data set, but you can also combine output objects from multiple procedures into a common data set. If you are running a single procedure repeatedly, it can be useful to be able to create a combined data set.

For example, let's say you are running a series of models to explore the relationships between your variables. This can generate pages and pages of printed output. It would be much nicer to be able to produce a simple summary table. This example looks at how to combine the odds ratio results from a series of PROC LOGISTIC runs. After running the procedure once as a test, you can see from the Results window in Output 7.13 that the output object you want is called "Odds Ratios." The code below asks for an output data set to be created from this object.

```
ODS OUTPUT "Odds Ratios"=FatalOdds;
proc logistic data=Traffic;
   model Fatal=MPH;
run;
proc logistic data=traffic;
   model Fatal=Location;
run;
proc logistic data=traffic;
   model Fatal=Location Highway;
run;
ODS OUTPUT CLOSE;
```

The resulting data set is shown in Output 7.14. It contains the odds ratios you want, but something is wrong. It only contains the results from the first model. This is because ODS output data set definitions only hold until the next procedure or DATA step starts. To keep the definition in place across multiple procedures, you need to add two options. The first option, MATCH_ALL, tells ODS to create a new data set for each of the multiple output objects. It has an optional parameter for a macro variable name to be used to hold the names of the data sets created. The second option is PERSIST, which forces the definition to hold for multiple procedures. These options are added to the first ODS OUTPUT statement as follows:

```
ODS OUTPUT "Odds Ratios"(MATCH_ALL=OddsDS PERSIST=PROC)=FatalOdds;
```

Now when the code is run, instead of getting just a single output data set called FatalOdds with just the results of the first procedure, you get two more data sets called FatalOdds1 and FatalOdds2 with the results of the next two procedures. Since it would be a hassle to have to figure out these data set names and write code to combine them, ODS also gives you the macro variable OddsDS, which is set to "FATALODDS  FATALODDS1 FATALODDS2." You can now use this variable to add a DATA step to combine your results. The new output is shown in Output 7.15. It has the results of all three models in one data set.

```
data AllOdds;
   set &OddsDS;
run;
```

**Output 7.13**

**Output 7.14**

| Obs | Effect | OddsRatioEst | LowerCL | UpperCL |
|-----|--------|--------------|---------|---------|
| 1 | MPH | 1.011 | 0.993 | 1.029 |

**Output 7.15**

| Obs | _Proc_ | _Run_ | Effect | OddsRatioEst | LowerCL | UpperCL |
|-----|--------|-------|--------|--------------|---------|---------|
| 1 | Logistic | 1 | MPH | 1.011 | 0.993 | 1.029 |
| 2 | Logistic | 1 | Loc | 1.117 | 0.921 | 1.355 |
| 3 | Logistic | 1 | Loc | 1.118 | 0.921 | 1.357 |
| 4 | Logistic | 1 | Hig | 1.079 | 0.898 | 1.298 |

By default, when the MATCH_ALL option is used, ODS creates additional data sets by adding a digit to the end of the data set name you provide. If you give the name DS, then ODS creates the names DS1, DS2, etc., for the next data sets it creates. This can be confusing, since the second data set is number 1 and the third data set is number 2. If you would like ODS to start numbering from 1, just use DS1 for the data set name in your code. ODS will name the next ones DS2, DS3, etc.

This example used PERSIST=PROC to create a file for each procedure. You can also use PERSIST=RUN to create a file for each run group. This is useful when working with procedures like GLM.

## Creating Output Data Sets without Printed Output

When you're running a procedure to produce an output data set, you may want to get rid of the results displayed in the output window or listing file. Before ODS, you would use the NOPRINT option available on many procedures to eliminate the "printed" output.

For example, let's say you're running a single regression model with the REG procedure and you want to build a data set with the parameter estimates. After running the code once to find out the name of the output object ("Parameter Estimates"; see Output 7.16), you can set up the code as follows:

```
ODS OUTPUT "Parameter Estimates"=Params;
proc reg data=traffic NOPRINT;
   model mph=highway location;
quit;
ODS OUTPUT CLOSE;
```

The NOPRINT option has been turned on to eliminate the unnecessary listing output, since the data set "Params" will hold the results you need. Or does it? If you view Output 7.17, you can see from the warning message in the log that the output data set Params was never created. This is because in order for ODS to create an output data set (or HTML file, RTF file, or printer output), there has to be an output object. With NOPRINT turned on, the output object is never created.

This is a major difference between Version 6 output data sets and Version 8 ODS data sets. You cannot use the NOPRINT option on any procedure and still get an ODS output data set.

However, this does not mean that you can't get rid of the unwanted listing output. All you have to do is use ODS instead of the NOPRINT option. The listing output is just another form of ODS output. It can be turned on and off. By default, this output destination is turned on. If you don't want listing output, just turn it off with the ODS LISTING CLOSE statement.

For example, to revise our previous code to create an output data set without creating listing output, the new code is

```
ODS LISTING CLOSE;
ODS OUTPUT "Parameter Estimates"=Params;
proc reg data=traffic;
   model mph=highway location;
quit;
ODS OUTPUT CLOSE;
ODS LISTING;
```

The first ODS LISTING CLOSE statement shuts off the listing destination. Then the ODS OUTPUT statements capture the output data set called "Params." Finally, another ODS LISTING statement turns the listing back on. This time there's no warning message in the log. The "Params" data set is created, and is shown in Output 7.18.

**Output 7.16**

```
Results                              ☒
  Results
  ⊟ Reg
     ⊟ MODEL1
        ⊟ Fit
           ⊟ MPH
                 Analysis of Variance
                 Fit Statistics
                 Parameter Estimates
```

**Output 7.17**

```
19   ODS OUTPUT "Parameter Estimates"=Params;
20   proc reg data=traffic noprint;
21       model mph=highway location;
22   quit;

NOTE: 189 observations read.
NOTE: 189 observations used in computations.
WARNING: Output '"Parameter Estimates"' was not created.
NOTE: There were 189 observations read from the data set WORK.TRAFFIC.
NOTE: PROCEDURE REG used:
      real time            0.04 seconds

23   ODS OUTPUT CLOSE;
```

**Output 7.18**

| Obs | Model | Dependent | Variable | DF | Estimate | StdErr | tValue | Probt | Label |
|---|---|---|---|---|---|---|---|---|---|
| 1 | MODEL1 | MPH | Intercept | 1 | 26.22363 | 3.20828 | 8.17 | <.0001 | Intercept |
| 2 | MODEL1 | MPH | Highway | 1 | 0.09636 | 0.78172 | 0.12 | 0.9020 | |
| 3 | MODEL1 | MPH | Location | 1 | 0.47083 | 0.82264 | 0.57 | 0.5678 | |

In addition to the TRACE procedure and the Results window, another way to look up the names of output objects for statistical procedures is to use the "SAS/STAT User's Guide" in SAS OnlineDoc. The ODS table names are listed in the documentation for each procedure.

## Opening and Closing Output Data Sets

You might think that the results of every procedure between two ODS OUTPUT statements are sent to an output data set, but that's not quite true. Once you open the ODS OUTPUT destination, it captures every specified output object that is created before the next ODS OUTPUT CLOSE statement.

The difference between these two statements may not be clear, so let's look at an example. This code runs two TTEST procedures (see Output 7.19 for the output objects created), captures the t-test results, and then prints their output data sets. The MATCH_ALL and PERSIST options create two data sets: "TTests" and "TTests1."

```
ODS OUTPUT "T-Tests"(MATCH_ALL PERSIST=PROC)=TTests;
proc ttest data=traffic;
   class fatal;
   var MPH;
run;
proc ttest data=traffic;
   class fatal;
   var MPH;
ODS OUTPUT CLOSE;
proc print data=TTests;
run;
proc print data=TTests1;
run;
```

However, if this code is run as is, the result is the error log shown in Output 7.20. The second data set was not created. This is not the result of any errors in specifying the ODS OUTPUT statements. The problem is caused by the lack of a RUN or QUIT statement after the second TTEST procedure.

Because SAS never came to another procedure, DATA step, RUN, or QUIT before it came to the ODS OUTPUT CLOSE statement, the procedure was not finished when the output destination was closed. The output objects for the second procedure were not created until the PROC PRINT statement was reached, which was too late. So both TTEST procedures produced listing output, but only one produced an output data set. To correct this, just add a RUN or QUIT before the ODS OUTPUT CLOSE statement.

```
ODS OUTPUT "T-Tests"(MATCH_ALL PERSIST=PROC)=TTests;
proc ttest data=traffic;
   class fatal;
   var MPH;
proc ttest data=traffic;
   class fatal;
   var MPH;
run;
ODS OUTPUT CLOSE;
proc print data=TTests;
run;
proc print data=TTests1;
run;
```

**Output 7.19**

```
Results                                    ☒
  📋 Results
  └─ 📋 T test
        📄 Statistics
        📄 T-Tests
        📄 Equality of Variances
```

**Output 7.20**

```
17    ODS OUTPUT "T-Tests"(MATCH_ALL PERSIST)=TTests;
18    proc ttest data=traffic;
19       class fatal;
20       var MPH;

NOTE: The data set WORK.TTESTS has 2 observations and 8 variables.
NOTE: There were 189 observations read from the data set WORK.TRAFFIC.
NOTE: PROCEDURE TTEST used:
      real time              0.11 seconds


21    proc ttest data=traffic;
22       class fatal;
23       var MPH;
24    ODS OUTPUT CLOSE;

NOTE: There were 189 observations read from the data set WORK.TRAFFIC.
NOTE: PROCEDURE TTEST used:
      real time              0.17 seconds
25    proc print data=TTests;
26    run;

NOTE: There were 2 observations read from the data set WORK.TTESTS.
NOTE: PROCEDURE PRINT used:
      real time              0.11 seconds


27    proc print data=TTests1;
ERROR: File WORK.TTESTS1.DATA does not exist.
28    run;

NOTE: The SAS System stopped processing this step because of errors.
NOTE: PROCEDURE PRINT used:
      real time              0.00 seconds
```

The problem illustrated in this example is not limited to ODS output data sets. You can run into the same problem with HTML, RTF, or printer output. Be sure to put a RUN or QUIT statement before every ODS CLOSE statement.

## Using Data Set Options with Output Data Sets

In each of the previous examples, we've selected specific output data sets. The data sets were chosen from the list of available output objects in the Results window. The contents of each of these data sets are determined by ODS.

For example, if you run the RSREG procedure and request a data set with the parameter estimates (see Output 7.21), you automatically get the data shown in Output 7.22.

```
ODS OUTPUT "Parameter Estimates"=Params;
proc rsreg data=traffic;
   model fatal=mph;
run;
ODS OUTPUT CLOSE;
```

This data set has eight variables. Every time you request this data set, you get the same variables with the same names. However, you may not always want all eight variables, and you may not like their default names. For example, let's say you want only three of the variables, and you would like to rename "Probt" as "Pvalue." One way to achieve this would be to write a DATA step like the following:

```
data Params2;
   set Params (keep=Parameter Estimate Probt
                 rename=(Probt=Pvalue));
run;
```

This code will do the trick, and it could be used to create the data set shown in Output 7.23. However, this is an extra processing step. A better way to do this is to specify these changes in the ODS OUTPUT statement. When you ask for a data set in an ODS OUTPUT statement, all of the usual data set options apply. By adding parentheses after the SAS data set name, you can use all of the usual data set options like KEEP, RENAME, and DROP.

The following code accomplishes the same thing as the combination of ODS and DATA step code above. However, this code does it in a single pass of the data, so you save resources.

```
ODS OUTPUT "Parameter Estimates"=Params
   (KEEP=Parameter Estimate Probt RENAME=(Probt=Pvalue));
proc rsreg data=traffic;
   model fatal=mph;
run;
ODS OUTPUT CLOSE;
```

This code will also produce the data set shown in Output 7.23.

**Output 7.21**

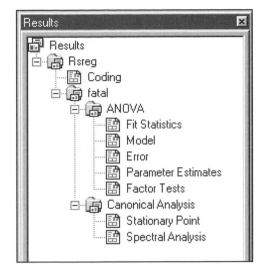

**Output 7.22**

| Obs | Dependent | Parameter | DF | Estimate | StdErr | tValue | Probt | CodedEstimate |
|---|---|---|---|---|---|---|---|---|
| 1 | fatal | Intercept | 1 | 0.427698 | 0.084652 | 5.05 | <.0001 | 0.247315 |
| 2 | fatal | MPH | 1 | -0.009171 | 0.006216 | -1.48 | 0.1418 | -0.062710 |
| 3 | fatal | MPH*MPH | 1 | 0.000111 | 0.000095659 | 1.16 | 0.2457 | 0.117672 |

**Output 7.23**

| Obs | Parameter | Estimate | Pvalue |
|---|---|---|---|
| 1 | Intercept | 0.427698 | <.0001 |
| 2 | MPH | -0.009171 | 0.1418 |
| 3 | MPH*MPH | 0.000111 | 0.2457 |

# Chapter 8

# *Limiting ODS Output*

It used to be that when you ran a SAS procedure, output was pretty much an all-or-nothing proposition. Either you got pages of output, or you used the NOPRINT option and got no output at all except a data set.

Some procedures had options to give you a little control over the output. For example, in the FREQ procedure you can request certain statistics (CHISQ option) or remove some of the frequencies (NOROW or NOCOL options). However, this ability was limited to a few procedures.

Now, with ODS, you can get exactly the output you want, in exactly the formats you want, for any procedure you want.

For example, you can request a complete output data set, one table from the results as RTF, and another table of the results in listing format. Plus, you can request these things for virtually any procedure.

## Selecting a Subset of Your Results

If you're using ODS to create output data sets, you have to specify each output object you want. With HTML, RTF, printer, and listing output, by default you get everything the procedure can produce. You can change what you get in limited ways by using certain procedure options. For example, the CHISQ option adds some results to PROC FREQ output, and the NOSIMPLE option removes some results from PROC CORR output.

However, the best way to customize the content of your results is to use ODS. For example, if you have the following code that creates RTF output from some univariate statistics, you get the standard UNIVARIATE procedure output shown in Output 8.1.

```
ODS RTF FILE='Univariate.rtf';
proc univariate data=voters;
   var income;
run;
ODS RTF CLOSE;
```

This procedure produces a lot of output. So much, in fact, that there isn't room to show it all on the facing page. If what you really want is just the basic statistics like mean, median, and mode, you can save a lot of space by getting rid of the other information.

One way to get these statistics is to use ODS to create an output data set from the BasicMeasures output object, and then print the results to an RTF file. A better way is to use the ODS SELECT statement. This statement allows you to list the names of the output objects you want to select. The syntax is

```
ODS SELECT output-object(s)-to-include;
```

These are the only objects that will be sent to your open output destinations. In this example, you can use ODS SELECT to request that the output be limited to the BasicMeasures object.

```
ODS SELECT BasicMeasures;
ODS RTF FILE='UnivariateSelect.rtf';
proc univariate data=voters;
   var income;
run;
ODS RTF CLOSE;
```

Now the results easily fit into just a portion of the page, as shown in Output 8.2. You can use this technique with any output destination except ODS OUTPUT. This example used RTF output and the UNIVARIATE procedure, but the RTF specification could be traded for HTML or PRINTER, and the result would be the same. If listing output is turned on, then the selection applies to that output too.

**Output 8.1**

| Moments | | | |
|---|---|---|---|
| N | 276 | Sum Weights | 276 |
| Mean | 120433.087 | Sum Observations | 33239532 |
| Std Deviation | 60089.207 | Variance | 3610712795 |
| Skewness | -0.0637537 | Kurtosis | -1.2638647 |
| Uncorrected SS | 4.99609E12 | Corrected SS | 9.92946E11 |
| Coeff Variation | 49.8942678 | Std Error Mean | 3616.94522 |

| Basic Statistical Measures | | | |
|---|---|---|---|
| Location | | Variability | |
| Mean | 120433.1 | Std Deviation | 60089 |
| Median | 124862.0 | Variance | 3610712795 |
| Mode | . | Range | 198416 |
| | | Interquartile Range | 106549 |

| Tests for Location: Mu0=0 | | | | |
|---|---|---|---|---|
| Test | | Statistic | p Value | |
| Student's t | t | 33.29691 | Pr > \|t\| | <.0001 |
| Sign | M | 138 | Pr >= \|M\| | <.0001 |
| Signed Rank | S | 19113 | Pr >= \|S\| | <.0001 |

*(results truncated to save space)*

**Output 8.2**

| Basic Statistical Measures | | | |
|---|---|---|---|
| Location | | Variability | |
| Mean | 120433.1 | Std Deviation | 60089 |
| Median | 124862.0 | Variance | 3610712795 |
| Mode | . | Range | 198416 |
| | | Interquartile Range | 106549 |

## Selecting Multiple Output Objects

The SELECT statement does not limit you to selecting just a single output object for display. You can choose among all of the output objects that a procedure produces.

For example, if you've run a simple regression model, you may look over the results and decide that you'd like to create a report that includes just part of the output. You may find the R-square statistic and the parameter estimates useful, but you don't need things like the sum of squares or the root MSE (mean square error).

By running an ODS TRACE, you discover that the R-square statistic is in the FitStatistics output object and the parameter estimates are in the ParameterEstimates object. So those two objects go in the ODS SELECT statement. The code for these selections follows, and the output is displayed in Output 8.3.

```
ODS SELECT FitStatistics ParameterEstimates;
ODS HTML BODY='SelectReg.htm';
proc reg data=Turnout;
    model PctTurnout = Gender Age Party;
quit;
ODS HTML CLOSE;
```

That was easy, so let's look at another example. When you explore a data set for the first time, one of the first things you want to do is run a PROC CONTENTS to find out what's in the data set. The default output has a header with information such as the number of observations and the number of variables. It also has a detailed listing of each variable. However, there is no option to view just the header information. If you have a large data set, the PROC CONTENTS output can be unwieldy.

ODS SELECT can solve this problem. If you run an ODS TRACE on a PROC CONTENTS, you will discover that the header and the list of variables are two separate output objects. This means that you can select one but not the other.

So to get a PROC CONTENTS with just the header information, use ODS SELECT to request just the Attributes object. The code is as follows, and the output is displayed in Output 8.4.

```
ODS SELECT Attributes;
ODS HTML BODY='SelectContents.htm';
proc contents data=voters;
run;
ODS HTML CLOSE;
```

**Output 8.3**

| Root MSE | 0.80889 | R-Square | 0.0644 |
|---|---|---|---|
| Dependent Mean | 2.03890 | Adj R-Sq | 0.0006 |
| Coeff Var | 39.67296 | | |

| Parameter Estimates | | | | | | |
|---|---|---|---|---|---|---|
| Variable | Label | DF | Parameter Estimate | Standard Error | t Value | Pr > \|t\| |
| Intercept | Intercept | 1 | 2.58077 | 0.37083 | 6.96 | <.0001 |
| Gender | | 1 | 0.03704 | 0.23351 | 0.16 | 0.8747 |
| Age | | 1 | -0.00910 | 0.00713 | -1.28 | 0.2089 |
| Party | Political Affiliation | 1 | -0.04517 | 0.03852 | -1.17 | 0.2473 |

**Output 8.4**

| Data Set Name: | WORK.VOTERS | Observations: | 276 |
|---|---|---|---|
| Member Type: | DATA | Variables: | 6 |
| Engine: | V8 | Indexes: | 0 |
| Created: | 17:05 Monday, November 27, 2000 | Observation Length: | 48 |
| Last Modified: | 17:05 Monday, November 27, 2000 | Deleted Observations: | 0 |
| Protection: | | Compressed: | NO |
| Data Set Type: | | Sorted: | NO |
| Label: | | | |

## Excluding the Output You Don't Want

If you're working with a procedure that produces many output objects, you may find it easier to exclude the ones you don't want rather than select all of the ones you do want. ODS provides an EXCLUDE statement in addition to the SELECT statement. The syntax is the same:

```
ODS EXCLUDE output-object(s)-to-exclude;
```

To compare the two statements, let's look at a sample program. First, we'll identify our chosen output objects using the SELECT statement, and then we'll repeat the program using the EXCLUDE statement.

For this example, we will modify the output from the UNIVARIATE procedure to eliminate the Extreme Observations table. To code this using the SELECT statement, you need to name every output object that you want except for the ExtremeObs object. The code follows:

```
ODS SELECT Moments BasicMeasures TestsForLocation Quantiles;
ODS PDF FILE='SelectUniv.pdf';
proc univariate data=voters;
    var income;
run;
ODS PDF CLOSE;
```

Since PROC UNIVARIATE produces five output objects, to exclude one you need to select the other four. This code produces the output shown in Output 8.5.

You can produce exactly the same output using the EXCLUDE statement. With EXCLUDE, all you have to do is list the one object you want to exclude: the ExtremeObs object. The code is shown below.

```
ODS EXCLUDE ExtremeObs;
ODS PDF FILE='SelectUniv2.pdf';
proc univariate data=voters;
    var income;
run;
ODS PDF CLOSE;
```

This code also produces the output shown in Output 8.5. The output files from these two versions of the code are identical.

It's up to you whether to use SELECT or EXCLUDE. You can achieve exactly the same results with either statement. Generally, you will want to use the statement that involves the least typing. So if you have more objects to keep than to remove, use EXCLUDE. But if you have more objects to get rid of than to keep, use SELECT.

Another consideration is documentation. If you want your code to be self-documenting, you may find it helpful to have a list of the selected output objects hard-coded into your program. SELECT will do this for you, while EXCLUDE shows only what was left out.

**Output 8.5**

| Moments | | | |
|---|---|---|---|
| N | 276 | Sum Weights | 276 |
| Mean | 521967.149 | Sum Observations | 144062933 |
| Std Deviation | 273132.444 | Variance | 7.46013E10 |
| Skewness | -0.0085717 | Kurtosis | -0.978514 |
| Uncorrected SS | 9.57115E13 | Corrected SS | 2.05154E13 |
| Coeff Variation | 52.3275162 | Std Error Mean | 16440.6411 |

| Basic Statistical Measures | | | |
|---|---|---|---|
| Location | | Variability | |
| Mean | 521967.1 | Std Deviation | 273132 |
| Median | 523693.5 | Variance | 7.46013E10 |
| Mode | . | Range | 995746 |
| | | Interquartile Range | 425758 |

| Tests for Location: Mu0=0 | | | | |
|---|---|---|---|---|
| Test | | Statistic | p Value | |
| Student's t | t | 31.74859 | Pr > |t| | <.0001 |
| Sign | M | 138 | Pr >= |M| | <.0001 |
| Signed Rank | S | 19113 | Pr >= |S| | <.0001 |

| Quantiles (Definition 5) | |
|---|---|
| Quantile | Estimate |
| 100% Max | 1011495 |
| 99% | 1003082 |
| 95% | 971833 |
| 90% | 913008 |
| 75% Q3 | 727653 |
| 50% Median | 523694 |
| 25% Q1 | 301895 |
| 10% | 146641 |
| 5% | 56402 |
| 1% | 22111 |
| 0% Min | 15749 |

Avoid using ODS SELECT and ODS EXCLUDE in the same program. These two statements can interact and generate unexpected results.

## Selecting Output for Multiple Procedures

The ability to limit your output is especially handy when you're doing repeated runs of the same procedure. For example, you may be running a series of models or a series of tables. If you're forced to keep all of the output from all of the procedures, your results can get unwieldy.

Using SELECT or EXCLUDE allows you to build a concise summary report from your results. For example, let's say you are running a bunch of crosstabulations, trying to identify variables with significant relationships. You can do this with a series of FREQ procedures. Since you only want to know which variables are significantly related, you can save space in the output by reporting just the statistics, not the actual crosstabs. The following code uses the SELECT statement to request only the ChiSq output object. It has two FREQ procedures that are used to create an RTF report.

```
ODS SELECT ChiSq;
ODS RTF FILE='SelectFreq.rtf';
proc freq data=voters;
   table voted*party / chisq;
run;
proc freq data=voters;
   table voted*age / chisq;
run;
ODS RTF CLOSE;
```

However, you need to make a couple of additions before running this code. To use SELECT or EXCLUDE with multiple procedures, you need to add a new option. Following the output object, you need to add the option PERSIST. The syntax calls for this option to be placed in parentheses after each output object.

Another change comes at the end of the code. To keep this selection from continuing until the end of the SAS session, it's best to follow your procedures with an ODS SELECT ALL to reset the select list. If you used ODS EXCLUDE with the PERSIST option, add an ODS EXCLUDE NONE at the end to reset the selections.

```
ODS SELECT ChiSq (PERSIST);
ODS RTF FILE='SelectFreq.rtf';
proc freq data=voters;
   table voted*party / chisq;
run;
proc freq data=voters;
   table voted*age / chisq;
run;
ODS RTF CLOSE;
ODS SELECT ALL;
```

If you look at the Results window shown in Output 8.6, you can see that only the ChiSq output object has been created by each procedure. The resulting RTF file is shown in Output 8.7.

**Output 8.6**

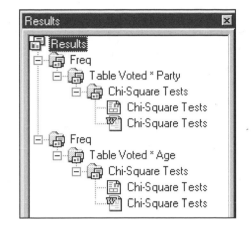

**Output 8.7**

| Statistic | DF | Value | Prob |
|---|---|---|---|
| Chi-Square | 2 | 0.7567 | 0.6850 |
| Likelihood Ratio Chi-Square | 2 | 0.7573 | 0.6848 |
| Mantel-Haenszel Chi-Square | 1 | 0.4935 | 0.4824 |
| Phi Coefficient | | 0.0524 | |
| Contingency Coefficient | | 0.0523 | |
| Cramer's V | | 0.0524 | |

| Statistic | DF | Value | Prob |
|---|---|---|---|
| Chi-Square | 5 | 7.1965 | 0.2064 |
| Likelihood Ratio Chi-Square | 5 | 7.2814 | 0.2005 |
| Mantel-Haenszel Chi-Square | 1 | 0.5756 | 0.4480 |
| Phi Coefficient | | 0.1615 | |
| Contingency Coefficient | | 0.1594 | |
| Cramer's V | | 0.1615 | |

## Customizing Your Selections for Each Output Destination

Using the SELECT or EXCLUDE statement to summarize your results can be helpful, but you need to be careful. By dropping some of the output, you may miss something important. For example, what if the frequency table in the previous example contained some unexpected missing data? You might not spot the problem by just looking at the ChiSq output object.

The best way to avoid this problem is to produce summary reports using HTML, RTF, or printer output; but be sure to keep the full output in the listing. This way you can review the detailed listing before you start using the summary report.

Both the SELECT and EXCLUDE statements can be applied to a specific output destination. All of the previous examples have omitted the output destination option, causing the statements to apply to all output objects. If you want the selections or exclusions to apply to only one output destination, you just need to add the appropriate destination. For example, to exclude an object from the RTF destination, the syntax is

```
ODS RTF EXCLUDE output-object-name;
```

Alternatively, to select an object for the HTML destination, you use

```
ODS HTML SELECT output-object-name;
```

As an example, you can create a summary report with just the correlation coefficients from PROC CORR but keep the full listing output for detailed review. This allows you to review the basic statistics shown in the listing to be sure that the data is what you expected. The code is shown below:

```
ODS HTML BODY='SelectCorr.html';
ODS HTML SELECT PearsonCorr;
proc corr data=voters;
   var income;
   with age;
run;
ODS HTML CLOSE;
```

The HTML file created by this code is shown in Output 8.8. Notice that it contains only the correlation coefficients. The listing output, shown in Output 8.9, contains the full results. By using SELECT or EXCLUDE with a specific output destination, you get the best of both worlds: a short summary report and a detailed listing for review.

The SELECT statement must come after the HTML destination has been opened. When you issue a general SELECT that does not apply to any one destination, you can list it before or after a destination is opened, as long as it comes before the statements that generate the results you want to capture. When you specify a single output destination, that destination must be open in order for the SELECT or EXCLUDE to work. Otherwise, you will get a warning message in your log, and the SELECT or EXCLUDE will have no effect.

**Output 8.8**

### The CORR Procedure

| Pearson Correlation Coefficients, N = 276 Prob > \|r\| under H0: Rho=0 | |
|---|---|
| | Income |
| Age | 0.01250 0.8362 |

**Output 8.9**

```
The CORR Procedure

    1 With Variables:    Age
    1      Variables:    Income


                              Simple Statistics

Variable        N        Mean      Std Dev        Sum      Minimum      Maximum

Age           276    54.59420     22.59578      15068     18.00000     92.00000
Income        276      521967       273132  144062933        15749      1011495


Pearson Correlation Coefficients, N = 276
         Prob > |r|  under HO: Rho=0

            Income

Age       0.01250
          0.8362
```

## Selecting Complex Combinations of Output Objects

In Chapter 6, you saw several examples of identifying output objects by their labels. In this chapter, you have seen several examples of identifying output objects by their names. These are the simplest ways to identify an output object when you are creating an output data set or using SELECT or EXCLUDE. However, these are not the only ways.

The code below uses a number of approaches to identify the output objects in its SELECT statements. To see how these methods relate to the output objects, you will need to review the ODS TRACE output shown in Output 8.10. This is not a complete trace of the code, but rather a selection of tracings, one for each type of output object.

```
ODS LISTING CLOSE;
ODS HTML BODY='SelectMany.htm';
ODS HTML SELECT Freq.Table1.OneWayFreqs
                Table2.OneWayFreqs
                "Table Party"."One-Way Frequencies"
                "One-Way Chi-Square Test";
proc freq data=voters;
   tables gender age party / chisq;
run;
ODS HTML SELECT ExtremeObs#1 Quantiles#2;
proc univariate data=voters;
   var income age;
run;
ODS HTML CLOSE;
```

First, let's look at the selections for the PROC FREQ. The first selection, Freq.Table1.OneWayFreqs, is an example of selecting an object by its path. You can also identify an object by a partial path, as in the second selection, Table2.OneWayFreqs. When using a partial path, you can start with any portion of the path, but then you have to include everything to the right of where you start. Therefore, OneWayFreqs is a legal path, but Freq.Table1 is not.

The next two selections demonstrate the use of the label path. You can see the label path in Output 8.10, but you can also find this path by looking at the Results window. If you combine the labels at each level of the results in the Results window, you get the label path. The third and fourth selections in the code above demonstrate the use of partial label paths (you can also use a full label path, but those can get pretty long).

The net effect of the four selections that precede the PROC FREQ is to select all of the output objects available. The three frequency tables are picked individually by the first three selections, and the three chi-square tables are picked by the fourth selection.

The second SELECT statement applies to the PROC UNIVARIATE. It shows one more way to identify output. If you have an output object that will be created more than once, you can identify each occurrence by number. ExtremeObs#1 is the extreme observations table for the variable income, and Quantiles#2 is the quantiles table for the variable age.

To see how all of these selections work, take a look at the Results window from this run in Output 8.11.

**Output 8.10  Sample Output Tracings**

```
------------
Name:        OneWayFreqs
Label:       One-Way Frequencies
Template:    Base.Freq.OneWayFreqs
Path:        Freq.Table1.OneWayFreqs
Label Path: "The Freq Procedure"."Table Gender"."One-Way Frequencies"
------------


------------
Name:        OneWayChiSq
Label:       One-Way Chi-Square Test
Template:    Base.Freq.StatFactoid
Path:        Freq.Table2.OneWayChiSq
Label Path: "The Freq Procedure"."Table Age"."One-Way Chi-Square Test"
------------


------------
Name:        Quantiles
Label:       Quantiles
Template:    base.univariate.Quantiles
Path:        Univariate.Income.Quantiles
Label Path: "The Univariate Procedure"."Income"."Quantiles"
------------


------------
Name:        ExtremeObs
Label:       Extreme Observations
Template:    base.univariate.ExtObs
Path:        Univariate.Income.ExtremeObs
Label Path: "The Univariate Procedure"."Income"."Extreme Observations"
------------
```

**Output 8.11**

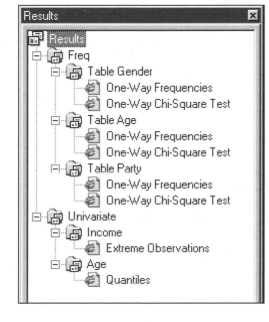

## Identifying the Current Selections and Exclusions

The examples so far have been simple. You could easily see what was being selected and excluded. However, as you start to create complex production jobs with thousands of lines of code, you may start running into problems. The following example shows how to debug a problem with your ODS output. This code should create an RTF file with two chi-square results tables. The EXCLUDE statement blocks the display of the crosstabs. However, if you view Output 8.12, you can see that the resulting RTF file is empty.

```
ODS RTF FILE='selectshow.rtf';
ODS RTF EXCLUDE CrossTabFreqs(Persist);
proc freq data=voters;
    tables party*gender / chisq;
run;
proc freq data=voters;
    tables party*age / chisq;
run;
ODS RTF CLOSE;
```

What happened to the results? The first thing to do is check the log for error messages. In this case, the log shows no error messages. It indicates that the requested RTF file was created. The next thing to do is look at the listing output. This output is not shown, but it contains only crosstabs and not the chi-square results.

So what's wrong? These lines of code are actually part of a larger program, and at this point you should be suspicious of the preceding code. The SELECT and EXCLUDE statements are powerful tools, but if you aren't careful, they can get you into trouble. To find out if that is the case, you need to use a new ODS statement, the SHOW statement:

**ODS RTF SHOW;**

This allows you to see the current selection and exclusion lists. This statement is added after the other ODS RTF statements and right before the procedures are called. The SHOW statement sends its results to the log window, as shown in Output 8.13. According to these results, our exclusion list is exactly as expected. The only item being excluded is the CrossTabFreqs object. So this does not solve the problem. The solution comes from adding a second SHOW statement. The ODS RTF SHOW statement lists the current selection and exclusion lists for the RTF destination. However, it is also possible to select and include objects across all destinations. To see what's going on, you need to add a SHOW statement for all destinations.

**ODS SHOW;**

Now you have your answer. Output 8.14 contains the lines written to the log file, and you can see that the problem is that you have an overall exclusion in effect, in addition to your exclusion for the RTF destination. The overall exclusion removed the ChiSq output object from all destinations. What's going on is that somewhere in the preceding code, we used an ODS EXCLUDE with a PERSIST option and forgot to clear the exclusion with a subsequent ODS EXCLUDE NONE statement. This allowed the earlier code to affect output later in the program.

**Output 8.12**

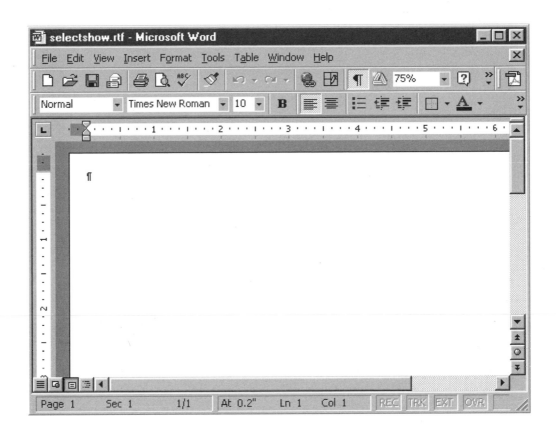

**Output 8.13**

```
Current RTF exclude list is:
1. CrossTabFreqs(PERSIST)
```

**Output 8.14**

```
Current OVERALL exclude list is:
1. ChiSq(PERSIST)
Current RTF exclude list is:
1. CrossTabFreqs(PERSIST)
```

 If you use the PERSIST option, be careful to follow it with an ODS SELECT ALL or ODS EXCLUDE NONE to keep it from affecting other parts of your program. If you do get into trouble, remember the ODS SHOW statement.

# Chapter
# 9

*Style Definitions*

ODS is a major step forward in giving you the power to customize output. The earlier chapters in this book looked at how to send output to various destinations and how to control which output objects you get.

The next few chapters are all about appearances. ODS gives you the power to customize virtually every aspect of how your results look. You can make a title bigger, make the detail data bolder, or even change the entire color scheme.

To make these customizations easier, Version 8 comes with a number of built-in output style definitions. This chapter shows how to use these existing style definitions. We will switch from one style definition to another, and make minor changes in an existing style definition. Subsequent chapters will go over style definition modifications in more detail, and show how you can build your own custom style definitions.

## Viewing a List of Available Style Definitions

You may not have realized it, but each of the preceding examples that produced HTML, RTF, or printer output used a style definition. By default, ODS uses a standard style definition for each output destination. This is a nice-looking style definition, which uses simple fonts and various shades of blue, gray, and black (HTML) or gray and black (printer and RTF). When you issue an ODS statement like

```
ODS HTML BODY='DefaultStyle.html';
```

you're really issuing the following:

```
ODS HTML BODY='DefaultStyle.html' STYLE=Default;
```

So if you want to switch to another style definition, all you have to do is add a STYLE= option and specify the name of a different style definition.

What are these other style definitions? There are two ways to get a list of the style definitions on your system. The first way is to select **Tools** from the menu bar in the Display Manager window. Next, select **Options** and then **Preferences**. In the window that pops up, select the **Results** tab. In the middle of this window is a pull-down list labeled Style. This list shows you the various style definitions available on your system, as shown in Figure 9.1.

The other way to get a list of style definitions it to use a new procedure released as part of ODS. The TEMPLATE procedure is used to review, modify, and create style definitions. To use TEMPLATE to get a list of available style definitions, run the following code:

```
PROC TEMPLATE;
    LIST STYLES;
RUN:
```

Sample output from this procedure is shown in Output 9.1. The first item on the list is simply the locations of the style definitions being listed (Styles directory). The style definitions themselves are listed next, and all are of type Style. Notice the style definition called Default. This style definition is used whenever you specify HTML output. The style definition called Printer is used by default when you ask for printer output, and the style definition called RTF is used by default when you ask for RTF output.

You can guess the uses of some of the other style definitions. The style definition Minimal is just that, a bare-bones style definition you can use if you don't want anything elaborate. FancyPrinter is a more detailed printer style definition. The Brown and Beige style definitions use those colors. When you run this code yourself, your list may be different.

If you want a quick preview of each of the available style definitions, see Appendix 1, "Sample Programs." It contains code to generate annotated output that displays each of the style definitions on your system.

**Figure 9.1**

**Output 9.1**

| Listing of: SASHELP.TMPLMST | | |
|---|---|---|
| Path Filter is: Styles | | |
| Sort by: PATH/ASCENDING | | |
| Obs | Path | Type |
| 1 | Styles | Dir |
| 2 | Styles.BarrettsBlue | Style |
| 3 | Styles.Beige | Style |
| 4 | Styles.Brick | Style |
| 5 | Styles.Brown | Style |
| 6 | Styles.D3d | Style |
| 7 | Styles.Default | Style |
| 8 | Styles.Minimal | Style |
| 9 | Styles.NoFontDefault | Style |
| 10 | Styles.Printer | Style |
| 11 | Styles.Rtf | Style |
| 12 | Styles.Statdoc | Style |
| 13 | Styles.Theme | Style |
| 14 | Styles.fancyPrinter | Style |
| 15 | Styles.sansPrinter | Style |
| 16 | Styles.sasdocPrinter | Style |
| 17 | Styles.serifPrinter | Style |

## Changing Style Definitions

Switching from one style definition to another is quite simple. Making up your mind about which one to use is the hard part.

To switch to a new style definition during your current SAS session, you can manually change the style definition using the Preferences window, as shown in the previous example. However, you have to remember to do this for each session. A better approach is to include the style definition name in your program.

To switch from the default style definition for a given output destination, just add the STYLE= option to your ODS statement when you open the output destination. For example, if you want to create HTML output using the Brick style definition, add STYLE="Brick" to your code. The following example shows how to use the same procedure to create a variety of output style definitions for the HTML and printer destinations.

```
ODS PRINTER STYLE=Brick;
proc means data=fashions maxdec=0 sum;
   class Skirts;
   var Sales;
run;
ODS PRINTER CLOSE;
```

The resulting printer output is shown in Output 9.2. It uses various shades of gray, plus brick red for the headings. If you have a color printer, this is an attractive style definition to use.

You can also use the same style definition for HTML output by changing the ODS statement in the previous example. The HTML version of the output is shown in Output 9.3. It looks almost identical to the printer output.

```
ODS HTML BODY='StyleSampler1.htm' STYLE=Brick;
```

Now let's look at another style definition by revising the code again to pick the Brown style definition.

```
ODS PRINTER STYLE=Brown;
```

Output 9.4 shows the new style definition. Unlike Brick, this style definition has both a color table background and a color page background. As a result, it is best suited to HTML output. For printer output, you will find that the style definitions with white backgrounds work best.

As a final example, let's look at a style definition that is meant for the printer. The FancyPrinter style definition is selected using the code below, and the results are shown in Output 9.5.

```
ODS PRINTER STYLE=FancyPrinter;
```

Experiment with each style definition in each of the output formats, and learn which ones you like best for each type of output.

**Output 9.2**

| Analysis Variable : Sales | | |
|---|---|---|
| Skirt length | N Obs | Sum |
| Mini | 73 | 3975498 |
| Above knees | 194 | 11767742 |
| Below knees | 168 | 10068671 |
| Maxi | 75 | 4777235 |

For a color version of Output 9.2, see page 283 in Appendix 3.

**Output 9.3**

| Analysis Variable : Sales | | |
|---|---|---|
| Skirt length | N Obs | Sum |
| Mini | 73 | 3975498 |
| Above knees | 194 | 11767742 |
| Below knees | 168 | 10068671 |
| Maxi | 75 | 4777235 |

For a color version of Output 9.3, see page 283 in Appendix 3.

**Output 9.4**

| Analysis Variable : Sales | | |
|---|---|---|
| Skirt length | N Obs | Sum |
| Mini | 73 | 3975498 |
| Above knees | 194 | 11767742 |
| Below knees | 168 | 10068671 |
| Maxi | 75 | 4777235 |

For a color version of Output 9.4, see page 283 in Appendix 3.

**Output 9.5**

| *Analysis Variable : Sales* | | |
|---|---|---|
| *Skirt length* | *N Obs* | *Sum* |
| Mini | 73 | 3975498 |
| Above knees | 194 | 11767742 |
| Below knees | 168 | 10068671 |
| Maxi | 75 | 4777235 |

## Examining the Components of an ODS Style Definition

You don't have to know how style definitions work to be able to use them. However, you do need to learn something about them if you want to be able to modify them. One of the most important features of ODS is the ability to customize a style to meet your needs.

The first thing you need to know about style definitions is how to look at the details. To do this, use the TEMPLATE procedure. To get a printout of the source code for a style definition, submit the following code:

```
PROC TEMPLATE;
   SOURCE Styles.Default;
RUN;
```

This example code requests a source listing for the Default style definition. The resulting printout is hundreds of lines long. To keep things simple, we're just going to look at a small sample of the code. Output 9.6 shows the lines of source code that affect the titles in your output. This includes the default SAS title ("The SAS System...") and any titles you add with a TITLE statement.

The code begins with a DEFINE statement that names the style definition it creates. The first section of code, headed with "style fonts," defines the fonts to be used for titles and regular document text. This section is called a *style statement* and it defines a *style element*, which is in turn composed of a number of *style attributes*. In the Default style definition, both the titles and the document text are set to the Arial font. Helvetica and Helv are listed as backup fonts in case your system does not have the preferred font. The only difference between the title and document fonts is size (5 and 4 versus 3) and weight (bold italic versus regular).

The second style element, "color_list," sets up the colors that will be used in this style definition. The colors are assigned to names ("fgA," "bgA") that will be used later in the code. The colors themselves are indicated using RGB values given in hexadecimal. These values represent dark blue and light gray. The third style element, "colors," applies these colors to the foreground and background color settings for titles and document text.

The fourth style element, "Container," is used for overall settings. Here the fonts and colors for regular document text are assigned. This "Container" is also the main organizing element of the style definition.

The fifth style element, "TitlesAndFooters from Container," is the specific part of the style definition that defines what makes titles and footnotes different from other parts of the style definition. This style element is listed as "from Container" because it inherits its basic settings from the Container style element. Then, in the TitlesAndFooters section, we have a series of settings that are used to describe the things that need to be different from Container. This includes the font specification (TitleFont2) and the colors.

The final style element, "SystemTitle from TitlesAndFooters," inherits its basic settings from the TitlesAndFooters and Container style elements. It has a special setting that applies only to titles. The font is changed from the TitleFont2 that was defined in TitlesAndFooters to the larger Title-Font.

Together, all of these style elements create a title with a particular font and colors. This is only an introduction, but it should give you a basic feel for how style definitions work.

**Output 9.6  Selected Sections of Style Definition Source Code**

```
define style Styles.Default;

   style fonts
      "Fonts used in the default style" /
      'TitleFont' = ("Arial, Helvetica, Helv",5,Bold Italic
      'TitleFont2' = ("Arial, Helvetica, Helv",4,Bold Italic)
      'docFont' = ("Arial, Helvetica, Helv",3);

   style color_list
      "Colors used in the default style" /
      'fgA' = cx002288
      'bgA' = cxE0E0E0;

   style colors
      "Abstract colors used in the default style" /
      'systitlefg' = color_list('fgA')
      'systitlebg' = color_list('bgA')
      'docfg' = color_list('fgA')
      'docbg' = color_list('bgA');

   style Container
      "Abstract. Controls all container oriented elements." /
      font = Fonts('DocFont')
      foreground = colors('docfg')
      background = colors('docbg');

   style TitlesAndFooters from Container
      "Abstract. Controls system page title text and system page footer text." /
      font = Fonts('TitleFont2')
      background = colors('systitlebg')
      foreground = colors('systitlefg');

   style SystemTitle from TitlesAndFooters
      "Controls system title text." /
      font = Fonts('TitleFont');

run;
```

The code in Output 9.6 does not represent a complete style definition. Major required portions of the code have been left out due to space considerations. Do not attempt to use this code with PROC TEMPLATE to create a style definition.

Although the complete style definition source code is long and intimidating, you may want to spend a little time reviewing it just to get a better feel for how a style definition works. Don't worry about understanding all of the details, but take the time to explore the basics. This effort will pay off as you start to modify style definitions in Chapters 10–12.

## Modifying a Style Definition: A Simple Example

Now that you've seen a simple example of how a style definition works, let's look at a simple example of modifying one. We're going to create a new style definition that looks just like the Default style definition, except that it uses a different font for the titles. This new style definition is stored and can be used repeatedly.

You may remember from the previous example that the fonts were defined in a style element called fonts. The previous example showed just a couple of the fonts. The full list is shown in Output 9.7. To modify the font, you use PROC TEMPLATE. This time you use a DEFINE statement to name your new style definition, and a PARENT statement to indicate that the new style definition will be based on the Default style definition.

```
PROC TEMPLATE;
   DEFINE STYLE DefaultNewTitle;
   PARENT=styles.default;
```

The PARENT statement makes it easy to create a new style definition, because you don't have to rewrite the whole style definition. You just have to indicate the parts you want to change. The rest of the style definition is inherited from the parent. A REPLACE statement is used for the part you want to change. In this example, we're going to replace the fonts style element shown in Output 9.7 with the code below. The only line that is changed is the definition for "TitleFont," which is now set to the Times New Roman font. The rest of the fonts are left as is. They must all be listed, because the REPLACE statement overwrites the previous fonts style element in the definition. Finally, to mark the end of the style definition changes, you need an END statement. The RUN statement executes the procedure.

```
     REPLACE fonts /
         'TitleFont2' = ("Arial, Helvetica, Helv",4,Bold Italic)
         'TitleFont' = ("Times New Roman, Times",5,Bold Italic)
         'StrongFont' = ("Arial, Helvetica, Helv",4,Bold)
         'EmphasisFont' = ("Arial, Helvetica, Helv",3,Italic)
         'FixedEmphasisFont' = ("Courier",2,Italic)
         'FixedStrongFont' = ("Courier",2,Bold)
         'FixedHeadingFont' = ("Courier",2)
         'BatchFixedFont' = ("SAS Monospace, Courier",2)
         'FixedFont' = ("Courier",2)
         'headingEmphasisFont' = ("Arial,Helvetica,Helv",4,Bold Italic)
         'headingFont' = ("Arial, Helvetica, Helv",4,Bold)
         'docFont' = ("Arial, Helvetica, Helv",3);
     END;
   RUN;
```

To use the new style definition, just name it in your ODS statement using the STYLE= option. Output 9.8 shows HTML output with the original style definition. Output 9.9 shows the output with the new style definition. Notice the font change in the title. That's all there is to modifying a style definition. You use PROC TEMPLATE with a SOURCE statement to find the code you want to change, and then you use PROC TEMPLATE with a DEFINE statement and a REPLACE statement to submit your modifications. For more examples, see Chapters 10–12.

**Output 9.7**

```
style fonts
   "Fonts used in the default style" /
   'TitleFont2' = ("Arial, Helvetica, Helv",4,Bold Italic)
   'TitleFont' = ("Arial, Helvetica, Helv",5,Bold Italic)
   'StrongFont' = ("Arial, Helvetica, Helv",4,Bold)
   'EmphasisFont' = ("Arial, Helvetica, Helv",3,Italic)
   'FixedEmphasisFont' = ("Courier",2,Italic)
   'FixedStrongFont' = ("Courier",2,Bold)
   'FixedHeadingFont' = ("Courier",2)
   'BatchFixedFont' = ("SAS Monospace, Courier",2)
   'FixedFont' = ("Courier",2)
   'headingEmphasisFont' = ("Arial, Helvetica, Helv",4,Bold Italic)
   'headingFont' = ("Arial, Helvetica, Helv",4,Bold)
   'docFont' = ("Arial, Helvetica, Helv",3);
```

**Output 9.8**

**Output 9.9**

## Finding Your Custom Style Definitions

Where do style definitions go once you've created them? In the previous example, we created a style definition called DefaultNewTitle. We were then able to use that style definition for ODS output using the STYLE=DefaultNewTitle option.

However, if you look at the style definitions listed when you select **Tools ➔ Options ➔ Preferences ➔ Results** from the menu bar, you will see that DefaultNewTitle is not listed (see Output 9.10). Also, if you run PROC TEMPLATE with a LIST STYLES statement, the DefaultNewTitle statement is not on that list either (see Output 9.11).

The reason is that your custom style definition has been saved in a SAS itemstore called SASUSER.TEMPLAT. The built-in style definitions are saved in an itemstore called SASHELP.TMPLMST. When you submit an ODS statement with a STYLE option, SAS looks in both places to find the style definition you have requested. How does this work? ODS has a PATH statement that defines the locations for all style definitions. By default, the PATH statement is set to

```
ODS PATH SASUSER.TEMPLAT(UPDATE) SASHELP.TMPLMST(READ);
```

This tells SAS to look in these two locations for style definitions. In addition, this default setting identifies the TMPLMST itemstore as read-only (to protect the built-in style definitions) and the TEMPLAT itemstore as updatable (so you can create new style definitions). When you use a style definition in your code, SAS will find it in either of these locations. However, the list of style definitions you can select from the Results tab looks only at the location for the built-in style definitions. And the default for the LIST STYLES statement in PROC TEMPLATE is also the location of the built-in style definitions.

What do you do when you want to see a list of your custom style definitions? You can view these style definitions with PROC TEMPLATE, but you need to change one option. Instead of using the LIST STYLES statement, you drop "STYLES" and instead add a location using the STORE option.

```
PROC TEMPLATE;
    LIST / STORE=SASUSER.TEMPLAT;
RUN;
```

The results of this procedure are shown in Output 9.12. Now you can see that our new style definition is listed. Anytime you need to see a list of your custom style definitions, just run this code.

In general, you don't need to change the default PATH setting shown above, so you don't need to use the ODS PATH statement. However, if you start building a number of style definitions, you may want to organize them into separate itemstores. You can do this by using a PATH statement with a new itemstore name in the PROC TEMPLATE when you create the new style definitions. Then you can add an ODS PATH statement to your code when you need to use the new style definitions.

Another reason to create a new location for your custom style definitions is that the SASUSER.TEMPLAT itemstore will be overwritten if you reinstall SAS. To keep your style definitions safe, either save the code that created them or set up a different location for the itemstore.

**Output 9.10**

**Output 9.11**

| Listing of: SASHELP.TMPLMST | | |
|---|---|---|
| Path Filter is: Styles | | |
| Sort by: PATH/ASCENDING | | |
| Obs | Path | Type |
| 1 | Styles | Dir |
| 2 | Styles.BarrettsBlue | Style |
| 3 | Styles.Beige | Style |
| 4 | Styles.Brick | Style |
| 5 | Styles.Brown | Style |
| 6 | Styles.D3d | Style |
| 7 | Styles.Default | Style |
| 8 | Styles.Minimal | Style |
| 9 | Styles.NoFontDefault | Style |
| 10 | Styles.Printer | Style |
| 11 | Styles.Rtf | Style |
| 12 | Styles.Statdoc | Style |
| 13 | Styles.Theme | Style |
| 14 | Styles.fancyPrinter | Style |
| 15 | Styles.sansPrinter | Style |
| 16 | Styles.sasdocPrinter | Style |
| 17 | Styles.serifPrinter | Style |

**Output 9.12**

| Listing of: SASUSER.TEMPLAT | | |
|---|---|---|
| Path Filter is: * | | |
| Sort by: PATH/ASCENDING | | |
| Obs | Path | Type |
| 1 | DefaultNewTitle | Style |

# *Modifying Output Fonts*

This is the first of three chapters that show you how to modify the built-in style definitions in ODS to suit your needs. Understanding how style definitions work is a complex topic that could be an entire book all by itself.

Rather than attempt to cover everything, these chapters focus on simple examples of basic style definition modifications. The examples are all things you can put to use right away, without having to take time to get a comprehensive understanding of style definitions.

To keep things simple, we'll deal with one aspect of style definitions at a time, starting with fonts.

In this chapter, a series of examples show you how to change the fonts in various parts of your results—titles, table headings, table cells, and footnotes. We will change typefaces, font sizes, and font weights.

## Identifying the Font Definitions in Each Part of Your Output

In the last chapter, you used the font definitions to modify the font used for a title. In fact, you can modify the fonts anywhere in your output.

If you run PROC TEMPLATE with a SOURCE statement, you can generate the following list of the font definitions contained in the fonts style element of the Default style definition.

```
'TitleFont2' = ("Arial, Helvetica, Helv",4,Bold Italic)
'TitleFont' = ("Arial, Helvetica, Helv",5,Bold Italic)
'StrongFont' = ("Arial, Helvetica, Helv",4,Bold)
'EmphasisFont' = ("Arial, Helvetica, Helv",3,Italic)
'FixedEmphasisFont' = ("Courier",2,Italic)
'FixedStrongFont' = ("Courier",2,Bold)
'FixedHeadingFont' = ("Courier",2)
'BatchFixedFont' = ("SAS Monospace, Courier",2)
'FixedFont' = ("Courier",2)
'headingEmphasisFont' = ("Arial, Helvetica, Helv",4,Bold Italic)
'headingFont' = ("Arial, Helvetica, Helv",4,Bold)
'docFont' = ("Arial, Helvetica, Helv",3);
```

For some of these fonts, it's clear which parts of the output they control. TitleFont sounds like it is used to control the titles. However, for most of the others, it's not very clear. The way to find out which parts of the output each definition controls is to read the rest of the style definition. For example, if you search for the definition EmphasisFont, you find it used in the following style elements:

```
IndexTitle
ExtendedPage
DataEmphasis
HeaderEmphasis
RowHeaderEmphasis
FooterEmphasis
RowFooterEmphasis
```

To save you the hassle of figuring out which part of the output is affected by each of the font definitions, Table 10.1 shows how the fonts in the Default style definition are used. Most of the time, you will be working with the Default style definition, or with style definitions based on the Default style definition, so you can use this table as a reference.

If you are working with a different style definition, such as the Printer or RTF style definition, the font definitions will be slightly different. However, in general, the font definitions are used in similar ways in all of the built-in style definitions. Go ahead and use Table 10.1 as a guide. If you run into problems, you'll need to review the source code for the style definition to identify the difference that is causing the problem.

If you are trying to modify a custom style definition created by another user, it is likely to be based on the Default style definition, and the information in Table 10.1 will still apply. If the custom style definition has substantial modifications, you may find that you need to review the source code in detail to learn how the font definitions are used.

**Table 10.1**

| *Output Part Controlled* | *Font Names Used* |
|---|---|
| Titles generated with TITLE statement | TitleFont |
| Titles for table of contents and table of pages | EmphasisFont |
| Titles for procedures ("The _____ Procedure") | TitleFont2 |
| Titles for procedures that use fixed-width fonts | FixedStrongFont |
| Page numbers | StrongFont |
| Footnotes generated with FOOTNOTE statement | TitleFont |
| Table headings and footers | headingFont, FixedFont |
| Emphasized table headings and footers | EmphasisFont, FixedEmphasisFont |
| Strong (more emphasized) table headings and footers | StrongFont, FixedStrongFont |
| Table column and row headings and footers | headingFont, FixedFont |
| Emphasized table column and row headings and footers | EmphasisFont, FixedEmphasisFont |
| Strong (more emphasized) table column and row headings and footers | StrongFont, FixedStrongFont |
| BY group headings | headingFont |
| Data in table cells | docFont |
| Emphasized data in table cells | EmphasisFont, FixedEmphasisFont |
| Strong (more emphasized) data in table cells | StrongFont, FixedStrongFont |
| Batch mode output for procedures that use fixed-width font | BatchFixedFont |
| NOTE, WARNING, ERROR, and FATAL messages for procedures that use fixed-width font | FixedFont |
| Message when page overflows | EmphasisFont |

You'll notice that many of the output sections listed in Table 10.1 have two font definitions listed. The first definition is used for most of the procedures you will encounter. However, a few procedures, such as CHART and PLOT, still require fixed-width fonts in order to create their results correctly. For those procedures, a second set of fonts is provided. If you modify the font definitions, be sure to only use fixed-width fonts for these definitions.

## Modifying the Default Font Sizes in HTML Output

The default style definition for ODS HTML output (which happens to be the style definition called Default) uses large fonts for titles and table headings. This is great if you want a bold look and if your titles and labels are short. However, if you have a lot of output to present, you may want to create a style definition that uses a little less space.

If you run the TEMPLATE procedure with a SOURCE statement to get the font definitions for the Default style definition, you will see the list of font definitions shown at the top of page 150. The first item listed in each definition is the font typeface. The second item is a number indicating the font size, ranging from 2 for the smaller items in the output to 5 for the largest title.

Changing the font sizes is easy. You start by running a PROC TEMPLATE with a SOURCE statement to get the font list from the style definition you are trying to modify. Then you set up your code to define your new style definition. You'll need another PROC TEMPLATE, this time with a DEFINE statement to name the new style definition, a PARENT statement to name the style definition it is based on, and a REPLACE statement to supply the new fonts. After the REPLACE statement, you copy the old font definitions. Finally, you edit these font definitions to make your desired changes.

If you want to make your output smaller, all you have to do is reduce these numbers. If you adjust each font size downward by 1, you should end up with output consistent with the original Default style definition, but smaller.

```
PROC TEMPLATE;
   DEFINE STYLE DefaultSmaller;
      PARENT=Styles.Default;
      REPLACE fonts /
         'TitleFont2'=("Arial, Helvetica, Helv",3,Bold Italic)
         'TitleFont'=("Arial, Helvetica, Helv",4,Bold Italic)
         'StrongFont'=("Arial, Helvetica, Helv",3,Bold)
         'EmphasisFont'=("Arial, Helvetica, Helv",2,Italic)
         'FixedEmphasisFont'=("Courier",1,Italic)
         'FixedStrongFont'=("Courier",1,Bold)
         'FixedHeadingFont'=("Courier",1)
         'BatchFixedFont'=("SAS Monospace, Courier",1)
         'FixedFont'=("Courier",1)
         'headingEmphasisFont'=("Arial,Helvetica,Helv",3,Bold Italic)
         'headingFont'=("Arial, Helvetica, Helv",3,Bold)
         'docFont'=("Arial, Helvetica, Helv",2);
   END;
RUN;
```

To see the difference these new sizes make, compare Output 10.1 with Output 10.2. The first output was created with the default HTML sizes. The second was created using the new style definition DefaultSmaller.

Notice how the overall look of the two style definitions remains the same, but the font size in Output 10.2 has been scaled down. The table dimensions have also automatically been scaled down to correspond to the reduced text size.

**Output 10.1**

### This is an extremely wordy title that is too large to fit on this line

| Department | | | | |
|---|---|---|---|---|
| Department | Frequency | Percent | Cumulative Frequency | Cumulative Percent |
| Administration | 157 | 20.21 | 157 | 20.21 |
| Sales | 338 | 43.50 | 495 | 63.71 |
| Technical | 282 | 36.29 | 777 | 100.00 |

**Output 10.2**

### This is an extremely wordy title that is too large to fit on this line

| Department | | | | |
|---|---|---|---|---|
| Department | Frequency | Percent | Cumulative Frequency | Cumulative Percent |
| Administration | 157 | 20.21 | 157 | 20.21 |
| Sales | 338 | 43.50 | 495 | 63.71 |
| Technical | 282 | 36.29 | 777 | 100.00 |

The font sizes used in the Default style definition range from 2 to 5. You can actually set them to values ranging from 1 to 7. What do these numbers represent? They are font size codes used by HTML. ODS just passes these codes through to your output, where they are interpreted by a browser.

## Modifying the Default Font Sizes in Printer Output

To change the font sizes used in Printer output, you need to look at a different style definition. The default style definition used for Printer output is called Printer, not Default.

By running the TEMPLATE procedure with a SOURCE statement on the Printer style definition, you can find out how the font definitions work for that style definition. A partial listing of the source code is shown in Output 10.3.

There are two important things to note. First, the Printer style definition is based on the Default style definition, as shown by the PARENT= attribute. Second, it has its own list of font definitions, which are different from those of the Default style definition.

If you want to create a style definition that reduces the size of your output, as in the previous example, all you have to do is modify the font sizes. However, you will note that the font sizes in the Printer style definition are given in points. This is different from the HTML style definition, where HTML font size numbers were used.

To create a new style definition with smaller fonts, all you need to do is copy the old font definition, assign smaller point sizes, and create a new style definition. In the HTML example, each of the font sizes was reduced by 1. For the Printer example, you'll want to reduce each font size by a couple of points to achieve the same proportional effect.

```
PROC TEMPLATE;
   DEFINE STYLE PrinterSmaller;
      PARENT=Styles.Printer;
   REPLACE fonts /
      'TitleFont2' = ("Times",10pt,Bold Italic)
      'TitleFont' = ("Times",11pt,Bold Italic)
      'StrongFont' = ("Times",8pt,Bold)
      'EmphasisFont' = ("Times",8pt,Italic)
      'FixedEmphasisFont' = ("Courier New, Courier",7pt,Italic)
      'FixedStrongFont' = ("Courier New, Courier",7pt,Bold)
      'FixedHeadingFont' = ("Courier New, Courier",7pt,Bold)
      'BatchFixedFont' = ("SAS Monospace,Courier New,Courier",6pt)
      'FixedFont' = ("Courier New, Courier",7pt)
      'headingEmphasisFont' = ("Times",9pt,Bold Italic)
      'headingFont' = ("Times",9pt,Bold)
      'docFont' = ("Times",8pt);
   END;
RUN;
```

To see the difference these new definitions make, compare Output 10.4 with Output 10.5. The first output was created with the default Printer definitions. The second was created using the new style definition PrinterSmaller. Notice how the overall look of the two style definitions remains the same, but the font size in Output 10.5 has been scaled down. The table dimensions have also automatically been scaled down to correspond to the reduced text size.

**Output 10.3**

```
define style Styles.Printer;
  parent = styles.default;
  replace fonts /
   'TitleFont2' = ("Times",12pt,Bold Italic)
   'TitleFont' = ("Times",13pt,Bold Italic)
   'StrongFont' = ("Times",10pt,Bold)
   'EmphasisFont' = ("Times",10pt,Italic)
   'FixedEmphasisFont' = ("Courier New, Courier",9pt,Italic)
   'FixedStrongFont' = ("Courier New, Courier",9pt,Bold)
   'FixedHeadingFont' = ("Courier New, Courier",9pt,Bold)
   'BatchFixedFont' = ("SAS Monospace, Courier New, Courier",6.7pt)
   'FixedFont' = ("Courier New, Courier",9pt)
   'headingEmphasisFont' = ("Times",11pt,Bold Italic)
   'headingFont' = ("Times",11pt,Bold)
   'docFont' = ("Times",10pt);
```

**Output 10.4**

| Department | | | | |
|---|---|---|---|---|
| Department | Frequency | Percent | Cumulative Frequency | Cumulative Percent |
| Administration | 157 | 20.21 | 157 | 20.21 |
| Sales | 338 | 43.50 | 495 | 63.71 |
| Technical | 282 | 36.29 | 777 | 100.00 |

**Output 10.5**

| Department | | | | |
|---|---|---|---|---|
| Department | Frequency | Percent | Cumulative Frequency | Cumulative Percent |
| Administration | 157 | 20.21 | 157 | 20.21 |
| Sales | 338 | 43.50 | 495 | 63.71 |
| Technical | 282 | 36.29 | 777 | 100.00 |

## Modifying the Default Font Sizes in RTF Output

To change the font sizes used in RTF output, you also need to look at a different style definition. The default style definition used for RTF output is called RTF.

By running the TEMPLATE procedure with a SOURCE statement on the RTF style definition, you can find out how the font definitions work for that style definition. A partial listing of the source code is shown in Output 10.6.

There are two important things to note. First, the RTF style definition is based on the Printer style definition, as shown by the PARENT= statement. (The Printer style definition, in turn, is based on the Default style definition.) Second, the RTF style definition does not have its own list of font definitions.

So how do you change the font size definitions if this style definition doesn't have any? Actually, the RTF style definition does have font definitions. Because this style definition is based on the Printer style definition, it picks up its font definitions from that style definition. This means that if you want to modify the font definitions of the RTF style definition, you can use exactly the same code you used in the Printer style definition.

```
PROC TEMPLATE;
   DEFINE STYLE RTFSmaller;
      PARENT=Styles.RTF;
   REPLACE fonts /
      'TitleFont2' = ("Times",10pt,Bold Italic)
      'TitleFont' = ("Times",11pt,Bold Italic)
      'StrongFont' = ("Times",8pt,Bold)
      'EmphasisFont' = ("Times",8pt,Italic)
      'FixedEmphasisFont' = ("Courier New, Courier",7pt,Italic)
      'FixedStrongFont' = ("Courier New, Courier",7pt,Bold)
      'FixedHeadingFont' = ("Courier New, Courier",7pt,Bold)
      'BatchFixedFont' = ("SAS Monospace,Courier New,Courier",6pt)
      'FixedFont' = ("Courier New, Courier",7pt)
      'headingEmphasisFont' = ("Times",9pt,Bold Italic)
      'headingFont' = ("Times",9pt,Bold)
      'docFont' = ("Times",8pt);
   END;
RUN;
```

When this code is run, it replaces the font definitions in the RTF style definition (which were inherited from the Printer style definition) with these new values.

To see the difference these new sizes make, compare Output 10.7 with Output 10.8. The first output was created with the default RTF definition. The second was created using the new style definition RTFSmaller.

Notice how the overall look of the two style definitions remains the same, but the font size in Output 10.8 has been scaled down. The table dimensions have also automatically been scaled down to correspond to the reduced text size.

**Output 10.6**

```
parent = styles.printer;
```

**Output 10.7**

| Department | | | | |
|---|---|---|---|---|
| Department | Frequency | Percent | Cumulative Frequency | Cumulative Percent |
| Administration | 157 | 20.21 | 157 | 20.21 |
| Sales | 338 | 43.50 | 495 | 63.71 |
| Technical | 282 | 36.29 | 777 | 100.00 |

**Output 10.8**

| Department | | | | |
|---|---|---|---|---|
| Department | Frequency | Percent | Cumulative Frequency | Cumulative Percent |
| Administration | 157 | 20.21 | 157 | 20.21 |
| Sales | 338 | 43.50 | 495 | 63.71 |
| Technical | 282 | 36.29 | 777 | 100.00 |

## Modifying the Default Typefaces

Modifying the typefaces used in your output is simple. Just as with the font sizes, all you have to do to change the typefaces is copy the old font definitions into a PROC TEMPLATE and then use a REPLACE statement to change the font names to the ones you want. The example below uses a wide variety of fonts to give you an idea of how they affect your output. The results are shown in Output 10.9.

```
PROC TEMPLATE;
   DEFINE STYLE DefaultNewFonts;
      PARENT=Styles.Default;
      REPLACE fonts /
      'TitleFont2' = ("Algerian",4,Bold Italic)
      'TitleFont' = ("Brittanic Bold",5,Bold Italic)
      'StrongFont' = ("Comic Sans MS",4,Bold)
      'EmphasisFont' = ("Desdemona",3,Italic)
      'FixedEmphasisFont' = ("Lucida Typewriter",2,Italic)
      'FixedStrongFont' = ("Letter Gothic MT",2,Bold)
      'FixedHeadingFont' = ("QuickType Mono",2)
      'BatchFixedFont' = ("SAS Monospace",2)
      'FixedFont' = ("Courier New",2)
      'headingEmphasisFont' = ("Eras Demi ITC",4,Bold Italic)
      'headingFont' = ("Franklin Gothic Medium",4,Bold)
      'docFont' = ("Goudy Old Style",3);
   END;
RUN;
```

There are several important things to note about this example. First, when you are replacing fonts in a style definition, you need to pay attention to which fonts are supposed to be fixed-width fonts. Those fonts should only be replaced with other fixed-width fonts. In the original version of this style definition, the five fixed-width font definitions were all set to Courier or SAS Monospace, which are both good, reliable fixed-width fonts. Depending on your system, you may have other fixed-width fonts available. A few examples have been listed here.

Second, you can't list just any font. It needs to be a font available on your system, and for HTML output it needs to be a font commonly available to users who will view your Web page. The next example gets into this in more detail.

Finally, you need to be careful about fonts used in special ways. If you look at the tables of contents and pages in Output 10.9, you see that instead of bullets for the items listed, there's an odd-looking box. That's because the font used for these items (Goudy Old Style) does not have the same symbols as the original font used in the Default style definition (Arial).

This example covered how to change the typefaces for HTML output. To change the typefaces for Printer or RTF output, the technique is the same. Just select the correct PARENT style definition, copy its font definitions, and modify them as needed.

**Output 10.9**

*Title1*

*Title2*

*Title3*

**THE RSREG PROCEDURE**

| Coding Coefficients for the Independent Variables | | |
|---|---|---|
| **Factor** | **Subtracted off** | **Divided by** |
| **Title** | 5.500000 | 4.500000 |

| Response Surface for Variable Salary: Annual Compensation | |
|---|---|
| **Response Mean** | 103174 |
| **Root MSE** | 54878 |
| **R-Square** | 0.0062 |
| **Coefficient of Variation** | 53.1895 |

## Identifying Available Fonts

If you are creating HTML output, you may select any font that you believe will be available to people who view your Web page. If you want to use a slightly unusual font, you can list alternative fonts in the definitions so that viewers who do not have the first-choice font can still view your output properly. The Default definition does this, listing Helvetica and Helv as alternate fonts for systems that do not have the Arial font. If none of the fonts listed in your definition are available, the viewer's browser will substitute a default font, which is generally not very attractive. Table 10.2 has a list of good fonts to use in HTML output.

If you are creating RTF or PDF output, you may select any typeface that is available in your system. To quickly view the available fonts, open a new document in Word and select the font pull-down list from the toolbar (shown in Figure 10.1), or select **Format** and then **Font** from the menu bar. If you plan to share your document with other users, you may want to limit yourself to the common fonts shown in Table 10.2.

If you are creating printer output in Windows, you can use the default host printer drivers.[1] This means that you have access to any font in your system. To get a list of these fonts, open your word processor and look up the font list using the steps described above.

For printer output on any other platform, the issue of determining available typefaces is much trickier. On these platforms, you cannot use host drivers. By default, you are using the SAS drivers. The default SAS font list includes Times, Helvetica, Courier, Symbol, Bookman, New Century Schoolbook, Palatino, Chancery, and Dingbats. Each of these fonts will be available if your printer supports them. At a minimum, your printer should support the standard PostScript fonts (Courier, Times, and Helvetica) or the standard PCL font (Courier).

For non-Windows systems, you may be able to use additional fonts besides this basic list. Each printer has a list of supported fonts, most of which the SAS System can support. Your SAS software comes with a number of printer prototypes, with the correct fonts for that specific printer already installed. What you have to do is select the appropriate prototype and create a local printer. For more information, consult the SAS manual for your operating system.

Whichever operating system you are using, if you're not sure which fonts your printer supports, the best thing to do is experiment. Create a series of style definitions that use a variety of fonts. Generate some test output and review the results. The fonts that are not supported on your system and/or printer will be displayed as one of the standard fonts (probably Courier). Start a list of the fonts that work and don't work and use it as a reference when you are building style definitions.

---

[1]   Unless you have added the SAS or PS option to your ODS PRINTER statement, you are using the host drivers. If you are on the Windows platform, it is recommended that you not change this setting unless you are having trouble printing.

**Figure 10.1**

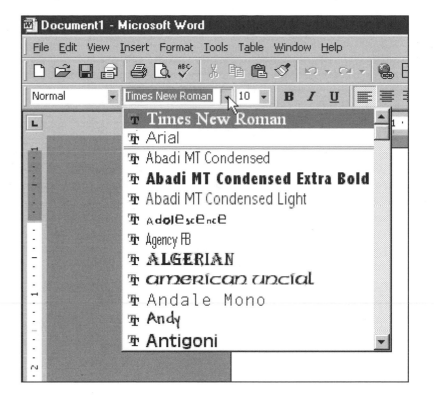

**Table 10.2**

| "Safe" Fonts to Use on the Internet[1] | "Unsafe" Fonts[2] |
| --- | --- |
| Times New Roman, Times | SAS Monospace, Courier |
| Arial, Helvetica | **SAS Monospace Bold,** Courier |
| Courier New, Courier | |
| Comic Sans MS, Arial, Helvetica | |
| Verdana, Arial, Helvetica | |
| **Impact, Arial Black,** Helvetica | |
| Georgia, Times New Roman, Times | |
| Trebuchet MS, Arial, Helvetica | |

[1] Although these fonts are fairly safe, good alternate fonts are also listed for each item.

[2] These fonts should always be used with alternates.

## Modifying the Default Font Weights, Font Styles, and Font Widths

The previous examples looked at how to modify font typefaces and sizes. These are the first two items listed in each font definition. The third item is a list of keywords that defines the font weight (bold,[2] for instance), the font style (italic, for instance), and the font width (compressed, for instance). These font weights and styles can be modified just as you modified the typefaces and sizes.

The RTF style definition uses four different combinations of font weight, font style, and font width: none, bold only, italic only, and bold italic. To see how to change these font definitions, we will change the style element so that it does not use italics. All we have to do is delete the word "Italic" from each definition. Output 10.10 shows the original font definitions for the RTF style definition. The revised style element, with the new font definitions, is shown below:

```
PROC TEMPLATE;
   DEFINE STYLE RTFNoItalics;
      PARENT=Styles.RTF;
   REPLACE fonts /
      'TitleFont2' = ("Times",12pt,Bold)
      'TitleFont' = ("Times",13pt,Bold)
      'StrongFont' = ("Times",10pt,Bold)
      'EmphasisFont' = ("Times",10pt)
      'FixedEmphasisFont' = ("Courier New, Courier",9pt)
      'FixedStrongFont' = ("Courier New, Courier",9pt,Bold)
      'FixedHeadingFont' = ("Courier New, Courier",9pt,Bold)
      'BatchFixedFont' = ("SAS Monospace,Courier New,Courier",6.7pt)
      'FixedFont' = ("Courier New, Courier",9pt)
      'headingEmphasisFont' = ("Times",11pt,Bold)
      'headingFont' = ("Times",11pt,Bold)
      'docFont' = ("Times",10pt);
   END;
RUN;
```

To see the impact of these changes, compare Output 10.11 with Output 10.12. In these examples, you can see that the two titles, which were italicized, have had the italics removed. For this simple MEANS procedure, these titles are the only place where italics were applied. In a more complex example, these changes would have affected other headings, as well as any emphasized results.

This example covered how to change the font style element for RTF output. To change the fonts weights, styles, or widths for printer or HTML output, the technique is the same. Just select the correct PARENT style definition, copy its font definitions, and modify them as needed.

---

[2]   There are other font weights you can use, such as "Light" and "Extra-Bold," but these may not be supported by all fonts. A list of font weights, as well as font styles and font widths, is included in the "Guide to the Output Delivery System" in SAS OnlineDoc.

**Output 10.10**

```
'TitleFont2' = ("Times",12pt,Bold Italic)
'TitleFont' = ("Times",13pt,Bold Italic)
'StrongFont' = ("Times",10pt,Bold)
'EmphasisFont' = ("Times",10pt,Italic)
'FixedEmphasisFont' = ("Courier New, Courier",9pt,Italic)
'FixedStrongFont' = ("Courier New, Courier",9pt,Bold)
'FixedHeadingFont' = ("Courier New, Courier",9pt,Bold)
'BatchFixedFont' = ("SAS Monospace, Courier New, Courier",6.7pt)
'FixedFont' = ("Courier New, Courier",9pt)
'headingEmphasisFont' = ("Times",11pt,Bold Italic)
'headingFont' = ("Times",11pt,Bold)
'docFont' = ("Times",10pt);
```

**Output 10.11**   *The SAS System*

*The FREQ Procedure*

| | | Experience Level | | |
|---|---|---|---|---|
| Grade | Frequency | Percent | Cumulative Frequency | Cumulative Percent |
| I | 273 | 35.14 | 273 | 35.14 |
| II | 256 | 32.95 | 529 | 68.08 |
| III | 132 | 16.99 | 661 | 85.07 |
| IV | 116 | 14.93 | 777 | 100.00 |

**Output 10.12**   The SAS System

The FREQ Procedure

| | | Experience Level | | |
|---|---|---|---|---|
| Grade | Frequency | Percent | Cumulative Frequency | Cumulative Percent |
| I | 273 | 35.14 | 273 | 35.14 |
| II | 256 | 32.95 | 529 | 68.08 |
| III | 132 | 16.99 | 661 | 85.07 |
| IV | 116 | 14.93 | 777 | 100.00 |

## Creating a New Font Definition

The easiest way to change font definitions is to just edit the existing font definitions. However, sometimes you'd like to have more flexibility.

For example, if you want to assign a new font to specific parts of your output, you can't do that with the existing font definitions. In the Default style definition, the same font definition is used for both titles and footnotes. So if you want to use a small, unobtrusive font for the footnotes, you have to use the same font for the titles.

There are a couple of ways to create a style definition with large, bold titles and small, subtle footnotes. One way is to create a new font definition. In the code below, a new font definition for FootnoteFont has been added.

```
PROC TEMPLATE;
   DEFINE STYLE DefaultNewFonts2;
      PARENT=Styles.Default;
      REPLACE fonts /
      'TitleFont2' = ("Arial, Helvetica, Helv",4,Bold Italic)
      'TitleFont' = ("Arial, Helvetica, Helv",5,Bold Italic)
      'StrongFont' = ("Arial, Helvetica, Helv",4,Bold)
      'EmphasisFont' = ("Arial, Helvetica, Helv",3,Italic)
      'FixedEmphasisFont' = ("Courier",2,Italic)
      'FixedStrongFont' = ("Courier",2,Bold)
      'FixedHeadingFont' = ("Courier",2)
      'BatchFixedFont' = ("SAS Monospace, Courier",2)
      'FixedFont' = ("Courier",2)
      'headingEmphasisFont' = ("Arial,Helvetica,Helv",4,Bold Italic)
      'headingFont' = ("Arial, Helvetica, Helv",4,Bold)
      'docFont' = ("Arial, Helvetica, Helv",3)
➡     'FootnoteFont'= ("Arial, Helvetica, Helv", 1, Italic);
```

Next, the new font definition has to be applied to the footnotes. To do this, you need to run a PROC TEMPLATE and find the part of the code that sets the font for footnotes. This code is shown in Output 10.13. To use your new font definition, just replace the original font definition of TitleFont with the new font definition FootnoteFont, and change the STYLE statement to a REPLACE statement.

```
      REPLACE SystemFooter from TitlesAndFooters /
         font = Fonts('FootnoteFont');
      END;
   RUN;
```

After creating this new style definition, you can now create output like Output 10.14, which has large titles and tiny footnotes. You can use this technique anytime you want to control the fonts used for a particular part of the output. Just because the Default style definition reuses the same fonts for a number of output sections, this doesn't mean you are limited to using those fonts. Just create a new font definition, and then apply it to the part of the output you want to change.

**Output 10.13**

```
style SystemFooter from TitlesAndFooters
    "Controls system footer text." /
    font = Fonts('TitleFont');
```

**Output 10.14**

*Title1*

*Title2*

**The MEANS Procedure**

| Analysis Variable : Salary Annual Compensation | | | | | | |
|---|---|---|---|---|---|---|
| Position Title | N Obs | N | Mean | Std Dev | Minimum | Maximum |
| Trainee | 71 | 71 | 103019 | 57999 | 28749 | 208074 |
| Specialist | 316 | 316 | 97834 | 52481 | 25632 | 209861 |
| Manager | 160 | 160 | 104254 | 55461 | 25002 | 209673 |
| Associate | 146 | 146 | 110226 | 57109 | 26035 | 209648 |
| VP | 84 | 84 | 109077 | 56082 | 26945 | 205293 |

*Footnote 1*

*Footnote 2*

If you only want to change the font in one place, and don't plan to use that font style anywhere else, you can create a new font definition inside the System-Footer style element, and avoid changing the Font style element. The syntax is

```
REPLACE SystemFooter from TitlesAndFooters /
        font=("Arial, Helvetica, Helv", 1, Italic);
```

## Modifying Fonts in Procedures That Use Fixed-Width Fonts

In each of the previous examples, we've been ignoring the definitions for the fixed-width fonts. For most SAS procedures, these fonts are never used. However, there are a few procedures where these fonts matter. For example, the PLOT, CHART, TIMEPLOT, and CALENDAR procedures all use fixed-width fonts to get their output to line up properly. It is possible to modify the style attributes for these fonts. However, do this carefully, and review your results. Because these fonts are so integral to the appearance of these procedures' results, changes to the font definitions can cause serious problems.

If you are creating HTML output, be aware that the output from these procedures may not look correct even if you use the Default style definition. Some parts of the output of these procedures use the SAS Monospace font. If this font is not available on your browser, it will default to Courier. The problem with this is that the output uses some special characters available in the SAS Monospace font. When your browser substitutes Courier, you end up with strange characters in your output. To fix the problem, use the FORMCHAR option to specify safer characters:

```
OPTIONS FORMCHAR="|----|+|---+=|-/\<>*";
```

If you are creating printer output, be wary about changing the font definitions. If you make the font sizes larger, your output may not line up correctly. In addition, if you change typefaces, you may get strange characters in your output because the procedure was expecting the SAS Monospace font. The only settings you can safely change are the font weight and style. You can switch from regular to bold, italic to roman, and so on.

With RTF output, changing the typeface to something other than SAS Monospace will cause problems with the alignment of your output, but you can safely change the font sizes and weights. This example code changes the font size and weight for BatchFixedFont, which is the font used for PROC CHART output.

```
PROC TEMPLATE;
  DEFINE STYLE RTFFixed;
    PARENT=Styles.RTF;
  REPLACE fonts /
    'TitleFont2' = ("Times",12pt,Bold Italic)
    'TitleFont' = ("Times",13pt,Bold Italic)
    'StrongFont' = ("Times",10pt,Bold)
    'EmphasisFont' = ("Times",10pt,Italic)
    'FixedEmphasisFont' = ("Courier New, Courier",9pt,Italic)
    'FixedStrongFont' = ("Courier New, Courier",9pt,Bold)
    'FixedHeadingFont' = ("Courier New, Courier",9pt,Bold)
➜   'BatchFixedFont' = ("SAS Monospace,Courier New,Courier",12pt, Bold)
    'FixedFont' = ("Courier New, Courier",9pt)
    'headingEmphasisFont' = ("Times",11pt,Bold Italic)
    'headingFont' = ("Times",11pt,Bold)
    'docFont' = ("Times",10pt);
  END;
RUN;
```

By using this font, you can make the bar chart stand out a bit more. Compare the readability of Output 10.15, which uses a regular 9-point font, with that of Output 10.16, which uses a bold 12-point font.

**Output 10.15**

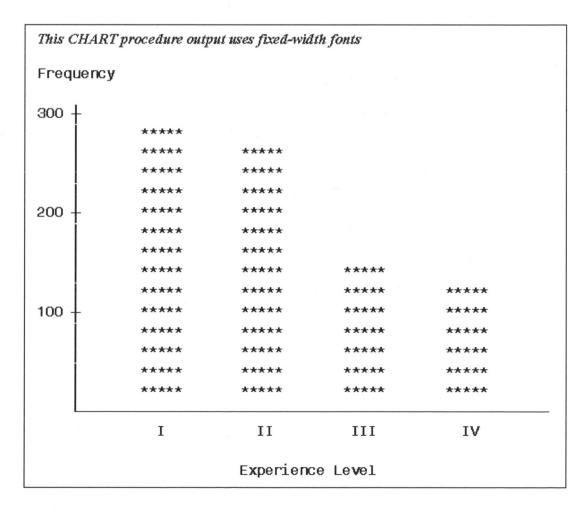

**Output 10.16**

# Chapter

# 11

*Modifying Output Structure*

The previous chapter was just the beginning. Modifying the fonts gives you control over all of the text portions of your output. However, surrounding all of that text are things like tables, borders, bullets, and headings.

ODS allows you to change each of these items as well. You can change the shape of a table or modify its borders. You can change or remove the bullets in a table of contents or pages. You can change page and procedure headings.

The possibilities are infinite. This chapter gives you some of the basic code building blocks you need to make these kinds of changes. After that, it's up to you. You can reuse and combine these bits of code to create the look you desire.

## Modifying Table Borders

Most ODS output is rendered in the form of tables. This allows your output to be well organized and easy to read. The appearance of these tables is controlled by the style definition.

To see how different table designs can affect your output, just compare the HTML output created with the D3D style definition in Output 11.1 to the same output created with the Default style definition in Output 11.2. The borders in the Default setting are flat looking and narrow. The D3D style definition has wide borders that achieve a three-dimensional appearance using shading.

You can change the borders on your output tables by switching style definitions with a STYLE= option. You can also change the border settings of existing style definitions. For example, if you like the general appearance of the Default style definition, but you also like the wider borders of the D3D style definition, you can create a new style definition that combines these characteristics.

To do this, you need to run PROC TEMPLATE with a SOURCE statement on the Default style definition so you can identify the part of the style definition that controls the border widths. It turns out that there are a number of border settings. The Output style element is where the settings for the main table borders are located. The original attributes and settings of this style element are

```
Style Output from Container /
   background = colors('tablebg')
   rules = GROUPS
   frame = BOX
   cellpadding = 7
   cellspacing = 1
   bordercolor = colors('tableborder')
   borderwidth = 1;
```

To make the border wider, you simply change the BORDERWIDTH attribute setting and switch the STYLE statement to a REPLACE statement. The following code creates a new style definition called DefaultBorder, which has a BORDERWIDTH setting of 10.

```
PROC TEMPLATE;
   DEFINE STYLE DefaultBorder;
      PARENT=Styles.Default;
      REPLACE Output from Container /
         background = colors('tablebg')
         rules = GROUPS
         frame = BOX
         cellpadding = 7
         cellspacing = 1
         bordercolor = colors('tableborder')
➡        borderwidth = 10;
   END;
RUN;
```

Output 11.3 shows the results of applying this new style definition to the same table used in the previous examples.

**Output 11.1**

| Analysis Variable : CostSqFt Cost per square foot | | | | | | |
|---|---|---|---|---|---|---|
| **Building type** | **N Obs** | **N** | **Mean** | **Std Dev** | **Minimum** | **Maximum** |
| Retail | 29 | 29 | 184.62 | 60.71 | 84.00 | 280.00 |
| Residential | 118 | 118 | 171.75 | 56.46 | 81.00 | 278.00 |
| Office | 135 | 135 | 180.12 | 56.19 | 82.00 | 280.00 |
| Warehouse | 60 | 60 | 177.97 | 57.68 | 82.00 | 278.00 |

**Output 11.2**

| Analysis Variable : CostSqFt Cost per square foot | | | | | | |
|---|---|---|---|---|---|---|
| **Building type** | **N Obs** | **N** | **Mean** | **Std Dev** | **Minimum** | **Maximum** |
| Retail | 29 | 29 | 184.62 | 60.71 | 84.00 | 280.00 |
| Residential | 118 | 118 | 171.75 | 56.46 | 81.00 | 278.00 |
| Office | 135 | 135 | 180.12 | 56.19 | 82.00 | 280.00 |
| Warehouse | 60 | 60 | 177.97 | 57.68 | 82.00 | 278.00 |

**Output 11.3**

| Analysis Variable : CostSqFt Cost per square foot | | | | | | |
|---|---|---|---|---|---|---|
| **Building type** | **N Obs** | **N** | **Mean** | **Std Dev** | **Minimum** | **Maximum** |
| Retail | 29 | 29 | 184.62 | 60.71 | 84.00 | 280.00 |
| Residential | 118 | 118 | 171.75 | 56.46 | 81.00 | 278.00 |
| Office | 135 | 135 | 180.12 | 56.19 | 82.00 | 280.00 |
| Warehouse | 60 | 60 | 177.97 | 57.68 | 82.00 | 278.00 |

## Removing Table Borders and Rules

The previous example created a style definition for tables with wider borders. You can also make the borders and rules go away altogether. All you have to do is modify a few other settings in the style element you worked with in the previous example.

We are working again with the Output style element of the Default style definition. As a reminder, the original settings of the Output style element are shown below.

```
Style Output from Container /
    background = colors('tablebg')
    rules = GROUPS
    frame = BOX
    cellpadding = 7
    cellspacing = 1
    bordercolor = colors('tableborder')
    borderwidth = 1;
```

There are three settings that need to be changed if you want to create a table without borders or rules. The first one is the RULES attribute setting. The Default style definition uses the setting GROUPS. This calls for rules to be placed between the table header and the table body, and between the table body and the table footer. If you want to get rid of these rules, the setting must be changed to NONE. Output 11.4 shows the revised HTML output with this setting in place.

The second setting used to control borders is the FRAME attribute setting. The Default style definition uses BOX. This setting calls for borders around the outside of the table. To get rid of these borders, the setting must be changed to VOID. Output 11.5 shows what the table borders look like with this second change in place.

At this point, you may think that the task is complete. But if you look closely at Output 11.5, you will see thin white rules between the table cells. These are not actually rules, but spaces between the table cells. However, they look like rules, so we'd like to remove them. To do this you need to change the CELLSPACING attribute setting from 1 to 0. The final code is shown below. It creates Output 11.6.

```
PROC TEMPLATE;
    DEFINE STYLE DefaultNoBorderRule;
        PARENT=Styles.Default;
        REPLACE Output from Container /
            background = colors('tablebg')
            rules = NONE
            frame = VOID
            cellpadding = 7
            cellspacing = 0
            bordercolor = colors('tableborder')
            borderwidth = 1;
    END;
RUN;
```

**Output 11.4**

| Analysis Variable : CostSqFt Cost per square foot | | | | | | |
|---|---|---|---|---|---|---|
| Building type | N Obs | N | Mean | Std Dev | Minimum | Maximum |
| Retail | 29 | 29 | 184.62 | 60.71 | 84.00 | 280.00 |
| Residential | 118 | 118 | 171.75 | 56.46 | 81.00 | 278.00 |
| Office | 135 | 135 | 180.12 | 56.19 | 82.00 | 280.00 |
| Warehouse | 60 | 60 | 177.97 | 57.68 | 82.00 | 278.00 |

**Output 11.5**

| Analysis Variable : CostSqFt Cost per square foot | | | | | | |
|---|---|---|---|---|---|---|
| Building type | N Obs | N | Mean | Std Dev | Minimum | Maximum |
| Retail | 29 | 29 | 184.62 | 60.71 | 84.00 | 280.00 |
| Residential | 118 | 118 | 171.75 | 56.46 | 81.00 | 278.00 |
| Office | 135 | 135 | 180.12 | 56.19 | 82.00 | 280.00 |
| Warehouse | 60 | 60 | 177.97 | 57.68 | 82.00 | 278.00 |

**Output 11.6**

| Analysis Variable : CostSqFt Cost per square foot | | | | | | |
|---|---|---|---|---|---|---|
| Building type | N Obs | N | Mean | Std Dev | Minimum | Maximum |
| Retail | 29 | 29 | 184.62 | 60.71 | 84.00 | 280.00 |
| Residential | 118 | 118 | 171.75 | 56.46 | 81.00 | 278.00 |
| Office | 135 | 135 | 180.12 | 56.19 | 82.00 | 280.00 |
| Warehouse | 60 | 60 | 177.97 | 57.68 | 82.00 | 278.00 |

You may have noticed that in the final code, the BORDERWIDTH attribute was still set to 1. Since we used the FRAME and RULES option to get rid of all borders, it does not matter that the width is still set to 1, since no borders will be created.

## Removing Table Borders and Rules from Printer Output

So far in this chapter, the examples have been based on the Default style definition, and the output destination has been HTML. This time you will work with the Printer style definition and create printed output. Again, you will be removing the table borders and rules. In the code below, you can see that the modifications are quite different from those in the previous example. First, the parent style definition is now listed as Styles.Printer. Second, instead of replacing the Output style element, you are replacing the Table style element. Output 11.7 shows the source code with the attributes and settings for the Table style element.

Why do we have to replace a different style element? In the Default style definition, the rules, frame, and cellspacing settings come from the Output style element. In the Printer style definition, the rules setting in the Output style element is overruled by the rules setting in the Table style element. Similarly, the cellspacing setting in the Output style element is overruled by the cellspacing setting in the Table style element. The frame setting still comes from the Output style element (see the tip below for an explanation).

In the code below, the modifications to the Table style element are the same as the modifications to the Output style element in the previous example. The rules attribute is set to NONE, the frame is set to VOID, and the cellspacing is set to zero. The frame attribute was not part of the Table style element you are updating, but it's a valid attribute for that style element.

If a style element you are modifying does not have all of the attributes you want to modify, you can often add them. Just check the "Guide to the Output Delivery System" in SAS OnlineDoc for that attribute to be sure it is valid for the style element you are trying to modify. However, if you accidentally specify an invalid attribute, it won't cause an error. ODS simply ignores extra attributes.

```
PROC TEMPLATE;
   DEFINE STYLE PrinterNoBorder;
      PARENT=Styles.Printer;
      REPLACE Table from Output /
         rules = NONE
         frame = VOID
         cellpadding = 4pt
         cellspacing = 0
         borderwidth = 1;
   END;
RUN;
```

Output 11.8 shows a sample table using the Printer style definition. Output 11.9 shows the same table again after applying the new PrinterNoBorder style definition.

TIP

This example may be a little confusing. If the Printer style definition doesn't have an Output style element, why does the Table style element refer to it? The answer is that STYLE and REPLACE statements in style definitions can refer to style elements in the parent style definition. Therefore, the source code in Output 11.7 can refer to the Output style element, even though it is in the Default style definition. Our new style definition can replace style elements in either the Printer style definition or its parent, the Default style definition.

**Output 11.7** Default Settings for the Table Style Element

```
style Table from Output /
    rules = ALL
    cellpadding = 4pt
    cellspacing = 0.25pt
    borderwidth = 0.75pt;
```

**Output 11.8**

| Analysis Variable : CostSqFt Cost per square foot | | | | | | |
|---|---|---|---|---|---|---|
| Building type | N Obs | N | Mean | Std Dev | Minimum | Maximum |
| Retail | 29 | 29 | 184.62 | 60.71 | 84.00 | 280.00 |
| Residential | 118 | 118 | 171.75 | 56.46 | 81.00 | 278.00 |
| Office | 135 | 135 | 180.12 | 56.19 | 82.00 | 280.00 |
| Warehouse | 60 | 60 | 177.97 | 57.68 | 82.00 | 278.00 |

**Output 11.9**

| Analysis Variable : CostSqFt Cost per square foot | | | | | | |
|---|---|---|---|---|---|---|
| Building type | N Obs | N | Mean | Std Dev | Minimum | Maximum |
| Retail | 29 | 29 | 184.62 | 60.71 | 84.00 | 280.00 |
| Residential | 118 | 118 | 171.75 | 56.46 | 81.00 | 278.00 |
| Office | 135 | 135 | 180.12 | 56.19 | 82.00 | 280.00 |
| Warehouse | 60 | 60 | 177.97 | 57.68 | 82.00 | 278.00 |

## Changing the Spacing inside Tables

ODS output is composed of tables, text, and the space between them. By default, a certain amount of space is left between the results and the table borders that surround them. If you want to create a more compressed table with less space, or a more open table with more space, you can create a style definition to do that.

The attribute setting you need to modify is called CELLPADDING. Like the table border settings, it's part of the Output style element of the Default style definition. By default, the setting is 7 pixels. This means that to the left and right of each number or label in the table, there are at least 7 pixels of space. There are also 7 pixels of space above and below each number or label.

If you want to create a more compressed table, simply reduce the value of the CELLPADDING setting. The following code sets CELLPADDING to 3 pixels.

```
PROC TEMPLATE;
  DEFINE STYLE DefaultSqueeze;
    PARENT=Styles.Default;
    REPLACE Output from Container /
      background = colors('tablebg')
      rules = GROUPS
      frame = BOX
      cellpadding = 3
      cellspacing = 1
      bordercolor = colors('tableborder')
      borderwidth = 1;
  END;
RUN;
```

The results of this change can be seen by comparing the HTML file for the Default style definition shown in Output 11.10 with this new style definition shown in Output 11.11. If you look at the column for the *N* statistic, you can see how much less space is used in the second version.

To see the opposite effect, look at Output 11.12. It was created using the same code as above, except for the following line:

```
cellpadding = 10
```

Again, looking at the column for the *N* statistic, you can see how much more space is allowed in this table. It now has 10 pixels of space around each number and label.

In general, you will find that the default setting is just fine. However, if you need to squeeze a bit more output onto a page, reducing the cell padding is one way to go. Similarly, if you want to leave a bit more room to make a crowded table easier to read, increase the cell padding.

This example is for HTML output. If you are creating RTF or printer output, the CELLPADDING attribute uses settings in points. The default value is 4pt for printer and 3pt for RTF.

**Output 11.10  Table with Default CELLPADDING Setting of 7**

| Analysis Variable : CostSqFt Cost per square foot | | | | | | |
|---|---|---|---|---|---|---|
| Building height | N Obs | N | Mean | Std Dev | Minimum | Maximum |
| 1 story | 117 | 117 | 170.75 | 58.34 | 81.00 | 278.00 |
| 2 stories | 122 | 122 | 180.83 | 55.87 | 82.00 | 280.00 |
| mid-rise | 54 | 54 | 184.65 | 57.63 | 82.00 | 280.00 |
| high-rise | 49 | 49 | 175.59 | 54.70 | 82.00 | 280.00 |

**Output 11.11  Table with CELLPADDING Setting Changed to 3**

| Analysis Variable : CostSqFt Cost per square foot | | | | | | |
|---|---|---|---|---|---|---|
| Building height | N Obs | N | Mean | Std Dev | Minimum | Maximum |
| 1 story | 117 | 117 | 170.75 | 58.34 | 81.00 | 278.00 |
| 2 stories | 122 | 122 | 180.83 | 55.87 | 82.00 | 280.00 |
| mid-rise | 54 | 54 | 184.65 | 57.63 | 82.00 | 280.00 |
| high-rise | 49 | 49 | 175.59 | 54.70 | 82.00 | 280.00 |

**Output 11.12  Table with CELLPADDING Setting Changed to 10**

| Analysis Variable : CostSqFt Cost per square foot | | | | | | |
|---|---|---|---|---|---|---|
| Building height | N Obs | N | Mean | Std Dev | Minimum | Maximum |
| 1 story | 117 | 117 | 170.75 | 58.34 | 81.00 | 278.00 |
| 2 stories | 122 | 122 | 180.83 | 55.87 | 82.00 | 280.00 |
| mid-rise | 54 | 54 | 184.65 | 57.63 | 82.00 | 280.00 |
| high-rise | 49 | 49 | 175.59 | 54.70 | 82.00 | 280.00 |

## Removing Numbers from the Table of Contents

Back in Chapter 3, "HTML Output," there was an example that showed how to remove the procedure labels from a HTML table of contents. By using the ODS PROCLABEL statement, you were able to remove the text labels like "The MEANS Procedure" and "The PRINT Procedure" from the table of contents listing.

Using a blank for the PROCLABEL setting, you can create the Web page shown in Output 11.13. The procedure labels have now been removed. The problem is that although the unwanted text in the table of contents is gone, the number for that item is still in place. The "1." is still displayed. To get rid of the "1." you can't use a simple ODS command. This functionality is controlled by the style definition. To remove the "1." you have to create a new definition that does not call for the item numbers.

For many style definition modifications, you can run PROC TEMPLATE with a SOURCE statement to get the source code listing. Then you can read through the code and identify the style element and style attribute that control the item you want to change. However, if you read through the Default style definition, you will quickly discover that there is no attribute called "TableOfContentsNumbers" or anything like that.

This is where the "Guide to the Output Delivery System" in SAS OnlineDoc comes in handy. Each of the style elements, style attributes, and their settings are explained in the section on the TEMPLATE procedure.

Here is how you use the documentation to find what you need. If you open the ODS documentation, and then select the Reference section, you will see a section on the TEMPLATE procedure. Open the Concepts section. This section has a helpful table titled "Style Elements That Are Available in the Default Style Definition." Reading this table, you will discover that the Content-ProcName style element controls the procedure labels in the table of contents.

If you look at the source code for the Default style definition, you will see that the Content-ProcName style element has no attributes. However, it comes from the IndexProcName style element. If you look at the IndexProcName style element, you see a number of attributes. There's no setting that is obviously the one you are looking for, but BULLET= "decimal" is a possibility. To be sure this is the right setting, you could run a test, or you could also look at the Index style element (on which IndexProcName is based) and the Container style element (on which Index is based). Neither of these style elements has anything more promising, so the BULLET attribute is probably what you need.

Now you can look up that style attribute in the documentation and learn how to change its value. It turns out that "NONE" is the setting to remove the bullet. Therefore, the code to solve the problem is

```
PROC TEMPLATE;
   DEFINE STYLE DefaultBlank;
      PARENT=Styles.Default;
      REPLACE ContentProcName FROM IndexProcName /
         BULLET=NONE;
   END;
RUN;
```

This code creates the Web page shown in Output 11.14. Notice that the "1." is no longer displayed. There's still a blank line, but at least the orphan number is gone.

**Output 11.13**

## Construction Materials

*The FREQ Procedure*

| Primary construction material | | | | |
|---|---|---|---|---|
| Material | Frequency | Percent | Cumulative Frequency | Cumulative Percent |
| Wood | 76 | 22.22 | 76 | 22.22 |
| Concrete | 115 | 33.63 | 191 | 55.85 |
| Brick | 69 | 20.18 | 260 | 76.02 |
| Steel | 82 | 23.98 | 342 | 100.00 |

**Output 11.14**

## Construction Materials

*The FREQ Procedure*

| Primary construction material | | | | |
|---|---|---|---|---|
| Material | Frequency | Percent | Cumulative Frequency | Cumulative Percent |
| Wood | 76 | 22.22 | 76 | 22.22 |
| Concrete | 115 | 33.63 | 191 | 55.85 |
| Brick | 69 | 20.18 | 260 | 76.02 |
| Steel | 82 | 23.98 | 342 | 100.00 |

## Hiding Procedure Titles

If you're creating your results for users who don't know SAS, they may find the procedure titles confusing. After all, "The FREQ Procedure" is meaningful to a SAS programmer, but it's not exactly common terminology. It would be nice to be able to get rid of these labels. In the table of contents and table of pages for HTML output, the ODS PROCLABEL statement allows you to modify these labels. They can be changed to something meaningful or removed entirely.

However, the ODS PROCLABEL statement does not affect the corresponding procedure labels in the body file of your output. If you want to get rid of that "The FREQ Procedure" that's displayed above your output, you have to use a different ODS statement. You need an ODS statement with a NOPTITLE option.

The option is NOPTITLE. Unlike the other examples in this chapter, this time you do not need to use PROC TEMPLATE to create a new style definition in order to use this setting. The syntax is

```
ODS NOPTITLE;
```

To see how it works, we'll create a simple PDF file. Output 11.15 shows the output before using the new option. The standard title "The FREQ Procedure" appears above the output table.

To get rid of this title, just add an ODS statement with a NOPTITLE option:

```
ODS PDF FILE='NoProcedure.pdf';
ODS NOPTITLE;
title 'Construction Materials';
proc freq data=Buildings;
    tables material*type / norow nocol nopercent;
run;
ODS PDF CLOSE;
```

Output 11.16 shows the same table with the new option in place. The procedure title has disappeared. Notice that the title "Construction Materials" that was created by the TITLE statement in the code has not been affected.

The ODS NOPTITLE statement persists until you change it back with an ODS PTITLE statement.

The PTITLE option affects only the procedure titles in the body of the output. If you use this technique with the HTML destination, you will still get the title "The FREQ Procedure" in the table of contents. To completely remove the title, you need to use the NOPTITLE option in conjunction with the PROCLABEL option (as shown in Chapter 3, "HTML Output") and a custom style definition to remove the blank lines from the table of contents (as shown in the previous example).

**Output 11.15**

*Construction Materials*

*The FREQ Procedure*

| Frequency | Table of Material by Type | | | | | |
|---|---|---|---|---|---|---|
| | Material(Primary construction material) | Type(Building type) | | | | Total |
| | | Retail | Residential | Office | Warehouse | |
| | Wood | 4 | 48 | 13 | 11 | 76 |
| | Concrete | 15 | 34 | 42 | 24 | 115 |
| | Brick | 7 | 36 | 14 | 12 | 69 |
| | Steel | 3 | 0 | 66 | 13 | 82 |
| | Total | 29 | 118 | 135 | 60 | 342 |

**Output 11.16**

*Construction Materials*

| Frequency | Table of Material by Type | | | | | |
|---|---|---|---|---|---|---|
| | Material(Primary construction material) | Type(Building  type) | | | | Total |
| | | Retail | Residential | Office | Warehouse | |
| | Wood | 4 | 48 | 13 | 11 | 76 |
| | Concrete | 15 | 34 | 42 | 24 | 115 |
| | Brick | 7 | 36 | 14 | 12 | 69 |
| | Steel | 3 | 0 | 66 | 13 | 82 |
| | Total | 29 | 118 | 135 | 60 | 342 |

## Setting the Width of HTML Output

The challenge to creating output for the Web is that the people who view your results will be using a variety of browsers on a variety of screen sizes and resolutions. HTML is a great tool for handling these variations, as it can adjust the width of various objects to the width of the browser window. This automatic behavior is great for fitting output on the screen, but it means that your results will look different, depending on the size of the browser window. For example, in Output 11.17, the table of contents is too narrow and some of the labels wrap awkwardly because the browser window was too small. This may be fine for your purposes. However, if you would like your output to look the same wherever it is viewed, you can change some settings.

This example shows how to set a fixed width for the table of contents and for the tables in the body of your output. Together, these changes ensure a standard look for your output. You will assign an overall width of 600 pixels to your results. The first 200 pixels will be used for the table of contents, and the remaining 400 will be used by the output tables. These results should be viewable by anyone with a screen resolution of at least 640x480, if they maximize the browser window.

We will work with the Default style definition for this example. There are two settings you need to change. First, you need to add a width setting to your output tables. This is done in the Table style element. If you look at that style element in the source code, you will see that it has no attributes. However, a review of the documentation[1] reveals that there is an OUTPUTWIDTH attribute you can use. Set the output width to 400.

Second, you need to fix the width of the table of contents. This width is controlled by the Frame style element. The attribute CONTENTSIZE can be set to a percentage of the screen or to a fixed width. Set it to a fixed width of 200 pixels.

```
PROC TEMPLATE;
   DEFINE STYLE DefaultWidth;
      PARENT=Styles.Default;
      REPLACE Table from Output /
         outputwidth=400;
      REPLACE Frame from Document /
         contentposition = L
         bodyscrollbar = auto
         bodysize = *
         contentscrollbar = auto
         contentsize = 200
         framespacing = 1
         frameborderwidth = 4
         frameborder = on;
   END;
RUN;
```

The revised output is shown in Output 11.18. Now the table of contents has enough room and the labels do not wrap so awkwardly, and there is still enough space for the tables. If the browser window were any smaller, however, you would have to use the scroll bar to view the right side of the tables.

---

[1] To learn which style attributes to use, go to the "Guide to the SAS Output Delivery System" in SAS OnlineDoc and find the section on the TEMPLATE procedure. Then go to the section on the DEFINE STYLE statement. It has a lengthy discussion of style attributes that lists each of the attributes and what parts of the output they affect.

**Output 11.17**

### The UNIVARIATE Procedure
### Variable: CostSqFt (Cost per square foot)

| Moments | | | |
|---|---|---|---|
| N | 342 | Sum Weights | 342 |
| Mean | 177.233918 | Sum Observations | 60614 |
| Std Deviation | 56.8410163 | Variance | 3230.90113 |
| Skewness | 0.08618204 | Kurtosis | -1.13331 |
| Uncorrected SS | 11844594 | Corrected SS | 1101737.29 |
| Coeff Variation | 32.0711842 | Std Error Mean | 3.07361015 |

**Output 11.18**

### The UNIVARIATE Procedure
### Variable: CostSqFt (Cost per square foot)

| Moments | | | |
|---|---|---|---|
| N | 342 | Sum Weights | 342 |
| Mean | 177.233918 | Sum Observations | 60614 |
| Std Deviation | 56.8410163 | Variance | 3230.90113 |
| Skewness | 0.08618204 | Kurtosis | -1.13331 |
| Uncorrected SS | 11844594 | Corrected SS | 1101737.29 |
| Coeff Variation | 32.0711842 | Std Error Mean | 3.07361015 |

## Hiding the Frame Border

When you create a Web page with a table of contents, ODS creates a border to separate the table of contents from the body of the output. You can modify this border to make it wider or narrower or to make it go away altogether.

If you look at a variety of Web sites, you will see that many designers choose to do away with frame borders. These distract from the design of the rest of the page. In this example, we will remove the frame border from ODS HTML output.

We will modify the Default style definition to remove the border. The section of code that controls the frame border is the Frame style element. In the previous example, we used this style element to change the space allowed for the contents frame. This time, we will use the FRAMEBORDER attribute to remove the border.

```
PROC TEMPLATE;
   DEFINE STYLE DefaultFrameBorder;
      PARENT=Styles.Default;
      REPLACE Frame from Document /
         contentposition = L
         bodyscrollbar = auto
         bodysize = *
         contentscrollbar = auto
         contentsize = 23%
         framespacing = 1
         frameborderwidth = 4
         frameborder = OFF;
   END;
RUN;
```

By changing the FRAMEBORDER attribute setting from ON to OFF, the results change from what you see in Output 11.19 to what you see in Output 11.20. The output is unchanged, except that there is no longer a frame border.

The effect of the change is that the page has a cleaner look. The frame border no longer distracts from the output. Because the contents frame has a darker background than the body frame, you still get the effect of a border between the two. That is the trick to using this technique: it works best when you have different colors for the two backgrounds. Otherwise, if both were the same color, the contents would run into the body and the result would be confusing.

There is one caveat to this technique. If you have a lengthy table of contents, ODS will add a scroll bar when the table of contents exceeds the length of the browser window. This can look a little odd, because the scroll bar floats between the two frames.

You can turn off the scroll bar if you want, by changing the CONTENTSCROLLBAR attribute setting from "auto" to "no," but then you might end up with a long table of contents and no way to get to the entries at the bottom. Changing the CONTENTSCROLLBAR setting is not recommended.

**Output 11.19**

**The UNIVARIATE Procedure**
**Variable: CostSqFt (Cost per square foot)**

| Moments | | | |
|---|---|---|---|
| N | 342 | Sum Weights | 342 |
| Mean | 177.233918 | Sum Observations | 60614 |
| Std Deviation | 56.8410163 | Variance | 3230.90113 |
| Skewness | 0.08618204 | Kurtosis | -1.13331 |
| Uncorrected SS | 11844594 | Corrected SS | 1101737.29 |
| Coeff Variation | 32.0711842 | Std Error Mean | 3.07361015 |

**Output 11.20**

**The UNIVARIATE Procedure**
**Variable: CostSqFt (Cost per square foot)**

| Moments | | | |
|---|---|---|---|
| N | 342 | Sum Weights | 342 |
| Mean | 177.233918 | Sum Observations | 60614 |
| Std Deviation | 56.8410163 | Variance | 3230.90113 |
| Skewness | 0.08618204 | Kurtosis | -1.13331 |
| Uncorrected SS | 11844594 | Corrected SS | 1101737.29 |
| Coeff Variation | 32.0711842 | Std Error Mean | 3.07361015 |

# Chapter
# 12

## *Modifying Output Colors and Graphics*

It used to be that you could only create color output from a limited number of graphics procedures. Now, with ODS, you can create color virtually anywhere you want it.

If you'd like a purple frequency distribution and an orange regression model, you can do it. You can create Web pages using psychedelic color schemes. You can also create output that matches the colors in your corporate logo.

This chapter describes how colors work in ODS. It covers how and where in the code to identify them, and shows how to create style definitions with custom color schemes.

In addition, because not all output is generated for the Web or for a color printer, we'll look at a color scheme designed for black and white output.

## Exploring the Style Elements That Control Color

The colors in an ODS style definition are organized much like the fonts. A style element creates a list of colors that are used elsewhere in the output.

To see how colors work, you need to run a PROC TEMPLATE with a SOURCE statement. Output 12.1 shows selected portions of the source code. The first style element shown is color_list. It contains a list of color codes, each of which is assigned to a name. The codes are RGB values given in hexadecimal. See "Identifying Colors" on page 192 for more information on these codes. The color names are just a convenience. Foreground colors all start with "fg" and background colors all start with "bg." The subsequent letters and numbers have no special meaning; they're just used to uniquely identify each color.

The second style element is called Colors, and it is used to assign color names to more descriptive names that will be used in various parts of the output. For example, in the color_list style element, there is a color called "fgA," which has a specific color of cx002288. In the Colors style element, this color is assigned to "notefg," "proctitlefg," "titlefg," "systitlefg," "Conentryfg," "Confolderfg," "Contitlefg," and "docfg."

So the color_list style element creates a list of colors, and the colors style element assigns these colors to a list of names representing various parts of your output. Thus far, all you have are two lists. The key to making this work is the third style element shown. See Output 12.2. It is an example of how colors are applied to output. In this case, the color defined by "systitlefg" is applied to the TitlesAndFooters style element as the foreground color, and the color defined by "systitlebg" is applied to the TitlesAndFooters style element as the background color. The net effect of all of this code is that the titles and footnotes in your output are colored royal blue and placed on a background of light gray.

If you want to modify the color scheme for the titles and footnotes, there are three ways to do it. First, you could create a new style definition with a different color_list. If you change "fgA" and "bgA" to different hex codes, the new colors are then assigned to the color names in the Colors style element. These names would then be assigned to the TitlesAndFooters style element. The problem with this approach is that the new colors will also apply everywhere else that "fgA" and "bgA" are used. If you want to create a consistent change in the color scheme across all parts of your output, modifying the color_list style element is the way to go.

The second way to modify the color scheme is to modify the Colors style element. You can change the color that is used by the "systitlefg" or "systitlebg" attributes. This approach works better if you want to change the color assignment for a particular part of your output.

The third way to modify the color scheme is to change the color name that is given in the style element that controls the part of the output you want to change. The TitlesAndFooters style element can be modified to request a color name other than "systitlefg" or "systitlebg."

You can also use a combination of these approaches. For example, if you want to create purple titles and footnotes, you can add a new color to the color_list style element, create a new color name for the new color in the Color style element, and assign the new color name to the appropriate attribute in the TitlesAndFooters style element.

The examples in this chapter show how these techniques work.

**Output 12.1**

```
style color_list
   "Colors used in the default style" /
   'fgB2' = cx0066AA
   'fgB1' = cx004488
   'fgA4' = cxAAFFAA
   'bgA4' = cx880000
   'bgA3' = cxD3D3D3
   'fgA2' = cx0033AA
   'bgA2' = cxB0B0B0
   'fgA1' = cx000000
   'bgA1' = cxF0F0F0
   'fgA' = cx002288
   'bgA' = cxE0E0E0;
style colors
   "Abstract colors used in the default style" /
   'headerfgemph' = color_list('fgA2')
   'headerbgemph' = color_list('bgA2')
   'headerfgstrong' = color_list('fgA2')
   'headerbgstrong' = color_list('bgA2')
   'headerfg' = color_list('fgA2')
   'headerbg' = color_list('bgA2')
   'datafgemph' = color_list('fgA1')
   'databgemph' = color_list('bgA3')
   'datafgstrong' = color_list('fgA1')
   'databgstrong' = color_list('bgA3')
   'datafg' = color_list('fgA1')
   'databg' = color_list('bgA3')
   'batchfg' = color_list('fgA1')
   'batchbg' = color_list('bgA3')
   'tableborder' = color_list('fgA1')
   'tablebg' = color_list('bgA1')
   'notefg' = color_list('fgA')
   'notebg' = color_list('bgA')
   'bylinefg' = color_list('fgA2')
   'bylinebg' = color_list('bgA2')
   'captionfg' = color_list('fgA1')
   'captionbg' = color_list('bgA')
   'proctitlefg' = color_list('fgA')
   'proctitlebg' = color_list('bgA')
   'titlefg' = color_list('fgA')
   'titlebg' = color_list('bgA')
   'systitlefg' = color_list('fgA')
   'systitlebg' = color_list('bgA')
   'Conentryfg' = color_list('fgA')
   'Confolderfg' = color_list('fgA')
   'Contitlefg' = color_list('fgA')
   'link2' = color_list('fgB2')
   'link1' = color_list('fgB1')
   'contentfg' = color_list('fgA2')
   'contentbg' = color_list('bgA2')
   'docfg' = color_list('fgA')
   'docbg' = color_list('bgA');
```

**Output 12.2**

```
style TitlesAndFooters from Container
   "Abstract. Controls system page title text and system page footer text." /
   font = Fonts('TitleFont2')
   background = colors('systitlebg')
   foreground = colors('systitlefg');
```

## Modifying the Color of Your Titles

Because there are so many ways to modify color settings, it can get a bit confusing. This first example is very simple so you can see what's going on.

The Default style definition uses dark text on a light background for titles and footnotes. For a different look, you can reverse those settings. In the Default style definition, "fgA" is set to the color cx002288, and "bgA" is set to the color cxE0E0E0. To reverse the settings, you just have to exchange those two values. The code that follows shows how to modify the Default style definition with the new settings.

```
PROC TEMPLATE;
   DEFINE STYLE DefaultTitle;
      PARENT=Styles.Default;
   REPLACE color_list /
      'fgB2' = cx0066AA
      'fgB1' = cx004488
      'fgA4' = cxAAFFAA
      'bgA4' = cx880000
      'bgA3' = cxD3D3D3
      'fgA2' = cx0033AA
      'bgA2' = cxB0B0B0
      'fgA1' = cx000000
      'bgA1' = cxF0F0F0
      'fgA' = cxE0E0E0
      'bgA' = cx002288;
   END;
RUN;
```

Output 12.3 shows a simple table in the Default style definition. Output 12.4 shows the same table with the new DefaultTitle style definition applied. Notice how the entire background has been reversed. This is because "fgA" and "bgA" apply to more than just the titles and footnotes.

Another way to write this code so only the titles and footnotes are affected is to just reverse the color assignments in the TitlesAndFooters style element, as shown in the code below.

```
PROC TEMPLATE;
   DEFINE STYLE DefaultTitle2;
      PARENT=Styles.Default;
   REPLACE TitlesAndFooters from Container /
      font = Fonts('TitleFont2')
      background = colors('systitlefg')
      foreground = colors('systitlebg');
   END;
RUN;
```

This code assigns the background color to the foreground and the foreground color to the background. The result is output with the title appearing in reverse, as shown in Output 12.5.

**Output 12.3**

**Paint Industry Statistics**

| Frequency | Table of Base by Type | | | |
| --- | --- | --- | --- | --- |
| | Type(Type of Finish) | | | |
| Base | Paint | Stain | Sealer | Total |
| Latex | 271 | 171 | 78 | 520 |
| Oil | 135 | 68 | 44 | 247 |
| Total | 406 | 239 | 122 | 767 |

For a color version of Output 12.3, see page 284 in Appendix 3.

**Output 12.4**

**Paint Industry Statistics**

| Frequency | Table of Base by Type | | | |
| --- | --- | --- | --- | --- |
| | Type(Type of Finish) | | | |
| Base | Paint | Stain | Sealer | Total |
| Latex | 271 | 171 | 78 | 520 |
| Oil | 135 | 68 | 44 | 247 |
| Total | 406 | 239 | 122 | 767 |

For a color version of Output 12.4, see page 284 in Appendix 3.

**Output 12.5**

**Paint Industry Statistics**

| Frequency | Table of Base by Type | | | |
| --- | --- | --- | --- | --- |
| | Type(Type of Finish) | | | |
| Base | Paint | Stain | Sealer | Total |
| Latex | 271 | 171 | 78 | 520 |
| Oil | 135 | 68 | 44 | 247 |
| Total | 406 | 239 | 122 | 767 |

For a color version of Output 12.5, see page 284 in Appendix 3.

## Identifying Colors

The Default style definition uses colors like "cx0066AA," "cx004488," and "cx002288." What do these stand for? The "cx" part indicates that this is a RGB color given in hexadecimal values. The numbers that follow are the red, green, and blue values that define the colors. For example, "cx0066AA" refers to red=00, green=66, and blue=AA. Those values produce a medium grayish blue. In this color scheme, "cxFFFFFF" refers to white, "cx000000" refers to black, and "cx0000FF" refers to blue.

If you want to change a color on the color list, you can simply replace the old RGB color code with the new RGB color code. For example, if you change the code for the "fgA" value, you can request green foreground text. The code change is

```
"fgA" = cx002288        to        "fgA" = cx00FF00
```

This creates the output shown in Output 12.6. If you look at the generated HTML code in detail, you will see the following color assignment for the title:

```
<font  face="Arial, Helvetica, Helv" size="5" color="#00FF00">
<b><i>Paint Industry Statistics</i></b></font>
```

The color code is passed through to the HTML code for your Web page. Instead of "cx00FF00," it is listed in the HTML format of "#00FF00," but the code is the same. If you create RTF or printer output, the same color is used, though you can't see the color code directly like this.

If you find these color codes confusing, you can also choose to identify your colors by name. This can make your style definition code more readable. For example, to get green foreground text, you can use the following code:

```
"fgA" = GREEN
```

Output 12.7 shows the results with the new color. This example illustrates the limitations of color names. The green color selected by "GREEN" is not the same as the green color selected by "cx00FF00." If you look at the HTML code, you can see why this is the case.

```
<font  face="Arial, Helvetica, Helv" size="5" color="#008000">
<b><i>Paint Industry Statistics</i></b></font>
```

SAS has assigned the color code "cx008000" instead of "cx00FF00" when creating the HTML output. This is the catch to using color names. SAS assigns the names to color values when it generates the output. For a list of the color names and their values, see the sections about SAS/GRAPH in SAS OnlineDoc.

If you're a stickler for getting the exact color you want, you may be happier using the RGB codes. You can download a tool from the Internet to help you pick colors. Just use any search engine and look for the term "Color Picker." These tools generally have a color palette you can click on to get the RGB code for that color. Output 12.8 shows an example of one of these tools. By clicking on the box with the desired shade of green, you can look up the code 009966 that will give you that shade of green.

**Output 12.6**

## Paint Industry Statistics

| Analysis Variable : Warranty Year of Warranty | | | | |
|---|---|---|---|---|
| N | Mean | Std Dev | Minimum | Maximum |
| 767 | 12.1 | 1.4 | 10.0 | 14.0 |

For a color version of Output 12.6, see page 285 in Appendix 3.

**Output 12.7**

## Paint Industry Statistics

| Analysis Variable : Warranty Year of Warranty | | | | |
|---|---|---|---|---|
| N | Mean | Std Dev | Minimum | Maximum |
| 767 | 12.1 | 1.4 | 10.0 | 14.0 |

For a color version of Output 12.7, see page 285 in Appendix 3.

**Output 12.8**

## ColorPicker

Custom BGCOLOR * :  #009966

For a color version of Output 12.8, see page 285 in Appendix 3.

Most color pickers will show you the 216 "safe" colors to use for HTML. These colors will generally be rendered correctly by all browsers. Other colors may look different in Netscape than they do in Internet Explorer.

## Modifying Background Colors

Each of the previous examples in this chapter looked at changing the color of the text in your output. This example focuses on the background.

If you expect that a lot of users will want to print your HTML output, the first thing you will want to change about the Default style definition is its background. The gray background looks fine when viewed in a browser, but it looks terrible when you print. Because your printer cannot print all the way to the edge of the paper, you get output on a gray background with a white border.

To make your HTML output easier to print, you can change the Default style definition to use a white background. In the code below, the "bgA" color is changed from "cxE0E0E0," the gray shade, to "cxFFFFFF," a pure white.

```
PROC TEMPLATE;
   DEFINE STYLE DefaultBack;
      PARENT=Styles.Default;
   REPLACE color_list /
      'fgB2' = cx0066AA
      'fgB1' = cx004488
      'fgA4' = cxAAFFAA
      'bgA4' = cx880000
      'bgA3' = cxD3D3D3
      'fgA2' = cx0033AA
      'bgA2' = cxB0B0B0
      'fgA1' = cx000000
      'bgA1' = cxF0F0F0
      'fgA' = cx002288
 ➡    'bgA' = cxFFFFFF;
   END;
 RUN;
```

This style definition changes your output from the color scheme shown in Output 12.9 to the color scheme shown in Output 12.10. Now the entire background, except the tables themselves, is shown in white.

If you want the background to be completely white, including the table, then you need to make a few more changes. Every color that starts with "bg" needs to be changed to "cxFFFFFF." The items to change are

```
'bgA4' = cxFFFFFF
'bgA3' = cxFFFFFF
'bgA2' = cxFFFFFF
'bgA1' = cxFFFFFF
'bgA' = cxFFFFFF
```

The revised output is shown in Output 12.11. Now everything is white except the foreground text and the table borders.

**Output 12.9**

## *Paint Industry Statistics*

| Analysis Variable : Warranty Year of Warranty | | | | | | |
|---|---|---|---|---|---|---|
| Type of Finish | N Obs | N | Mean | Std Dev | Minimum | Maximum |
| Paint | 406 | 406 | 6.7 | 2.8 | 2.0 | 11.0 |
| Stain | 239 | 239 | 6.7 | 2.9 | 2.0 | 11.0 |
| Sealer | 122 | 122 | 6.5 | 3.0 | 2.0 | 11.0 |

For a color version of Output 12.9, see page 286 in Appendix 3.

**Output 12.10**

## *Paint Industry Statistics*

| Analysis Variable : Warranty Year of Warranty | | | | | | |
|---|---|---|---|---|---|---|
| Type of Finish | N Obs | N | Mean | Std Dev | Minimum | Maximum |
| Paint | 406 | 406 | 6.7 | 2.8 | 2.0 | 11.0 |
| Stain | 239 | 239 | 6.7 | 2.9 | 2.0 | 11.0 |
| Sealer | 122 | 122 | 6.5 | 3.0 | 2.0 | 11.0 |

For a color version of Output 12.10, see page 286 in Appendix 3.

**Output 12.11**

## *Paint Industry Statistics*

| Analysis Variable : Warranty Year of Warranty | | | | | | |
|---|---|---|---|---|---|---|
| Type of Finish | N Obs | N | Mean | Std Dev | Minimum | Maximum |
| Paint | 406 | 406 | 6.7 | 2.8 | 2.0 | 11.0 |
| Stain | 239 | 239 | 6.7 | 2.9 | 2.0 | 11.0 |
| Sealer | 122 | 122 | 6.5 | 3.0 | 2.0 | 11.0 |

For a color version of Output 12.11, see page 286 in Appendix 3.

## Modifying Colors in Tables

If you want to change all of the table elements to the same color scheme, then you know from the previous example that modifying table colors is simple. You can just change all of the colors that start with "bg" to the same color. You can also do the same thing with all of the colors labeled "fg."

However, what makes tables interesting is the mix of colors used to define the table cells and headings. A better color scheme uses a variety of colors. Let's assume that you're creating a table for a company with a green and gold logo. This example creates a color scheme to match.

In order to change the colors used by the table, you first need to find out which colors are used in the table. The way to do this is to run PROC TEMPLATE with a source statement and to start tracking down each of the parts of the table. Starting with the header, if you look at the Headers-AndFooters style element, you find that the colors used are "headerfg" for the foreground text and "headerbg" for the background. If you then look these up in the color_list style element, you find that "headerfg" is assigned color "fgA2" and "headerbg" is assigned "bgA2."

Following the same steps, you learn that the table cells use "fgA1" for the foreground and "bgA3" for the background. The table border color is "fgA" and the table background (the color that shows through when cell spacing is greater than 0) is "bgA1."

To change the Default style definition to a new color scheme, you just have to change those five color settings to colors that match the green and gold logo. When replacing the colors, the main thing to keep in mind is to replace dark colors with dark colors and light colors with light colors. Otherwise, you may get output with text that is hard to distinguish from the background. The revised colors in the code below create a table color scheme with green text on a gold background. The table text and borders are a shade of dark green.

```
PROC TEMPLATE;
   DEFINE STYLE DefaultLogoColors;
      PARENT=Styles.Default;
   REPLACE color_list /
      'fgB2' = cx0066AA
      'fgB1' = cx004488
      'fgA4' = cxAAFFAA
      'bgA4' = cx880000
      'bgA3' = cxFFFF33
      'fgA2' = cx336600
      'bgA2' = cxFFCC00
      'fgA1' = cx003300
      'bgA1' = cxFFFF66
      'fgA' = cx002288
      'bgA' = cxE0E0E0;
   END;
RUN;
```

Compare Output 12.12 to Output 12.13 to see the change. Taking this color scheme a step further, you could also modify "fgA" and "bgA" to create titles and a page background in a similar color scheme, as shown in Output 12.14. The colors are cx336600 for the foreground and cxFFFF66 for the background.

**Output 12.12**

### Paint Industry Statistics

| Frequency | Table of Base by Color | | | | |
|---|---|---|---|---|---|
| | | | Color | | |
| Base | Gray | White | Tan | Yellow | Total |
| Latex | 55 | 244 | 118 | 103 | 520 |
| Oil | 21 | 108 | 52 | 66 | 247 |
| Total | 76 | 352 | 170 | 169 | 767 |

For a color version of Output 12.12, see page 287 in Appendix 3.

**Output 12.13**

### Paint Industry Statistics

| Frequency | Table of Base by Color | | | | |
|---|---|---|---|---|---|
| | | | Color | | |
| Base | Gray | White | Tan | Yellow | Total |
| Latex | 55 | 244 | 118 | 103 | 520 |
| Oil | 21 | 108 | 52 | 66 | 247 |
| Total | 76 | 352 | 170 | 169 | 767 |

For a color version of Output 12.13, see page 287 in Appendix 3.

**Output 12.14**

### Paint Industry Statistics

| Frequency | Table of Base by Color | | | | |
|---|---|---|---|---|---|
| | | | Color | | |
| Base | Gray | White | Tan | Yellow | Total |
| Latex | 55 | 244 | 118 | 103 | 520 |
| Oil | 21 | 108 | 52 | 66 | 247 |
| Total | 76 | 352 | 170 | 169 | 767 |

For a color version of Output 12.14, see page 287 in Appendix 3.

## Adding a New Color to the Color Scheme

If you would like to depart from the default color scheme and add a new color for some part of the output, you can do that by adding a new color to your style definition.

The following code creates a new purple color just for footnotes (the code has been abbreviated to save space, but the important changes are shown). First, the new color is added to the color list. A new color we'll call "fgNew" is set to cx660066, which is a dark purple. Second, the new color is assigned to the name "footnotefg." Finally, the new color name is applied to the SystemFooter style element. Previously, this style element contained only a font definition. The foreground setting has been added so that we can modify the color.

```
PROC TEMPLATE;
   DEFINE STYLE DefaultPurpleFN;
      PARENT=Styles.Default;
   REPLACE color_list /
                ... list standard colors here ...
      'fgNew'= cx660066;
   REPLACE colors /
                ... list standard colors here ...
      'footnotefg' = color_list('fgNew');
   REPLACE SystemFooter from TitlesAndFooters
      "Controls system footer text." /
      font = Fonts('TitleFont')
      foreground = colors('footnotefg');
   END;
RUN;
```

Using this style definition, you can change your output from the version shown in Output 12.15 to the version shown in Output 12.16. The only difference is that the second version has a purple footnote.

There is a simpler way to create the same effect. Instead of modifying the color_list and Colors style elements, you can assign the new color directly in the SystemFooter style element. All you have to do is list the color code as the foreground setting, as in the code below.

```
PROC TEMPLATE;
   DEFINE STYLE DefaultPurpleFN;
      PARENT=Styles.Default;
   REPLACE SystemFooter from TitlesAndFooters
      "Controls system footer text." /
      font = Fonts('TitleFont')
      foreground = cx660066;
   END;
RUN;
```

This code produces exactly the same output as the previous code. However, it makes your source code more confusing since it does not follow the convention of assigning colors in the color_list and Colors style elements. You can decide which approach you prefer.

**Output 12.15**

## *Paint Industry Statistics*

### *Variable: Price*

| Basic Statistical Measures | | | |
|---|---|---|---|
| **Location** | | **Variability** | |
| **Mean** | 11.07898 | **Std Deviation** | 2.86897 |
| **Median** | 11.01149 | **Variance** | 8.23099 |
| **Mode** | . | **Range** | 9.97714 |
| | | **Interquartile Range** | 5.00348 |

## *6/2000 monthly sales figures*

For a color version of Output 12.15, see page 288 in Appendix 3.

**Output 12.16**

## *Paint Industry Statistics*

### *Variable: Price*

| Basic Statistical Measures | | | |
|---|---|---|---|
| **Location** | | **Variability** | |
| **Mean** | 11.07898 | **Std Deviation** | 2.86897 |
| **Median** | 11.01149 | **Variance** | 8.23099 |
| **Mode** | . | **Range** | 9.97714 |
| | | **Interquartile Range** | 5.00348 |

## *6/2000 monthly sales figures*

For a color version of Output 12.16, see page 288 in Appendix 3.

## Color Techniques to Use with Black and White Output

If you know you will be printing your results in black and white, you need to be careful about creating color schemes. Some schemes look great in color, but when they are converted to grayscale, there isn't enough contrast between foreground and background and the results are hard to read. One solution to this problem is to use a black and white style definition. In fact, there are a couple of built-in style definitions that do not use color. For example, the D3D style definition uses no colors. This style definition has a nice three-dimensional effect (see Output 12.17), but the effect only works for HTML output.

The other solution is to use a style definition with colors but test it first in grayscale. For example, the Default style definition uses shades of blue and gray to create table headers that are distinct from the table body. However, when you print the output in grayscale, you get the uniformly gray table shown in Output 12.18. This example shows how to create a color scheme that also looks good when printed in grayscale.

The code below creates a color scheme in red and gold. The page background ("bgA") is set to white, the best setting for printed output. The titles and footnotes ("fgA") are set to a dark red. The table row and column header backgrounds ("bgA2") are set to the same red. For contrast, the row and column header foreground text ("fgA2") is set to white. The table cell backgrounds ("bgA3") are set to a gold shade. The table cell foreground text ("fgA1") is set to black. Finally, the table background ("bgA1") is set to black.

```
PROC TEMPLATE;
   DEFINE STYLE GraySafe;
      PARENT=Styles.Default;
   REPLACE color_list /
      'fgB2' = cx0066AA
      'fgB1' = cx004488
      'fgA4' = cxAAFFAA
      'bgA4' = cx880000
      'bgA3' = cxFFFF33
      'fgA2' = cxFFFFFF
      'bgA2' = cxFF2222
      'fgA1' = cx000000
      'bgA1' = cx000000
      'fgA' = cxFFFF22
      'bgA' = cxFFFFFF;
   END;
RUN;
```

The color version of this style definition is shown in Output 12.19. Now that the color version looks the way you want it, the next step is to look at how it turns out when printed in grayscale. To quickly view grayscale results, temporarily add an OPTIONS NOCOLORPRINTING statement to your code (put it before your first ODS statement). The grayscale version of our new style definition is shown in Output 12.20. This output is readable, but things have changed. The white reverse text in the row and column headers has been converted to black, and the gold cell background in the table has been converted to white. Each time you create a new style definition or use a built-in style definition, it's important to do this test to be sure you can live with the grayscale results. Even if you're only creating HTML output, the likelihood is high that some user will want to print it on a black and white printer.

**Output 12.17**

| Pearson Correlation Coefficients, N = 767 Prob > \|r\| under H0: Rho=0 | |
|---|---|
| | Price |
| Warranty Year of Warranty | 0.01597 0.6588 |

**Output 12.18**

| Pearson Correlation Coefficients, N = 767 Prob > \|r\| under H0: Rho=0 | |
|---|---|
| | Price |
| Warranty Year of Warranty | 0.01597 0.6588 |

**Output 12.19**

| Pearson Correlation Coefficients, N = 767 Prob > \|r\| under H0: Rho=0 | |
|---|---|
| | Price |
| Warranty Year of Warranty | 0.01597 0.6588 |

For a color version of Output 12.19, see page 289 in Appendix 3.

**Output 12.20**

| Pearson Correlation Coefficients, N = 767 Prob > \|r\| under H0: Rho=0 | |
|---|---|
| | Price |
| Warranty Year of  Warranty | 0.01597 0.6588 |

The same color schemes that make your color output look good in black and white are also easier for people who are colorblind to see, increasing the accessibility of your output.

## Adding a Logo to Your Output

Once you start customizing your style definition, one of the first things you will probably want to do is add a company logo to your page headings. This is a great way to add your corporate identity to any results you send out. This example shows how to add a logo, and then demonstrates the technique for HTML, RTF, and printer output.

First, you need to build a new style definition. You do this by using an attribute of the Body style element. The attribute is called PREIMAGE, and you use it to name the image file to be used. For HTML output, these images must be in a browser-compatible format like GIF or JPEG. For RTF output, the images need to be JPEG files. For printer output (PostScript, PDF), you can use virtually any image format.

```
PROC TEMPLATE;
   DEFINE STYLE DefaultLogo;
      PARENT=Styles.Default;
   REPLACE Body from Document /
      preimage="logo.gif";
   END;
RUN;
```

Output 12.21 shows the results from the new style definition in HTML. The logo is displayed at the top of the page.

Okay, you're probably thinking, *This is the ugliest design I have ever seen*. The red logo looks awful with the blue and gray Default style definition. This example is just the beginning. If you are going to develop a corporate style definition, you will want to work with the color settings as well as the PREIMAGE attribute in order to create an attractive look. But once it is created, you can use it repeatedly to ensure a consistent corporate look for all of your output.

**Output 12.21**

October Price Report

| Analysis Variable : Price | | | | |
|---|---|---|---|---|
| N | Mean | Std Dev | Minimum | Maximum |
| 767 | 11.08 | 2.87 | 6.01 | 15.99 |

For a color version of Output 12.21, see page 289 in Appendix 3.

## Adding a Logo and Custom Heading to Your HTML Output

Most style definition techniques work for all output formats, but if you are creating HTML output, there are a few extra tricks in your bag. HTML output allows you to add images and HTML code to your output.

As an example, we will set up a logo and company name as a default page heading. This time, instead of the PREIMAGE attribute, we'll use the PREHTML attribute of the Body style element. The attribute allows you to pass HTML code straight through to your output. In this case, the code being passed is the IMG tag used to display an image, some text and formatting tags to create a heading, and some table tags to organize the logo and text. The BORDER="0" hides the border of the image so that it blends in to the Web page. The SRC="logo.gif" names the image to be used. These images must be in a browser-compatible format like GIF or JPEG.

```
PROC TEMPLATE;
   DEFINE STYLE DefaultLogo2;
      PARENT=Styles.Default;
   REPLACE Body from Document /
      prehtml='<table width=100%><tr><td nowrap align=left>
         <img border="0" src="logo.gif">
         <font face="Arial" size=3><b>SprayTech Corp.</b></font>
         </tr></td></table>';
   END;
RUN;
```

The results are shown in Output 12.22. Now both the logo and the company name appear at the top of the page.

Using the PREHTML attribute, you can add anything you want to the top of your output. However, this technique only works for the HTML destination.

Also, a matching POSTHTML attribute allows you to add custom HTML code to the bottom of your output. This is a handy way to put a standard footer on all of your output pages.

**Output 12.22**

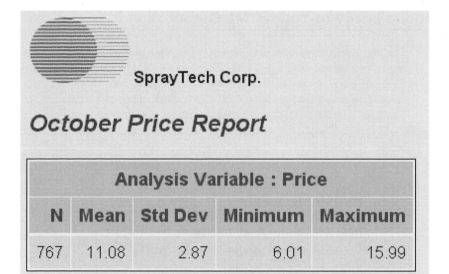

For a color version of Output 12.22, see page 289 in Appendix 3.

## Adding a Background Image to Your HTML Output

The previous example showed how to add a logo at the top of each output page. This example shows how to use an image for the background. We will build a style definition with a repeated image of the company logo as a background. Again, we will be working with the Body style element. This time, instead of the PREHTML attribute, we will take advantage of another attribute. The BACKGROUNDIMAGE attribute allows you to specify an image file to use as the page background. You do not have to write the HTML code yourself if all you want is a background image.

```
PROC TEMPLATE;
   DEFINE STYLE DefaultLogoBG;
      PARENT=Styles.Default;
   REPLACE Body from Document /
      backgroundimage="logobg.gif";
   END;
RUN;
```

The resulting Web output is shown in Output 12.23. The output is very ugly because the image clashes with the Default color scheme, but you get the idea. You can enhance this output by adding the company title to the page heading, and by fixing the ugly background behind the page title. The company title is added in exactly the same way as in the previous example. The PREHTML attribute is used to add the HTML needed to create the title. Next, you can fix the background for the titles. This requires removing the background setting from the TitlesAndFooters and Container style elements.

```
PROC TEMPLATE;
   DEFINE STYLE DefaultLogoBG2;
      PARENT=Styles.Default;
   REPLACE Body from Document /
      prehtml='<table width=100%><tr><td nowrap align=left>
         <font face="Arial" size=5><b>SprayTech Corp.</b></font>
         </tr></td></table>'
      backgroundimage='logobg.gif';
   REPLACE Container /
      font = Fonts('DocFont')
      foreground = colors('docfg');
   REPLACE TitlesAndFooters from Container /
      font = Fonts('TitleFont2')
      foreground = colors('systitlefg');
   END;
RUN;
```

Now you get the table shown in Output 12.24. It looks better, but it's still ugly. One solution to this problem would be to use the Minimal style definition as the parent, rather than the Default style definition. This requires an additional code tweak to change the table background to white, but it can yield results like Output 12.25. The bottom line is that no matter how you create your background image style definition, you'll have to tweak some settings (color scheme, background colors) to get the attractive look you want. This example is merely an introduction.

**Output 12.23**

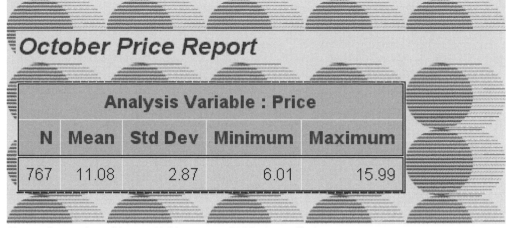

## October Price Report

| Analysis Variable : Price | | | | |
|---|---|---|---|---|
| N | Mean | Std Dev | Minimum | Maximum |
| 767 | 11.08 | 2.87 | 6.01 | 15.99 |

For a color version of Output 12.23, see page 290 in Appendix 3.

**Output 12.24**

## SprayTech Corp.

## October Price Report

| Analysis Variable : Price | | | | |
|---|---|---|---|---|
| N | Mean | Std Dev | Minimum | Maximum |
| 767 | 11.08 | 2.87 | 6.01 | 15.99 |

For a color version of Output 12.24, see page 290 in Appendix 3.

**Output 12.25**

## SprayTech Corp.

October Price Report

| Analysis Variable : Price | | | | |
|---|---|---|---|---|
| N | Mean | Std Dev | Minimum | Maximum |
| 767 | 11.08 | 2.87 | 6.01 | 15.99 |

For a color version of Output 12.25, see page 290 in Appendix 3.

# Special Cases: The REPORT, TABULATE, and PRINT Procedures

Chapter

13

For most procedures in the SAS System, the only way to change the appearance of the output is to change or modify the style definition. There are three exceptions: the REPORT, TABULATE, and PRINT procedures. These procedures allow you to change the output style attributes on the fly when the output is generated. With these three procedures, you can create almost any type of tabular report. Add in the extra control over style attributes that ODS gives you, and you have a reporting powerhouse.

This chapter shows how to change fonts, colors, and alignment of your output. It also shows how to use formats to highlight key results in special colors and use images in table headings.

For convenience, all of the examples are shown as HTML output. Except where noted, the examples all work for both RTF and printer output.

## Changing PROC REPORT Column Heading Style Attributes

Applying style attributes to PROC REPORT output is very simple. All you have to do is add STYLE= options to whichever part of the output you want to change.

STYLE= is a new option available for just the PRINT, REPORT, and TABULATE procedures. What it allows you to do is specify a number of different style attributes for specific parts of your output. These style attributes control things like typefaces, foreground and background colors, text alignment, and table borders.

There are a number of ways you can use STYLE= in PROC REPORT. We'll start out with one simple technique: using STYLE= to change the column headings. We'll start with a simple table.

```
ODS HTML BODY='tables.htm';
proc report data=tables nowd;
   column Type Material Price;
   define Type / group 'Table Type';
   define Material / group 'Construction';
   define Price / analysis mean 'Average Price' format=dollar8.;
run;
ODS HTML CLOSE;
```

This code produces the output shown in Output 13.1. It's a basic table using the Default style definition. The typeface used in the headings is Arial. As an example, we will change this typeface to Times New Roman.

This is done by adding a STYLE= option to the PROC REPORT statement. The STYLE keyword is followed by the name of the location you want to modify. In this case, the location is called Header. A list of the locations you can modify is in the SAS OnlineDoc section on the REPORT procedure.

Following the name of the location, use an equal sign and then list the style attributes you want to change. You can list a single attribute or a number of attributes. A list of the attributes you can modify is shown in Table 13.1, "Style Attributes for PROC REPORT, TABULATE, and PRINT," on page 247. Detailed documentation on these attributes and their settings can be found in the "Guide to the Output Delivery System" in SAS OnlineDoc.

The attribute must be enclosed in square brackets ([ ]) or curly brackets ({ }). The code below changes the font typeface to Times New Roman. Notice the use of quotes around the typeface name. Because "Times New Roman" contains spaces, these quotes are necessary.

```
ODS HTML BODY='tables.htm';
proc report data=tables nowd
   STYLE(Header)=[FONT_FACE='Times New Roman'];
   column Type Material Price;
   define Type / group 'Table Type';
   define Material / group 'Construction';
   define Price / analysis mean 'Average Price' format=dollar8.;
run;
ODS HTML CLOSE;
```

The results are shown in Output 13.2. This technique can be used to change any of the column header attributes.

**Output 13.1**

## Retail Stock Report

| Table Type | Construction | Average Price |
|---|---|---|
| Coffee | Glass/Metal | $101 |
| | Wood | $61 |
| Dining | Glass/Metal | $400 |
| | Wood | $196 |
| End | Glass/Metal | $104 |
| | Wood | $59 |

**Output 13.2**

## Retail Stock Report

| Table Type | Construction | Average Price |
|---|---|---|
| Coffee | Glass/Metal | $101 |
| | Wood | $61 |
| Dining | Glass/Metal | $400 |
| | Wood | $196 |
| End | Glass/Metal | $104 |
| | Wood | $59 |

## Changing PROC REPORT Table Cell Style Attributes

In addition to being able to control style attributes for PROC REPORT column headings, you can also control style attributes for the cells under a particular heading. This example shows how to change the background color for the table cells with the dollar amounts.

You do this by adding a STYLE= option to the DEFINE Price statement. The STYLE= option can be added anywhere after the slash (/). The code below changes the background color to white (cxFFFFFF).

In the last example, you used STYLE(Header) to specify that the new style attribute applied to the table headers. This time, you use STYLE(Column) to specify that the new style attribute is to be applied to the table cells in that column.

```
ODS HTML BODY='tables.htm';
proc report data=tables nowd;
   column Type Material Price;
   define Type / group 'Table Type';
   define Material / group 'Construction';
   define Price / analysis mean 'Average Price' format=dollar8.
      STYLE(Column)=[BACKGROUND=cxFFFFFF];
run;
ODS HTML CLOSE;
```

This code produces the output shown in Output 13.3. You can see that the table cells with the dollar amounts now have a white background. The column header retains its original color scheme.

If you want to change the style attribute of the column header for the Price column, add a STYLE(Header)= option to the DEFINE statement for Price.

**Output 13.3**

## Retail Stock Report

| Table Type | Construction | Average Price |
|---|---|---|
| Coffee | Glass/Metal | $101 |
| | Wood | $61 |
| Dining | Glass/Metal | $400 |
| | Wood | $196 |
| End | Glass/Metal | $104 |
| | Wood | $59 |

## Changing PROC REPORT Row Style Attributes

To change the style attributes of a column of a PROC REPORT table, you use a STYLE= option in the DEFINE statement that builds the column. To change the style attributes of a row, you use a different technique. This example shows how to modify the row style attributes to create rows of alternating colors. This can make your table much easier to read.

Instead of using STYLE=, you can use a CALL DEFINE statement inside a COMPUTE statement. This allows you to call up the row style element and modify its attributes. The CALL DEFINE has three parameters: the name of the element being modified (_ROW_), the description of what is being modified (STYLE), and the STYLE= code to make the change.

The following code shows how to create the alternating rows. The COMPUTE statement contains an IF statement that selects odd numbered rows. Those rows are then modified to change the background color to white.

```
ODS HTML BODY='tables.htm';
proc report data=tables nowd;
   column Type Material Price;
   define Type / group 'Table Type';
   define Material / group 'Construction';
   define Price / analysis mean 'Average Price' format=dollar8.;
   compute Material;
      count+1;
      if (mod(count,2)) then do;
         CALL DEFINE(_ROW_, "STYLE", "STYLE=[BACKGROUND=cxFFFFFF]");
      end;
   endcomp;
run;
ODS HTML CLOSE;
```

The resulting table is shown in Output 13.4. Notice how rows 1, 3, and 5 are now white. If you want to switch this around, you can change the code inside the COMPUTE statement to select the even rows instead.

```
if not (mod(count,2)) then do;
   CALL DEFINE(_ROW_, "STYLE", "STYLE=[BACKGROUND=cxFFFFFF]");
end;
```

The revised code creates the table shown in Output 13.5. Now rows 2, 4, and 6 are white. This is a fairly complex example for this introductory book, but the technique is very useful. Even if you don't understand all of the details in this example, you can copy the code and put it to use.

**Output 13.4**

## Retail Stock Report

| Table Type | Construction | Average Price |
|---|---|---|
| Coffee | Glass/Metal | $101 |
| | Wood | $61 |
| Dining | Glass/Metal | $400 |
| | Wood | $196 |
| End | Glass/Metal | $104 |
| | Wood | $59 |

**Output 13.5**

## Retail Stock Report

| Table Type | Construction | Average Price |
|---|---|---|
| Coffee | Glass/Metal | $101 |
| | Wood | $61 |
| Dining | Glass/Metal | $400 |
| | Wood | $196 |
| End | Glass/Metal | $104 |
| | Wood | $59 |

## REPORT Subtotals and Totals Style Attributes

A common technique in PROC REPORT is to create totals at the end of each group of results. PROC REPORT gives you some ability to control the format of these breaks in your listing output. You can add single or double overlines or underlines, and you can skip a row. If you want to do fancier formatting of your subtotals and totals, you will want to turn to ODS. Subtotals and totals are created using the BREAK and RBREAK statements, as shown in the code below.

```
ODS HTML BODY='tables.htm';
proc report data=tables nowd;
    column Type Material Price;
    define Type / group 'Table Type';
    define Material / group 'Construction';
    define Price / analysis mean 'Average Price' format=dollar8.;
    break after Type / summarize;
    rbreak after / summarize;
run;
ODS HTML CLOSE;
```

The resulting table is shown in Output 13.6. This table has all of the results you need, but it could be made easier to read. By adding some formatting to the subtotals and totals, you can make them stand out. A STYLE= option for the subtotals is used to add some space below each subtotal by increasing the cell height and vertically justifying the text. In addition, the font weight for both subtotals and totals is set to bold.

```
ODS HTML BODY='tables.htm';
proc report data=tables nowd;
    column Type Material Price;
    define Type / group 'Table Type';
    define Material / group 'Construction';
    define Price / analysis mean 'Average Price' format=dollar8.;
    break after Type / summarize STYLE=[VJUST=T CELLHEIGHT=5O
                                        FONT_WEIGHT=Bold];
    rbreak after / summarize STYLE=[FONT_WEIGHT=Bold];
run;
ODS HTML CLOSE;
```

The revised table is shown in Output 13.7.

**Output 13.6**

| Table Type | Construction | Average Price |
|---|---|---|
| Coffee | Glass/Metal | $101 |
| | Wood | $61 |
| *Coffee* | | *$79* |
| Dining | Glass/Metal | $400 |
| | Wood | $196 |
| *Dining* | | *$275* |
| End | Glass/Metal | $104 |
| | Wood | $59 |
| *End* | | *$77* |
| | | *$175* |

**Output 13.7**

| Table Type | Construction | Average Price |
|---|---|---|
| Coffee | Glass/Metal | $101 |
| | Wood | $61 |
| **Coffee** | | **$79** |
| Dining | Glass/Metal | $400 |
| | Wood | $196 |
| **Dining** | | **$275** |
| End | Glass/Metal | $104 |
| | Wood | $59 |
| **End** | | **$77** |
| | | **$175** |

## Adding Traffic Lighting to PROC REPORT Table Values

What do traffic lights have to do with SAS output? The answer is that the familiar red, yellow, and green lights can be used to highlight results in your output. You can use red for bad results, yellow for neutral results, and green for good results. If you're creating a large table, this technique is great for focusing the reader's attention on the key results.

In this example, we will take our familiar table and use traffic lighting to mark low prices in green, high prices in red, and prices in between in yellow. This is done with a COMPUTE block. The variable for the COMPUTE block is Price. Then a series of IF-THEN/ELSE statements assigns the foreground colors based on the value of Price.

What may be a little confusing is how the values are tested. You might think that each statement should be like "IF Price <=100 THEN ...," but the code uses _C3_ instead of Price. This refers to the third column, which happens to be Price. If you want to refer to a specific table cell within a column, then this is the syntax you have to use.

The three color settings are RGB values for red, yellow, and green. The shades of these colors were chosen to be a bit darker than a true red, green, or yellow so that they would stand out against the gray table background. The fonts were all changed to bold for the same reason.

```
ODS HTML BODY='tables.htm';
proc report data=tables nowd;
   column Type Material Price;
   define Type / group 'Table Type';
   define Material / group 'Construction';
   define Price / analysis mean 'Average Price' format=dollar8.;
   compute Price;
      if _C3_ <= 100 then
         CALL DEFINE(_COL_,"STYLE",
            "STYLE=[FOREGROUND=cx006633 FONT_WEIGHT=Bold]");
      else if _C3_ >= 300 then
         CALL DEFINE(_COL_,"STYLE",
            "STYLE=[FOREGROUND=cxCC0000 FONT_WEIGHT=Bold]");
      else
         CALL DEFINE(_COL_,"STYLE",
            "STYLE=[FOREGROUND=cxFF9900 FONT_WEIGHT=Bold]");
   endcomp;
run;
ODS HTML CLOSE;
```

The results are shown in Output 13.8. The prices are all colored to draw attention to the high and low values. You can also use this technique in reverse, coloring the backgrounds of the cells in red, yellow, and green. The only modifications you need to make to the code are to change the FOREGROUND attributes to BACKGROUND and to pick slightly lighter shades of the three colors (so they don't overwhelm the foreground text). Suggested colors are cx00CC33 for green, cxFFFF66 for red, and cxFF3300 for yellow. Keep the fonts in bold so that the text will stand out. This version of the table is shown in Output 13.9.

**Output 13.8**

| Table Type | Construction | Average Price |
|---|---|---|
| Coffee | Glass/Metal | $101 |
|  | Wood | $61 |
| Dining | Glass/Metal | $400 |
|  | Wood | $196 |
| End | Glass/Metal | $104 |
|  | Wood | $59 |

For a color version of Output 13.8, see page 291 in Appendix 3.

**Output 13.9**

| Table Type | Construction | Average Price |
|---|---|---|
| Coffee | Glass/Metal | $101 |
|  | Wood | $61 |
| Dining | Glass/Metal | $400 |
|  | Wood | $196 |
| End | Glass/Metal | $104 |
|  | Wood | $59 |

For a color version of Output 13.9, see page 291 in Appendix 3.

 If you are going to use this technique, you should probably also take the time to design a style definition with a color scheme that's a better match for the red, yellow, and green traffic lighting. A simpler black and white color scheme may be the best approach.

 Another way to create traffic lighting in PROC REPORT is to use a user-defined format to assign the colors. See "Adding Traffic Lighting to PROC TABULATE Table Values" on page 234.

## Adding Graphics to PROC REPORT Tables

Changing fonts and colors goes a long way to livening up your output, but adding graphics takes your results to a new level. This example shows how to add a heading with a graphic to your PROC REPORT results.

The first thing you need to do is set up the heading. This is done with a COMPUTE BEFORE _PAGE_ statement and a LINE statement. The result is that a new row is added to the top of the table, and it contains the text given in the LINE statement, as shown in Output 13.10. Unfortunately, the row is created using the default table cell style attributes, which makes it rather faint in appearance.

```
ODS HTML BODY='tables.htm';
proc report data=tables nowd;
   column Type Material Price;
   define Type / group 'Table Type';
   define Material / group 'Construction';
   define Price / analysis mean 'Average Price' format=dollar8.;
   compute before _page_ / LEFT;
      LINE "Totally Tables, Inc.";
   endcomp;
run;
ODS HTML CLOSE;
```

To fix the appearance of the title and add a graphic, you can use the STYLE= option on the COMPUTE statement. First, add the graphic using the PREIMAGE attribute. This example assumes that the graphic is stored in the same file location as the HTML page you are creating. The second fix is to make the font bolder and bigger, and to choose a color that coordinates with the graphic.

```
ODS HTML BODY='tables.htm';
proc report data=tables nowd;
   column Type Material Price;
   define Type / group 'Table Type';
   define Material / group 'Construction';
   define Price / analysis mean 'Average Price' format=dollar8.;
   compute before _page_ / LEFT
      STYLE=[PREIMAGE='dining.gif'
            FONT_WEIGHT=Bold FONT_SIZE=5 FOREGROUND=cx993300];
      LINE "Totally Tables, Inc.";
   endcomp;
run;
ODS HTML CLOSE;
```

The new results are shown in Output 13.11.

**Output 13.10**

| Totally Tables, Inc. | | |
|---|---|---|
| **Table Type** | **Construction** | **Average Price** |
| Coffee | Glass/Metal | $101 |
| | Wood | $61 |
| Dining | Glass/Metal | $400 |
| | Wood | $196 |
| End | Glass/Metal | $104 |
| | Wood | $59 |

For a color version of Output 13.10, see page 292 in Appendix 3.

**Output 13.11**

| Totally Tables, Inc. | | |
|---|---|---|
| **Table Type** | **Construction** | **Average Price** |
| Coffee | Glass/Metal | $101 |
| | Wood | $61 |
| Dining | Glass/Metal | $400 |
| | Wood | $196 |
| End | Glass/Metal | $104 |
| | Wood | $59 |

For a color version of Output 13.11, see page 292 in Appendix 3.

## Creating an Output Data Set from PROC REPORT

With other procedures, you use ODS OUTPUT to create an output data set. With the REPORT procedure, you can only create an output data set directly from the procedure.

A simple OUT= on the PROC REPORT statement is all you need. SAS will then generate a data set with one observation for each row in the report (including summary lines).

```
ODS LISTING;
proc report data=tables nowd out=tables1;
   column Type Material Price;
   define Type / group 'Table Type';
   define Material / group 'Construction';
   define Price / analysis mean 'Average Price' format=dollar8.;
run;
ODS HTML BODY='tables1.htm';
proc print data=tables1; run;
ODS HTML CLOSE;
```

The output data set generated by this code is shown in Output 13.12. You can see how closely the data set layout matches the table layout. There is one new column, called _BREAK_, which has no values in this example. This column holds information about summary rows. Since this table has no summary rows, _BREAK_ is not used. To see how the data set changes when subtotals and totals are added, the code can be modified as follows.

```
ODS LISTING;
proc report data=tables nowd out=tables2;
   column Type Material Price;
   define Type / group 'Table Type';
   define Material / group 'Construction';
   define Price / analysis mean 'Average Price' format=dollar8.;
   break after Type / summarize;
   rbreak after / summarize;
run;
ODS HTML BODY='tables2.htm';
proc print data=tables2; run;
ODS HTML CLOSE;
```

The new output data set is shown in Output 13.13. Notice that the data set has grown, with new rows added for the subtotals and totals. For each of the new rows, the _BREAK_ column shows what type of total it is. The three subtotals are labeled "Type," which is the name of the variable being subtotaled. The main total is labeled _RBREAK_ to indicate that it is the report total.

In order to create an output data set, you must have listing output turned on. Be sure to add an ODS LISTING statement before the REPORT procedure if you have previously turned off listing output.

**Output 13.12**

| Obs | Type | Material | Price | _BREAK_ |
|---|---|---|---|---|
| 1 | Coffee | Glass/Metal | 100.816 | |
| 2 | Coffee | Wood | 60.943 | |
| 3 | Dining | Glass/Metal | 400.483 | |
| 4 | Dining | Wood | 195.684 | |
| 5 | End | Glass/Metal | 103.892 | |
| 6 | End | Wood | 59.052 | |

**Output 13.13**

| Obs | Type | Material | Price | _BREAK_ |
|---|---|---|---|---|
| 1 | Coffee | Glass/Metal | 100.816 | |
| 2 | Coffee | Wood | 60.943 | |
| 3 | Coffee | . | 78.912 | Type |
| 4 | Dining | Glass/Metal | 400.483 | |
| 5 | Dining | Wood | 195.684 | |
| 6 | Dining | . | 275.000 | Type |
| 7 | End | Glass/Metal | 103.892 | |
| 8 | End | Wood | 59.052 | |
| 9 | End | . | 76.762 | Type |
| 10 | | . | 175.189 | _RBREAK_ |

## Changing PROC TABULATE Row and Column Heading Style Attributes

Applying style attributes to PROC TABULATE output is similar to applying them to PROC REPORT. All you have to do is add STYLE= options to whichever part of the output you want to change.

There are a number of ways you can use STYLE= in PROC TABULATE. To keep things simple, we'll just look at one technique: adding STYLE= options to the CLASS and VAR statements. We'll start with a table similar to the one in the previous examples.

```
ODS HTML BODY='tables.htm';
proc tabulate data=tables;
   class Type Material;
   var Price;
   table Type='Table Type'*
         Material='Construction',
         Price='Average Price'*Mean=" "*f=dollar8.;
run;
ODS HTML CLOSE;
```

This code produces the output shown in Output 13.14. It's a basic table using the Default style definition. The typeface used in the headings is Arial. As an example, we will change this typeface to Times New Roman.

You do this by adding a STYLE= option to the CLASS and VAR statements for each heading you want to change. Following the STYLE= option, list the attribute you want to change. A list of the attributes you can modify is shown in Table 13.1, "Style Attributes for PROC REPORT, TABULATE, and PRINT," on page 247.

The attribute must be enclosed in square brackets ([ ]) or curly brackets ({ }). The code below changes the font typeface to Times New Roman. Notice the use of quotes around the typeface name. Because "Times New Roman" contains spaces, these quotes are necessary.

```
ODS HTML BODY='tables.htm';
proc tabulate data=tables;
   class Type Material / STYLE=[FONT_FACE="Times New Roman"];
   var Price / STYLE=[FONT_FACE="Times New Roman"];
   table Type='Table Type'*
         Material='Construction',
         Price='Average Price'*Mean=" "*f=dollar8.;
run;
ODS HTML CLOSE;
```

The results are shown in Output 13.15. This technique can be used to change any of the row or column header attributes. You can also use different style attributes for each classification variable, by creating two CLASS statements, one for "Type" and one for "Material." Then you could use a different STYLE= option for each variable. The same technique also works when you have two analysis variables: you can use two VAR statements with two different STYLE= options.

**Output 13.14**

| Table Type | Construction | Average Price |
|---|---|---|
| Dining | Wood | $196 |
|  | Glass/Metal | $400 |
| Coffee | Wood | $61 |
|  | Glass/Metal | $101 |
| End | Wood | $59 |
|  | Glass/Metal | $104 |

**Output 13.15**

| Table Type | Construction | Average Price |
|---|---|---|
| Dining | Wood | $196 |
|  | Glass/Metal | $400 |
| Coffee | Wood | $61 |
|  | Glass/Metal | $101 |
| End | Wood | $59 |
|  | Glass/Metal | $104 |

## Changing PROC TABULATE BOX= Option Formatting

A common technique in PROC TABULATE is to use the BOX= option on the TABLE statement to put a title in the box at the top left corner of the table. The following code shows how the BOX= option is used.

```
ODS HTML BODY='tables.htm';
proc tabulate data=tables;
   class Type Material;
   var Price;
   table Type='Table Type'*
         Material='Construction',
         Price='Average Price'*Mean=" "*f=dollar8.
         / Box='Retail Stock Report';
run;
ODS HTML CLOSE;
```

The resulting table is shown in Output 13.16. Notice how the box label is centered in the box. The table might look better if the label was aligned with the left side of the table. That way it will match the row headings. To do this, you can apply a STYLE= option to the BOX= option.

First, you have to handle the BOX label ("Retail Stock Report"). In order to add a STYLE= option as well as a label, the label has to be specified in a slightly different way. The BOX= is followed by a bracket. Following the bracket, you have a LABEL= option and a STYLE= option.

The LABEL= is used to specify the label you want to place in the box. The STYLE= is used to change the justification from centered to left justified. A final bracket encloses the LABEL= and STYLE= settings.

```
ODS HTML BODY='tables.htm';
proc tabulate data=tables;
   class Type Material;
   var Price;
   table Type='Table Type'*
         Material='Construction',
         Price='Average Price'*Mean=" "*f=dollar8.
         / Box=[LABEL='Retail Stock Report' STYLE=[JUST=L]];
run;
ODS HTML CLOSE;
```

The revised table is shown in Output 13.17.

**Output 13.16**

| Retail Stock Report | | Average Price |
|---|---|---|
| Table Type | Construction | |
| Dining | Wood | $196 |
| | Glass/Metal | $400 |
| Coffee | Wood | $61 |
| | Glass/Metal | $101 |
| End | Wood | $59 |
| | Glass/Metal | $104 |

**Output 13.17**

| Retail Stock Report | | Average Price |
|---|---|---|
| Table Type | Construction | |
| Dining | Wood | $196 |
| | Glass/Metal | $400 |
| Coffee | Wood | $61 |
| | Glass/Metal | $101 |
| End | Wood | $59 |
| | Glass/Metal | $104 |

## Changing PROC TABULATE Table Cell Style Attributes

In addition to being able to control style attributes for PROC TABULATE column headings, you can also control style attributes for the cells under a particular heading. This example shows how to change the background color for the table cells with the dollar amounts.

You do this by adding a STYLE= option to the PROC TABULATE statement. The following code changes the background color to white (cxFFFFFF).

```
ODS HTML BODY='tables.htm';
proc tabulate data=tables
   STYLE=[BACKGROUND=cxFFFFFF];
   class Type Material;
   var Price;
   table Type='Table Type'*
         Material='Construction',
         Price='Average Price'*Mean=" "*f=dollar8.;
run;
ODS HTML CLOSE;
```

This code produces the output shown in Output 13.18. You can see that the table cells with the dollar amounts now have a white background. Another thing you can change is the font weight. The data values in the Default style definition are hard to read. You can fix this by adding another style attribute to the STYLE= option. The second attribute changes the font to bold.

```
ODS HTML BODY='tables.htm';
proc tabulate data=tables
   STYLE=[BACKGROUND=cxFFFFFF FONT_WEIGHT=bold];
   class Type Material;
   var Price;
   table Type='Table Type'*
         Material='Construction',
         Price='Average Price'*Mean=" "*f=dollar8.;
run;
ODS HTML CLOSE;
```

The results are shown in Output 13.19. This technique can be used to change many other attributes of TABULATE table cells.

**Output 13.18**

| | | Average Price |
|---|---|---|
| **Table Type** | **Construction** | |
| **Dining** | **Wood** | $196 |
| | **Glass/Metal** | $400 |
| **Coffee** | **Wood** | $61 |
| | **Glass/Metal** | $101 |
| **End** | **Wood** | $59 |
| | **Glass/Metal** | $104 |

**Output 13.19**

| | | Average Price |
|---|---|---|
| **Table Type** | **Construction** | |
| **Dining** | **Wood** | $196 |
| | **Glass/Metal** | $400 |
| **Coffee** | **Wood** | $61 |
| | **Glass/Metal** | $101 |
| **End** | **Wood** | $59 |
| | **Glass/Metal** | $104 |

## Changing PROC TABULATE Row Style Attributes

To change the style attributes of a row heading in a PROC TABULATE table, you can use a STYLE= option in the CLASS or VAR statements that build the heading. To change the style attributes of an entire row, you use a different technique. This example shows how to create rows of alternating colors.

First, you need to set up a format that contains the colors you want to use for each value. In this case, we want the first and third row to be gray and the second row to be white. The following PROC FORMAT code creates a SAS format that will be used to assign a color to each value of the variable Type.

```
proc format;
    value typecol 1,3='cxB0B0B0'
                    2='cxFFFFFF';
run;
```

Next, this format is used to define the BACKGROUND value for the variable Type. This is done by adding a CLASSLEV statement to the code. The CLASSLEV statement enables you to apply a STYLE= option to individual class variables.

```
ODS HTML BODY='tables.htm';
proc tabulate data=tables;
    class Type Material;
    classlev Type / STYLE=[BACKGROUND=typecol.];
    var Price;
    table Type='Table Type'*
            Material='Construction',
            Price='Average Price'*Mean=" "*f=dollar8.;
run;
ODS HTML CLOSE;
```

The resulting table is shown in Output 13.20. This output has alternating colors for the row headers. Now you can work on continuing that color scheme all the way across the rows. You need to apply a STYLE= option to the row headings for Material and to the data cells. To fix the row headings for Material, add another CLASSLEV statement for the variable Material, and set the STYLE= option to "<parent>." This means that these cells will pick up their formatting from the parent cells—the first heading in the row.

```
classlev Material / STYLE=<parent>;
```

To fix the table cells, you need to add a STYLE= option to the TABLE statement. To change the row style attributes, add this option to the row definition. This STYLE= option is also assigned to "<parent>."

```
table Type='Table Type'*
        Material='Construction'*[STYLE=<parent>],
        Price='Average Price'*Mean=" "*f=dollar8.;
```

The new results are shown in Output 13.21. Now the entire row picks up its formatting from the style attributes assigned to the variable TYPE. You can use this parent–child relationship to build complex row designs.

**Output 13.20**

| | | Average Price |
|---|---|---|
| **Table Type** | **Construction** | |
| **Dining** | Wood | $196 |
| | Glass/Metal | $400 |
| **Coffee** | Wood | $61 |
| | Glass/Metal | $101 |
| **End** | Wood | $59 |
| | Glass/Metal | $104 |

**Output 13.21**

| | | Average Price |
|---|---|---|
| **Table Type** | **Construction** | |
| **Dining** | Wood | **$196** |
| | Glass/Metal | **$400** |
| **Coffee** | Wood | **$61** |
| | Glass/Metal | **$101** |
| **End** | Wood | **$59** |
| | Glass/Metal | **$104** |

This technique works best if you have a row variable with a small number of values. Otherwise, you have to do a lot of typing to create the appropriate format. In this case, with only three values, it was easy to set up the PROC FORMAT code.

## Changing PROC TABULATE Subtotals and Totals Style Attributes

A common technique in PROC TABULATE is to create totals at the end of each group of results. PROC TABULATE gives you some basic control over these totals. You can change their labels and format their values. However, if you want to do fancier formatting of your subtotals and totals, you will want to turn to ODS. Subtotals and totals are created using the ALL keyword, as shown in the following code. This table uses ALL twice, once for the subtotals and once for the totals.

```
ODS HTML BODY='tables.htm';
proc tabulate data=tables;
   class Type Material;
   var Price;
   table Type='Table Type'*
         (Material='Construction' ALL)
         ALL,
         Price='Average Price'*Mean=" "*f=dollar8.;
run;
ODS HTML CLOSE;
```

The resulting table is shown in Output 13.22. This table has all of the results you need, but it could be made easier to read. By adding some formatting to the subtotals and totals, you can make them stand out. A STYLE= option for the subtotals is used to create bold type. A second STYLE= option is used to make the same change for the totals. The style attributes are applied in the TABLE statement, and an asterisk is used to link them to the desired part of the table.

```
ODS HTML BODY='tables.htm';
proc tabulate data=tables;
   class Type Material;
   var Price;
   table Type='Table Type'*
         (Material='Construction' ALL*[STYLE=[FONT_WEIGHT=bold]])
         ALL*[STYLE=[FONT_WEIGHT=bold]],
         Price='Average Price'*Mean=" "*f=dollar8.;
run;
ODS HTML CLOSE;
```

The revised table is shown in Output 13.23.

**Output 13.22**

|  |  | Average Price |
|---|---|---|
| Table Type | Construction |  |
| Dining | Wood | $196 |
|  | Glass/Metal | $400 |
|  | All | $275 |
| Coffee | Construction |  |
|  | Wood | $61 |
|  | Glass/Metal | $101 |
|  | All | $79 |
| End | Construction |  |
|  | Wood | $59 |
|  | Glass/Metal | $104 |
|  | All | $77 |
| All |  | $175 |

**Output 13.23**

|  |  | Average Price |
|---|---|---|
| Table Type | Construction |  |
| Dining | Wood | $196 |
|  | Glass/Metal | $400 |
|  | All | **$275** |
| Coffee | Construction |  |
|  | Wood | $61 |
|  | Glass/Metal | $101 |
|  | All | **$79** |
| End | Construction |  |
|  | Wood | $59 |
|  | Glass/Metal | $104 |
|  | All | **$77** |
| All |  | **$175** |

## Adding Traffic Lighting to PROC TABULATE Table Values

Just as in the earlier example for PROC REPORT, colors can be applied to PROC TABULATE table values based on their values. If you're creating a large table, this technique is great for focusing the reader's attention on the key results. You can use red for bad results, yellow for neutral results, and green for good results. In this example, we take our familiar table and use traffic lighting to mark low prices in green, high prices in red, and prices in between in yellow.

The first thing to do is create a format that assigns the value ranges for Price to the desired colors. This is very different from the PROC REPORT approach. The three color settings are RGB values for red, yellow, and green. The shades of these colors were chosen to be a bit darker than a true red, green, or yellow so that they would stand out against the gray table background.

```
proc format;
   value traffic low-100='cx006600'
                 100<-300='cxFF9900'
                 300<-high='cxCC0000';
run;
```

To apply these colors, you need to add a STYLE= option to the TABLE statement. Since you want to change the style attributes of the values for Price, the STYLE= option is added with an asterisk to the variable Price (the option is added to the end of a series of items linked to Price). The STYLE= option assigns the FOREGROUND attribute to the colors given by the format "traffic." To make the colored values easier to read, the type is changed to bold in the same STYLE= option.

```
ODS HTML BODY='tables.htm';
proc tabulate data=tables;
   class Type Material;
   var Price;
   table Type='Table Type'*
         Material='Construction',
         Price='Average Price'*Mean=" "*f=dollar8.*
         [STYLE=[FOREGROUND=traffic. FONT_WEIGHT=bold]];
run;
ODS HTML CLOSE;
```

The results are shown in Output 13.24. The prices are all colored to draw attention to the high and low values. You can also use this technique in reverse, coloring the backgrounds of the cells in red, yellow, and green. The only modifications you need to make to the code are to change the FOREGROUND attributes to BACKGROUND and to pick slightly lighter shades of the three colors (so they don't overwhelm the foreground text). Suggested colors are cx00CC33 for green, cxFFFF66 for red, and cxFF3300 for yellow. Keep the fonts in bold so that the text will stand out. This version of the table is shown in Output 13.25.

You can also use this technique with PROC PRINT and PROC REPORT, which also support user-defined formats for style attributes.

**Output 13.24**

| Table Type | Construction | Average Price |
|------------|--------------|--------------:|
| Dining     | Wood         | $196 |
|            | Glass/Metal  | $400 |
| Coffee     | Wood         | $61 |
|            | Glass/Metal  | $101 |
| End        | Wood         | $59 |
|            | Glass/Metal  | $104 |

For a color version of Output 13.24, see page 293 in Appendix 3.

**Output 13.25**

| Table Type | Construction | Average Price |
|------------|--------------|--------------:|
| Dining     | Wood         | $196 |
|            | Glass/Metal  | $400 |
| Coffee     | Wood         | $61 |
|            | Glass/Metal  | $101 |
| End        | Wood         | $59 |
|            | Glass/Metal  | $104 |

For a color version of Output 13.25, see page 293 in Appendix 3.

> **TIP**
>
> If you are going to use this technique, you should probably also take the time to design a style definition with a color scheme that's a better match for the red, yellow, and green traffic lighting. A simpler black and white color scheme may be the best approach.

## Adding Graphics to PROC TABULATE Tables

You have learned how to change fonts, colors, and other formatting aspects of PROC TABULATE output. However, so far you've just been working with the basic output. This example shows how to add something new to the output: a graphic.

In this example, we are going to place a graphic image in the table BOX. A graphic can be added in the same way you modified the style attributes for the BOX in a previous example. The style attribute information is added with a STYLE= suboption on the BOX= option. The PREIMAGE style attribute allows you to name an image that precedes the text in the cell.

```
ODS HTML BODY='tables.htm';
proc tabulate data=tables;
   class Type Material;
   var Price;
   table Type='Table Type'*
         Material='Construction',
         Price='Average Price'*Mean=" "*f=dollar8.
         / BOX=[LABEL='Totally Tables, Inc.'
                  STYLE=[PREIMAGE='dining.gif']];
run;
ODS HTML CLOSE;
```

This code creates the output shown in Output 13.26. The graphic has been added right before the label for the table BOX. However, the table looks a bit odd now, because the BOX label does not line up with the column label "Average Price."

To fix this, you can change the justification for the Price column. Since the BOX label is aligned with the bottom of the row, you can change the column label to do the same. This is done with a STYLE= option on the VAR statement for the variable Price. Setting the vertical justification to bottom (VJUST=B) should solve the problem.

```
ODS HTML BODY='tables.htm';
proc tabulate data=tables;
   class Type Material;
   var Price / STYLE=[VJUST=B];
   table Type='Table Type'*
         Material='Construction',
         Price='Average Price'*Mean=" "*f=dollar8.
         / BOX=[LABEL='Totally Tables, Inc.'
                  STYLE=[PREIMAGE='dining.gif']];
run;
ODS HTML CLOSE;
```

The revised table is shown in Output 13.27. Now the headings line up.

**Output 13.26**

| Totally Tables, Inc. | | Average Price |
|---|---|---|
| **Table Type** | **Construction** | |
| Dining | Wood | $196 |
| | Glass/Metal | $400 |
| Coffee | Wood | $61 |
| | Glass/Metal | $101 |
| End | Wood | $59 |
| | Glass/Metal | $104 |

For a color version of Output 13.26, see page 294 in Appendix 3.

**Output 13.27**

| Totally Tables, Inc. | Average Price | |
|---|---|---|
| **Table Type** | **Construction** | |
| Dining | Wood | $196 |
| | Glass/Metal | $400 |
| Coffee | Wood | $61 |
| | Glass/Metal | $101 |
| End | Wood | $59 |
| | Glass/Metal | $104 |

For a color version of Output 13.27, see page 294 in Appendix 3.

## Creating an Output Data Set from PROC TABULATE

With other procedures, you use ODS OUTPUT to create an output data set. With the TABULATE procedure, you can only create an output data set directly from the procedure.

A simple OUT= on the PROC TABULATE statement is all you need. SAS will then generate a data set with the same information as the tabular output.

```
proc tabulate data=tables OUT=tables1;
   class Type Material;
   var Price;
   table Type='Table Type'*
           Material='Construction',
           Price='Average Price'*Mean=" "*f=dollar8.;
run;
ODS HTML BODY='tables.htm';
proc print data=tables1; run;
ODS HTML CLOSE;
```

The output data set generated by this code is shown in Output 13.28. The data set closely matches the tabular output. There are three new columns (_TYPE_, _TABLE_, and _PAGE_) that show where each row of data came from. In this example, _TABLE_ and _PAGE_ do not come into play because you have only one table and only one page. The value of _TYPE_ indicates which combination of CLASS variables is in each row.

To see how the data set changes when subtotals and totals are added, the code can be modified as follows.

```
proc tabulate data=tables OUT=tables2;
   class Type Material;
   var Price;
   table Type='Table Type'*
           (Material='Construction' ALL) ALL,
           Price='Average Price'*Mean=" "*f=dollar8.;
run;
ODS HTML BODY='tables.htm';
proc print data=tables2; run;
ODS HTML CLOSE;
```

The new output data set is shown in Output 13.29. Notice that the data set has grown, with new rows added for the subtotals and totals. In addition, the order of the rows is quite different from the order in which they appear in the table. Unlike the output data set from PROC REPORT, this data set is not simply a copy of the results in the same order in which they appear in the table. Instead, the output data set has one row for every unique combination of the CLASS variables. This is similar to the output data sets created by the MEANS and SUMMARY procedures. If you have a very complex table with lots of nested classifications, the output data set can be very complex and confusing. Use PROC TABULATE output data sets with a good deal of caution and preparation.

**Output 13.28**

| Obs | Type | Material | _TYPE_ | _PAGE_ | _TABLE_ | Price_Mean |
|---|---|---|---|---|---|---|
| 1 | Dining | Wood | 11 | 1 | 1 | 195.684 |
| 2 | Dining | Glass/Metal | 11 | 1 | 1 | 400.483 |
| 3 | Coffee | Wood | 11 | 1 | 1 | 60.943 |
| 4 | Coffee | Glass/Metal | 11 | 1 | 1 | 100.816 |
| 5 | End | Wood | 11 | 1 | 1 | 59.052 |
| 6 | End | Glass/Metal | 11 | 1 | 1 | 103.892 |

**Output 13.29**

| Obs | Type | Material | _TYPE_ | _PAGE_ | _TABLE_ | Price_Mean |
|---|---|---|---|---|---|---|
| 1 | Dining | Wood | 11 | 1 | 1 | 195.684 |
| 2 | Dining | Glass/Metal | 11 | 1 | 1 | 400.483 |
| 3 | Coffee | Wood | 11 | 1 | 1 | 60.943 |
| 4 | Coffee | Glass/Metal | 11 | 1 | 1 | 100.816 |
| 5 | End | Wood | 11 | 1 | 1 | 59.052 |
| 6 | End | Glass/Metal | 11 | 1 | 1 | 103.892 |
| 7 | Dining | . | 10 | 1 | 1 | 275.000 |
| 8 | Coffee | . | 10 | 1 | 1 | 78.912 |
| 9 | End | . | 10 | 1 | 1 | 76.762 |
| 10 | . | . | 00 | 1 | 1 | 175.189 |

## Changing PROC PRINT Column Heading Style Attributes

Applying style attributes to PROC PRINT output is very simple. All you have to do is add STYLE= options to whichever part of the output you want to change.

There are a number of ways you can use STYLE= in the PRINT procedure. To keep things simple, we'll just look at one technique: adding a STYLE= option to the PROC PRINT statement. We'll start with the following code. It produces a listing of three variables.

```
ODS HTML FILE='tables.htm';
proc print data=tables noobs label;
    var Type Material Price;
run;
ODS HTML CLOSE;
```

This code produces the output shown in Output 13.30. It's a basic table in the Default style definition. The typeface used in the headings is Arial. As an example, we will change this typeface to Times New Roman.

This is done by adding a STYLE= option to the PROC PRINT statement. The STYLE keyword is followed by the name of the style element you want to modify. In this case, the element is called Header. A list of the elements you can modify is in the SAS OnlineDoc section on the PRINT procedure.

Following the name of the style element, use an equal sign and then list the attribute you want to change. Detailed documentation on these attributes and their settings can be found in the "Guide to the Output Delivery System" in SAS OnlineDoc.

The attribute must be enclosed in square brackets ([ ]) or curly brackets ({ }). The code below changes the font typeface to Times New Roman. Notice the use of quotes around the typeface name. Because "Times New Roman" contains spaces, these quotes are necessary.

```
ODS HTML BODY='tables.htm';
proc print data=tables noobs label
    STYLE(Header)=[FONT_FACE='Times New Roman'];
    var Type Material Price;
run;
ODS HTML CLOSE;
```

The results are shown in Output 13.31. This technique can be used to change any of the column header attributes.

**Output 13.30**

### Retail Stock Report

| Type | Material | Price |
|---|---|---|
| Dining | Wood | $195.68 |
| Dining | Glass/Metal | $400.48 |
| Coffee | Wood | $60.94 |
| Coffee | Glass/Metal | $100.82 |
| End | Wood | $59.05 |
| End | Glass/Metal | $103.89 |

**Output 13.31**

### Retail Stock Report

| Type | Material | Price |
|---|---|---|
| Dining | Wood | $195.68 |
| Dining | Glass/Metal | $400.48 |
| Coffee | Wood | $60.94 |
| Coffee | Glass/Metal | $100.82 |
| End | Wood | $59.05 |
| End | Glass/Metal | $103.89 |

## Changing PROC PRINT Table Cell Style Attributes

In addition to being able to control style attributes for PROC PRINT column headings, you can also control style attributes for the cells under a particular heading. This example shows how to change the background color for the table cells with the dollar amounts.

This is done by adding a STYLE= option to the VAR statement. However, since you only want to apply the style attributes to the variable Price, you need to create two VAR statements. The first VAR statement includes the first two variables. The style attributes for these variables will not be changed. The second VAR statement includes only the variable Price. At the end of the second VAR statement, add a slash and then follow it with a STYLE= option.

The following code changes the background color to white (cxFFFFFF). Notice that this time we are not using the name of a style element. In the last example, we used STYLE(Header) to specify that the new style attributes are to be applied to the table headers. This time, since we are applying the style attributes in the definition for Price, they will automatically be applied to that column. There is no need to specify a style element.

```
ODS HTML BODY='tables.htm';
proc print data=tables noobs label;
   var Type Material;
   var Price / STYLE=[BACKGROUND=cxFFFFFF];
run;
ODS HTML CLOSE;
```

This code produces the output shown in Output 13.32. You can see that the table cells with the dollar amounts now have a white background. The column heading also has a white background. When you apply a style attribute in the VAR statement, it applies to the entire column for that variable.

If you want only the column values to have the white background, you can achieve this by modifying your STYLE= option. Instead of applying a style attribute to the entire column, you can specify the location where you want the style attribute applied. The PRINT procedure has a style element called Data, which controls the appearance of the data in each column but does not affect the header.

```
ODS HTML BODY='tables.htm';
proc print data=tables noobs label;
   var Type Material;
   var Price / STYLE(Data)=[BACKGROUND=cxFFFFFF];
run;
ODS HTML CLOSE;
```

The results are shown in Output 13.33. This technique can be used to change the color of any of the table cells.

**Output 13.32**

## Retail Stock Report

| Type | Material | Price |
|---|---|---|
| Dining | Wood | $195.68 |
| Dining | Glass/Metal | $400.48 |
| Coffee | Wood | $60.94 |
| Coffee | Glass/Metal | $100.82 |
| End | Wood | $59.05 |
| End | Glass/Metal | $103.89 |

**Output 13.33**

## Retail Stock Report

| Type | Material | Price |
|---|---|---|
| Dining | Wood | $195.68 |
| Dining | Glass/Metal | $400.48 |
| Coffee | Wood | $60.94 |
| Coffee | Glass/Metal | $100.82 |
| End | Wood | $59.05 |
| End | Glass/Metal | $103.89 |

## Changing PROC PRINT Style Attributes for Totals

A common technique in PROC PRINT is to create totals at the end of your results. However, PROC PRINT does not give you any ability to control the formatting of this total.

To modify the appearance of your totals, you will want to turn to ODS. These totals are created by using the SUM statement and then listing the variable(s) you want to total, as shown in the following code.

```
ODS HTML BODY='tables.htm';
proc print data=tables noobs label;
   var Type Material Price;
   sum Price;
run;
ODS HTML CLOSE;
```

The resulting table is shown in Output 13.34. This table has all of the results you need, but it could be made easier to read. By adding some formatting to the total, you can make it stand out. A STYLE= option for the SUM statement is used to add some space before the total by increasing the cell height and vertically justifying or aligning the text with the bottom of the cell.

```
ODS HTML BODY='tables.htm';
proc print data=tables noobs label;
   var Type Material Price;
   sum Price / Style(Total)=[VJUST=B CELLHEIGHT=50];
run;
ODS HTML CLOSE;
```

The revised table is shown in Output 13.35. This technique can also be used to modify subtotals created by the SUMBY statement. The style elements in that case are Total (for the value) and ByLabel (for the label).

**Output 13.34**

## Retail Stock Report

| Type | Material | Price |
|------|----------|-------|
| Dining | Wood | $195.68 |
| Dining | Glass/Metal | $400.48 |
| Coffee | Wood | $60.94 |
| Coffee | Glass/Metal | $100.82 |
| End | Wood | $59.05 |
| End | Glass/Metal | $103.89 |
| | | $920.87 |

**Output 13.35**

## Retail Stock Report

| Type | Material | Price |
|------|----------|-------|
| Dining | Wood | $195.68 |
| Dining | Glass/Metal | $400.48 |
| Coffee | Wood | $60.94 |
| Coffee | Glass/Metal | $100.82 |
| End | Wood | $59.05 |
| End | Glass/Metal | $103.89 |
| | | $920.87 |

## Style Attributes for PROC REPORT, TABULATE, and PRINT

In general, the same style attributes are available for use with the STYLE= options for these three procedures. Table 13.1 lists these attributes and tells what they do.

The table has two columns to indicate where each attribute can be applied. The first column contains items that can be applied to individual cells, rows, columns, or headers within the table. The second column contains items that can be applied to the entire table.

If you look at the style attributes checked off for each column, the distinction makes sense. For example, the OUTPUTWIDTH attribute controls the width of the table. It's logical that it only applies to the entire table. On the other hand, CELLWIDTH is something that applies to a single cell or column, not the entire table.

The examples in this chapter showed how to modify individual cells, rows, columns, or headers. More examples of this type of modification are included in the "Guide to the SAS Output Delivery System" in SAS OnlineDoc.

This chapter has not covered how to apply a style attribute to the entire table or report. The syntax is actually quite simple. For PROC REPORT, use

```
PROC REPORT DATA=dataset STYLE=[style-attribute(s)];
```

For PROC PRINT, the syntax is very similar:

```
PROC PRINT DATA=dataset STYLE=[style-attribute(s)];
```

For PROC TABULATE, the syntax is different. You use a STYLE= option at the end of the TABLE statement:

```
TABLE <<page-definition,> row-definition,> column-definition
      / STYLE=[style-attribute(s)];
```

This is only a brief overview of the available style attributes. Detailed documentation of these attributes and their settings can be found in the "Guide to the Output Delivery System" in SAS OnlineDoc.

**Table 13.1  Style Attributes for PROC REPORT, TABULATE, and PRINT**

| Attribute | What it affects | Can be used for individual cells, columns, rows, and headings? | Can be used for entire table? |
|---|---|---|---|
| ASIS | leading/trailing spaces and line breaks | ✓ | |
| BACKGROUND= | background color | ✓ | ✓ |
| BACKGROUNDIMAGE= | background image | ✓ | ✓ |
| BORDERCOLOR= | border color | ✓ | ✓ |
| BORDERCOLORDARK= | dark border color for 3-D borders | ✓ | ✓ |
| BORDERCOLORLIGHT= | light border color for 3-D borders | ✓ | ✓ |
| BORDERWIDTH= | width of border | | ✓ |
| CELLHEIGHT= | height of table cell | ✓ | |
| CELLWIDTH= | width of table cell | ✓ | |
| CELLPADDING= | space between cell text and borders | | ✓ |
| CELLSPACING= | space between cells | | ✓ |
| FLYOVER | text to display for mouse over (HTML) | ✓ | |
| FONT= | font definition (face, size, weight/style) | ✓ | ✓* |
| FONT_FACE= | font typeface | ✓ | ✓* |
| FONT_SIZE= | font size | ✓ | ✓* |
| FONT_STYLE= | font style | ✓ | ✓* |
| FONT_WEIGHT= | font weight | ✓ | ✓* |
| FONT_WIDTH= | font width | ✓ | ✓* |
| FOREGROUND= | text color | ✓ | ✓* |
| FRAME= | table frame type | | ✓ |
| HREFTARGET= | window or frame to open for link | ✓ | |
| HTMLCLASS= | name of stylesheet to use | ✓ | ✓ |
| JUST= | horizontal justification | ✓ | ✓ |
| NOBREAKSPACE= | handling of spaces at line breaks | ✓ | |
| OUTPUTWIDTH= | width of table | | ✓ |
| POSTHTML= | HTML code to add at end of item | ✓ | ✓ |
| POSTIMAGE= | image to display at end of item | ✓ | ✓ |
| POSTTEXT= | text to display at end of item | ✓ | ✓ |
| PREHTML= | HTML code to add at beginning of item | ✓ | ✓ |
| PREIMAGE= | image to display at beginning of item | ✓ | ✓ |
| PRETEXT= | text to display at beginning of item | ✓ | ✓ |
| PROTECTSPECIALCHARS= | handling of <, >, and & characters | ✓ | |
| RULES= | lines between table cells | | ✓ |
| TAGATTR= | string to insert in HTML tag for the item | ✓ | |
| URL= | URL to link to when item is clicked | ✓ | |
| VJUST= | vertical justification | ✓ | |

*When applied to the entire table, these font definitions affect only the text that is added to the output with the PRETEXT, POSTTEXT, PREHTML, and POSTHTML attributes.

# Chapter

# 14

*Graphics Output*

---

So far, we've looked only at procedures that produce tabular output. However, ODS works with SAS/GRAPH output as well. This chapter explores the various options you have for creating graphs using ODS.

First, we'll look at ways to use graphs with HTML output. There are a number of options for creating Web-friendly graphs. These options include GIF files, JPEG files, animated GIF files, Java applets, and ActiveX controls. We'll also look at combining graphs with tabular output.

Then we'll look at creating graphs in printer and RTF output. Finally, we'll show how to import ODS graphs into a variety of other software packages.

## Creating HTML Output: Graphs as GIFs or JPEGs

Creating HTML output from SAS/GRAPH software is easy. All you have to do is write your usual SAS/GRAPH code and add two things: some ODS code and a GOPTIONS statement.

You need an ODS HTML statement, with at least a BODY= option to indicate the file to create. You also need a GPATH statement that points to the same location as the body file, as well as a URL=NONE to keep the path information from being used in the image tag. In the example code below, the body file is to be created in the directory "c:\temp," so the GPATH= option is set to "c:\temp."

The second bit of code to add is a GOPTIONS statement that defines the DEVICE as GIF or JPEG. These drivers create Web-friendly output from your SAS/GRAPH procedures. In this GOPTIONS statement, you also have the option of defining the resolution of the graph with the XPIXELS and YPIXELS options. Higher-resolution graphs are easier to read, but they also take up more storage space. Pick the settings that work for you.

```
ODS HTML BODY='c:\temp\PieStats.htm'
         GPATH='c:\temp\' (URL=NONE);
goptions DEVICE=GIF XPIXELS=480 YPIXELS=360;
title 'Pie Chart: Annual Sales by Flavor';
proc gchart data=PieStats;
     pie PieType / sumvar=Sales
                   other=0
                   midpoints='Blueberry' 'Apple' 'Cherry'
                             'Banana Creme' 'Pecan' 'Lemon Meringue'
                   cfill=gray
                   value=none
                   percent=arrow
                   slice=arrow
                   noheading;
run;
quit;
ODS HTML CLOSE;
```

This code produces the HTML output shown in Output 14.1. The pie chart is displayed in the middle of a Web page. If you look at the source code, you will see that the Web page contains an IMG tag that points to the GIF file created by the GCHART procedure. For more information on the HTML generated, see "Exploring the Body File: Graphics" on page 30.

This table was produced with the default ODS HTML settings for graph output. One setting you might think about changing is the GTITLE|NOGTITLE option. If you specify NOGTITLE, the titles for your Web page will appear in the Web page itself instead of in the graphic. Generally, the text is easier to read outside of the graphic. Output 14.2 shows the same graph with the NOGTITLE option.

If you close the Listing destination before creating your ODS graphs, you will save time and system resources. If the Listing destination is closed, the graph window will not open. Your graph will just go directly to a file.

**Output 14.1**

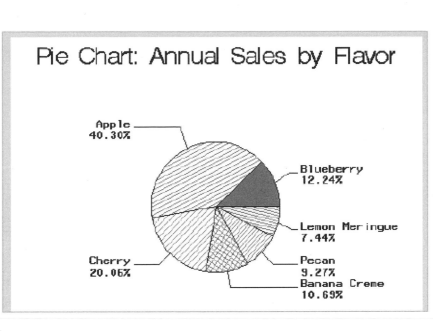

**Output 14.2**

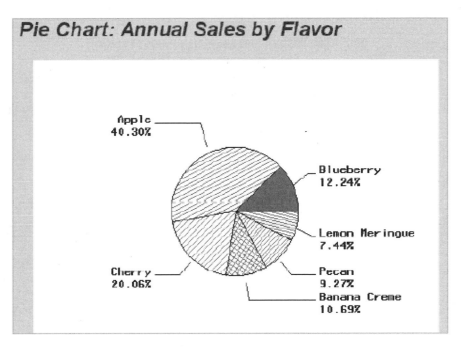

If you open your HTML page and the graph is not displayed, check the GPATH= option. This option must point to the same location as the BODY= option in order for the graph to be displayed properly. If you move the graph to a different location, the HTML page can no longer find its graphic. Another approach is to not include a path in the BODY= option and to drop the GPATH= option. Once your Web page and graphic are created, you can move them anywhere you like with no problems, since there's no path information embedded in the HTML.

## Creating HTML Output: Graphs as Java

GIF files are a quick and easy way to create simple output for the Web. They also have the advantage of being supported by virtually all Web browsers. However, if you want to impress your viewers, you might consider creating a Java graph.

The JAVA device driver allows you to produce a graph that is actually an application. Not only can it be viewed in a browser, but it can also be modified on the fly. Viewers can change the color or appearance, or drill down to more detailed information.

All you need to do to create a Java graph is to make two changes to your code and copy one extra file to your Web server. The code changes are shown below. You need to set DEVICE=JAVA in your GOPTIONS statement, and you need to add the code ARCHIVE='graphapp.jar' to your ODS HTML statement. Note: For Version 9.0 and later, do not add the ARCHIVE= option.

The file you need to move is called "graphapp.jar," and it contains the Java programs needed to run your graph. If you search the location where SAS is installed, you should be able to find this file. In Windows, it is stored in "Shared Files/applets" in the SAS root directory. Copy this file to the same directory as the file that is specified in your BODY= statement. Note: For Version 9.0 and later, you do not need to move or use this file.

```
ODS HTML BODY='JavaBar.htm' NOGTITLE
         ARCHIVE='graphapp.jar';
GOPTIONS DEVICE=JAVA GSFMODE=REPLACE XPIXELS=480 YPIXELS=360;
title 'Candy Bar Chart';
title2 'Annual Sales by Type of Chocolate and Filling';
proc gchart data=CandyBars;
   vbar3d Filling / sumvar=Sales
                    group=Chocolate;
run; quit;
ODS HTML CLOSE;
```

This code creates a single file, "JavaBar.htm." Unlike GIF output, the graph is not in a separate file from the HTML page. Instead, the HTML contains code that is used by Java to generate the graph. The resulting graph is shown in Output 14.3. Notice the pop-up box that appears when the mouse hovers over a graph bar. It contains detailed information about the point being graphed.

The most powerful feature of Java graphs is what happens when you right-click anywhere on the graph. This brings up a pop-up menu that allows you to select "Graph Properties." As shown in Output 14.4, you get a dialog box with a series of tabs that allows you to change the formatting of the graph. This example shows how you would change the bars from blocks to cylinders. Other options let you change the colors, switch the chart from vertical to horizontal, or change it to a pie or star chart. You can also click on any of the bar groups to drill down to a graph of just that group. Creating Java graphs allows you to have graphs that your users can customize as needed.

There are a couple of limitations to keep in mind. First, not all browsers support Java applets. If any of your users have outdated browsers, instead of the graph they will see the message, "Sorry, your browser does not support the applet tag." Another limitation is that this driver only works with the GCHART, GCONTOUR, GMAP, GPLOT, and G3D procedures. Finally, for Version 9.0 and later, if you do not remove the ARCHIVE= option, the graph will not display correctly. That option is for Version 8 only.

**Output 14.3**

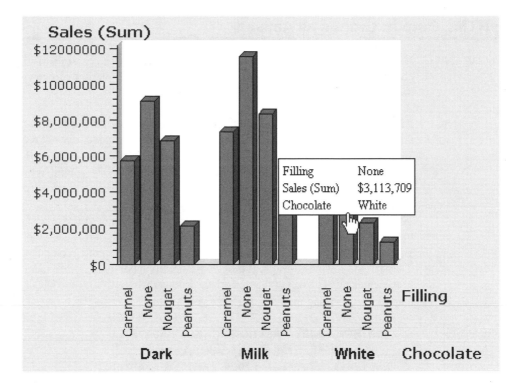

**Output 14.4**

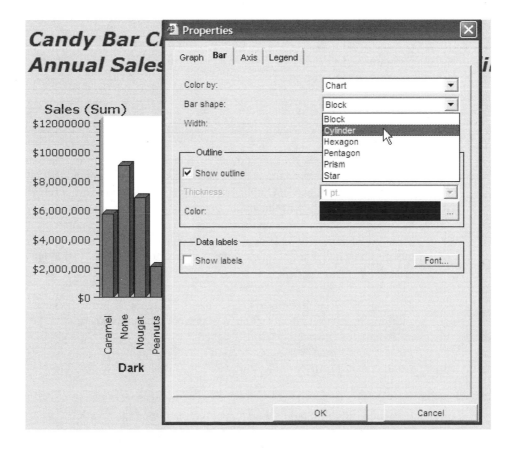

## Creating HTML Output: Graphs as ActiveX

Another option for creating interactive graphs is to use the ACTIVEX driver. This driver uses Microsoft's ActiveX technology to create an interactive graph that can be viewed on a Web site or inserted in a Microsoft Office document.

All you need to do to create an ActiveX graph is to make two code changes. The first is to change your DEVICE setting to ACTIVEX. Also, it is recommended, but not required, that you remove any XPIXELS or YPIXELS options from your GOPTIONS statement. If you try to make an ActiveX graph smaller, you get a graph with a scroll bar that you have to use to see the entire graph.

The second code change is to add an ARCHIVE= option to your ODS HTML statement, and then list the name of the SAS/GRAPH ActiveX control. This control can be downloaded from the SAS Web site. You then need to place it in the same location as the Web page you are creating. When users try to view your graph, if they don't already have this control installed, the ARCHIVE= option creates an HTML tag that tells their browser where to find the file. The control is then downloaded and installed and you can view your graph.

```
ODS HTML BODY='ActiveXBar.htm' NOGTITLE
         ARCHIVE='sasgraph.exe';
GOPTIONS DEVICE=ACTIVEX GSFMODE=REPLACE;
title 'Candy Bar Chart';
title2 'Annual Sales by Type of Chocolate and Filling';
proc gchart data=CandyBars;
   vbar3d Filling / sumvar=Sales
                    group=Chocolate;
run; quit;
ODS HTML CLOSE;
```

The resulting file is shown in Output 14.5. Notice the pop-up box that appears when the mouse hovers over a graph bar. It contains detailed information about the point being graphed.

As with Java graphs, the most powerful feature of ActiveX graphs is what happens when you right-click anywhere on the graph. This brings up a pop-up menu that allows you to select "Graph Properties." As shown in Output 14.6, you get a dialog box with a series of tabs that allows you to change the formatting of the graph. This example shows how you would change the bars from blocks to cylinders. Other options let you change the colors, switch the chart from vertical to horizontal, or change it to a pie or star chart. You can also click on any of the bar groups to drill down to a graph of just that group. Creating ActiveX graphs allows you to have graphs that your users can customize as needed.

There are a few limitations to keep in mind. First, not all browsers support ActiveX controls. In addition, many users disable ActiveX controls because of security concerns. If any of your users have outdated browsers or have disabled ActiveX, instead of the graph they will see the message, "Sorry, your browser does not support the object tag used for the ActiveX control." Another limitation is that this driver only works with the GCHART, GCONTOUR, GMAP, GPLOT, and G3D procedures.

If you are only producing Web output, you may find the JAVA driver easier for you and your users to work with. If you are creating a graph to import into a word processor, the ACTIVEX driver is a better choice (see the example on RTF and ActiveX on page 258).

**Output 14.5**

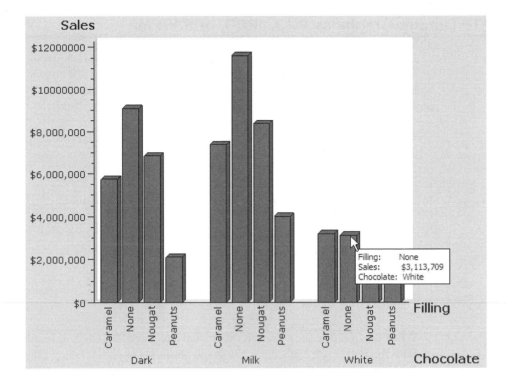

**Output 14.6**

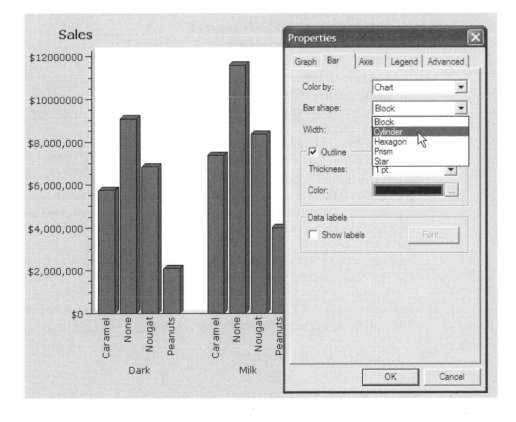

## Creating RTF Output: Graphs as PNG, JPEG, or SASEMF

If you are creating RTF output, you have four options for creating graphics output: PNG, JPEG, SASEMF, and ACTIVEX. The simplest to produce are PNG, JPEG, and SASEMF. All you have to do is add DEVICE=PNG, DEVICE=JPEG, or DEVICE=SASEMF to your GOPTIONS statement, and then create your ODS RTF statements as usual.

This first example shows how to create a PNG. The Portable Network Graphic file format is the public-domain version of the proprietary GIF format.

```
ODS RTF FILE='PNGplot.rtf';
GOPTIONS DEVICE=PNG;
title 'Movie Plots';
title2 'Ticket Sales by Theme';
proc gplot data=MoviePlots;
   plot Theaters*TicketsSold=Theme;
run; quit;
ODS RTF CLOSE;
```

When you run this code, the PNG is created and embedded in the RTF file. When you open the RTF file with a word processor, the graph appears. Output 14.7 shows how this graph appears in a word processor.

This next example shows how to create a SASEMF (the EMF stands for Extended Meta File). To create SASEMF output, the only change you need to make is in the DEVICE= option.

```
ODS RTF FILE='SASEMFplot.rtf';
GOPTIONS DEVICE=SASEMF;
title 'Movie Plots';
title2 'Ticket Sales by Theme';
proc gplot data=MoviePlots;
   plot Theaters*TicketsSold=Theme;
run; quit;
ODS RTF CLOSE;
```

When you run this code, the SASEMF graphic is created and embedded in the RTF file. When you open the RTF file with a word processor, the graph appears. Output 14.8 shows how this graph appears in a word processor. Notice the difference in the default graph size and resolution between the SASEMF version and the PNG version.

To create an RTF file with a JPEG graph, just change the DEVICE= option to DEVICE=JPEG. The resulting graph is not shown, but it's similar to Output 14.7.

Experiment with PNG, JPEG, and SASEMF graphics in your word processor. You will probably find that one works better for you than the others.

**Output 14.7**

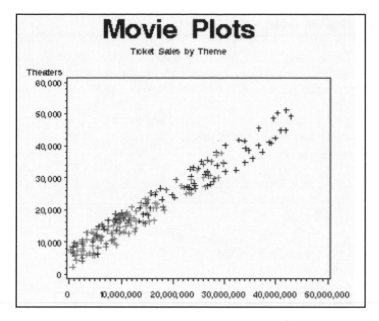

**Output 14.8**

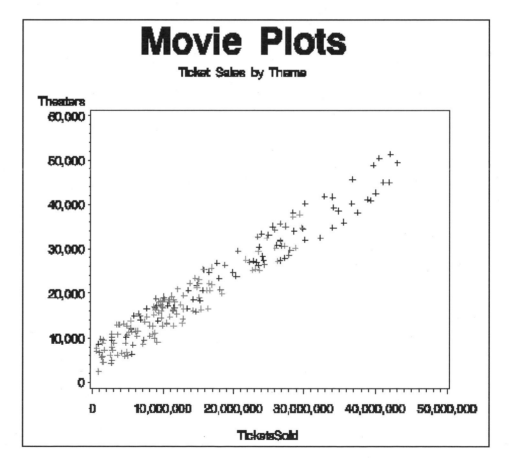

## Creating RTF Output: Graphs as ActiveX

Adding a graph to your RTF output lets you create impressive memos and reports. However, adding an interactive graph to a word processor document gives you even more impressive results. This allows the readers of your memo or report to modify the graph to suit their needs.

This technique is even more helpful if you're creating a graph for someone else's memo or report. You can send them an RTF file with a graph that they can adjust as needed before incorporating it into their report.

The code for ActiveX output for the RTF destination is simple. You use the same ODS RTF statements as with any other procedure. Then you need to add DEVICE=ACTIVEX to your GOPTIONS statement.

```
ODS RTF FILE='ActiveXPlot.rtf';
GOPTIONS DEVICE=ACTIVEX;
title 'Movie Plots';
title2 'Ticket Sales by Theme';
proc gplot data=MoviePlots;
   plot Theaters*TicketsSold=Theme;
run; quit;
ODS RTF CLOSE;
```

ODS takes it from there, creating an RTF file that contains the ActiveX graph object. When you open it in a word processor, you see the graph shown in Output 14.9. Instead of the ugly plus signs marking the plot points, the driver has substituted attractive spheres, cylinders, triangles, and squares. The color scheme has changed as well.

This graph is fully interactive from within your word processor. When the mouse hovers over a point, you get the pop-up box shown in Output 14.9 that describes the data point. If you right-click on the graph, you get a pop-up menu with options for modifying the graph. Since the graph was a bit hard to read because the large plot points were running into each other, the pop-up menu has been used to make the points smaller, as shown in Output 14.10.

ActiveX is an exciting new way to share SAS/GRAPH output, but it comes with a number of limitations. First, it only works with the GCHART, GCONTOUR, GMAP, GPLOT, and G3D procedures.

Second, it requires that you have the SAS/GRAPH ActiveX control installed. Unlike the HTML version of ActiveX output, there is no automated way to set up the driver so it can be downloaded and installed as needed.

The third weakness is that ActiveX is a Microsoft technology, and as such, it may only work with Microsoft Office products. This means that you can open the file with Microsoft Word, and you can copy and paste the graph into Microsoft Excel and Microsoft PowerPoint, but the graph may not work at all if you are using other products.

The fourth weakness is that many users may have ActiveX functionality turned off because it has proven to be a security risk. The technology can be used by hackers to insert a virus in your system. If you keep up with the latest security patches and anti-virus software, this should not be a problem. Nevertheless, as a safety measure, many sites choose to disable ActiveX.

**Output 14.9**

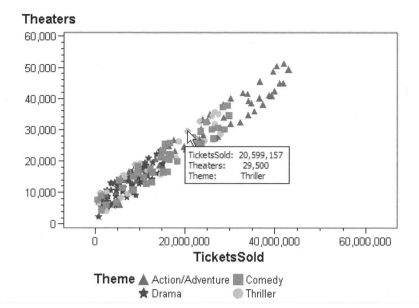

**Output 14.10**

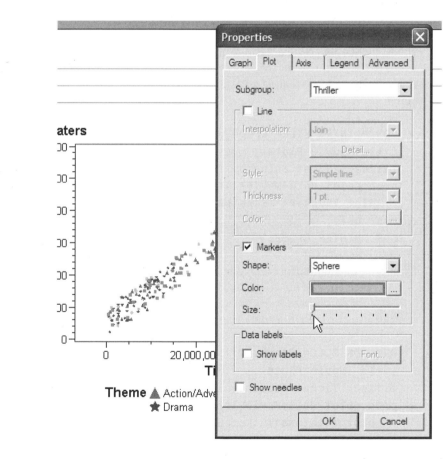

You may have noticed in the output examples above that the legend labels overlap the symbols. When you create ActiveX graphs, you may find that your output needs to be resized in your word processor in order to fit the axis and legend labels.

## Printer Output: Using the Internal Graphics Format

Creating graphics output using the printer destination is simple. You don't have to do anything special to your code.

You do not need to select an output graphics type using the DEVICE= option. Unlike HTML or RTF output, printer output does not require that you specify a format for the graphics file, because it doesn't create a graphics file. ODS uses an internal graphics format for printer output.

All you need to do is write your usual SAS/GRAPH code and enclose it in ODS PRINTER statements. For example, the following code produces the graph shown in Output 14.11.

```
ODS PRINTER;
title 'Movie Plots';
title2 'Ticket Sales by Theme';
proc gplot data=MoviePlots;
   plot Theaters*TicketsSold=Theme;
run; quit;
ODS PRINTER CLOSE;
```

This code creates the output, which contains the embedded graphic, and goes straight to the printer. It does not create a separate graphics file.

Alternatively, you can request a PostScript file instead of sending your output directly to the printer.

```
ODS PRINTER FILE='Graph.ps';
title 'Movie Plots';
title2 'Ticket Sales by Theme';
proc gplot data=MoviePlots;
   plot Theaters*TicketsSold=Theme;
run; quit;
ODS PRINTER CLOSE;
```

If you print the output from this code, it will look just like Output 14.11. Again, no separate graphics file is created. The image is embedded in the PostScript file.

You can also create PDF output using this same approach.

```
ODS PDF FILE='Graph.pdf';
title 'Movie Plots';
title2 'Ticket Sales by Theme';
proc gplot data=MoviePlots;
   plot Theaters*TicketsSold=Theme;
run; quit;
ODS PDF CLOSE;
```

This output also looks just like Output 14.11. The graphic image is embedded in the PDF file.

**Output 14.11**

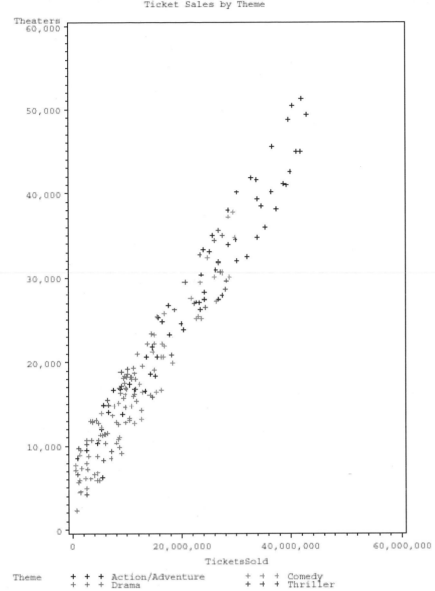

## Combining Graphs with Text Output

With ODS, it is possible to combine the output from a number of procedures into a single output file. This means that you can create an HTML page with a table from PROC FREQ and a bar chart from PROC GCHART. In HTML, because there are no page breaks, the output appears to be on the same "page." However, there are still large gaps between the procedures.

With RTF and printer output, multiple procedures appear on separate pages. You can use the STARTPAGE=NO option on your ODS RTF or ODS PRINTER statement to prevent these extra page breaks, but there will still be gaps between the procedures.

If you'd like to integrate your graphs and tabular output, there is a way to embed a graph in a row of a PROC REPORT table. The technique is simple. First, you need to create your graph and save it in a SAS catalog. The following code creates a bar chart called SalesBar and saves it in the Work library under the catalog name CandyBarChart.

```
GOPTIONS DEVICE=GIF XPIXELS=480 YPIXELS=360 GSFMODE=REPLACE;
title 'Candy Bar Chart';
title2 'Annual Sales by Chocolate Type and Filling';
proc gchart data=CandyBars GOUT=work.CandyBarChart;
   vbar3d Filling / name='SalesBar'
                    sumvar=Sales
                    group=Chocolate;
run; quit;
```

The next step is to create a PROC REPORT table. After you have the basic table set up, add a COMPUTE BEFORE _PAGE_ statement and a CALL DEFINE statement to insert a row at the top of the report and insert the graph you just created.

```
ODS HTML BODY='c:\temp\CandyBarReport.htm'
         GPATH='c:\temp\' (URL=NONE);
proc report data=CandyBars nowd;
   columns Chocolate Filling Sales;
   define Chocolate / group;
   define Filling / Group;
   define Sales / analysis sum format=dollar10.;
   compute before _page_ / center;
      call define( _ROW_, "GRSEG", "work.CandyBarChart.SalesBar" );
   endcomp;
run; quit;
ODS HTML CLOSE;
```

The resulting table is shown in Output 14.12. The graph is now part of the tabular report, so both appear together on the Web page. This output could have been created by enclosing both the GCHART and REPORT procedures in ODS HTML statements and removing the GOUT option and the COMPUTE block, but then there would be a gap between the chart and the table.

**Output 14.12**

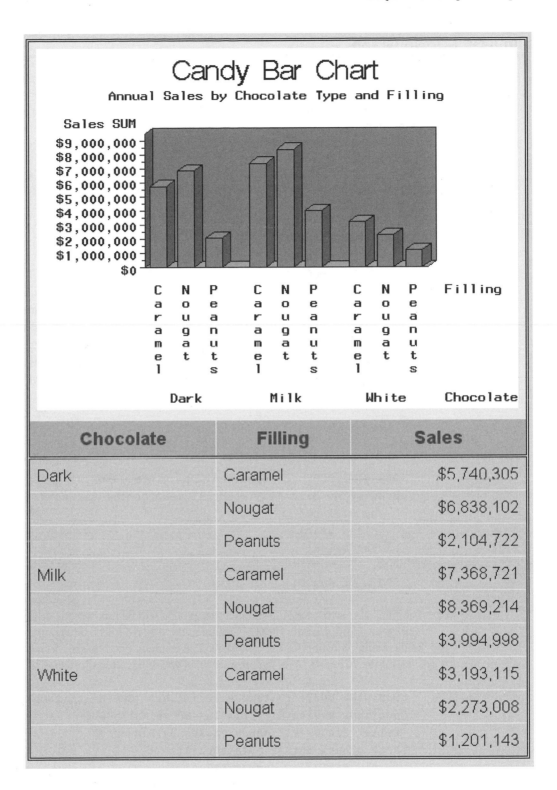

| Chocolate | Filling | Sales |
|-----------|---------|-------|
| Dark | Caramel | $5,740,305 |
| | Nougat | $6,838,102 |
| | Peanuts | $2,104,722 |
| Milk | Caramel | $7,368,721 |
| | Nougat | $8,369,214 |
| | Peanuts | $3,994,998 |
| White | Caramel | $3,193,115 |
| | Nougat | $2,273,008 |
| | Peanuts | $1,201,143 |

## Creating a Drill-Down Graph

Drill-down graphs allow you to present a summary graph, and then make detailed data available for interested viewers. The way it works is that you create a graph with HTML "hot spots." When you click on one of these spots, your browser links them to the detail data associated with that part of the graph. This example shows how to create drill-down graphs. More detailed information is available in the "Guide to the Output Delivery System" in SAS OnlineDoc.

The first step is to create a data set with a variable to hold the location of the HTML pages with the detail information. In this case, it is a single page with a separate anchor (pie1, pie2, ...) for each detail table.

```
Data PieStatsDrill;
   set PieStats;
   format rpt $40.;
   if PieType='Apple' then rpt='href="DrillDowns.htm#pie1"';
   else if PieType='Banana Creme' then rpt='href="DrillDowns.htm#pie2"';
   else if PieType='Blueberry' then rpt='href="DrillDowns.htm#pie3"';
   else if PieType='Cherry' then rpt='href="DrillDowns.htm#pie4"';
   else if PieType='Lemon Meringue' then rpt='href="DrillDowns.htm#pie5"';
   else if PieType='Pecan' then rpt='href="DrillDowns.htm#pie6"';
run;
```

The second step is to create the detail pages. Notice the ANCHOR= option that creates the anchors used above.

```
ODS HTML BODY='c:\temp\DrillDowns.htm' ANCHOR='pie1';
proc means data=PieStatsDrill mean nonobs maxdec=0;
   by PieType;
   class year;
   var Sales;
run;
ODS HTML CLOSE;
```

The final step is to create the summary graph that will be used for the drill-down. The only change here is the addition of the HTML= option in the PIE statement. This points to the variable that holds the link location for each pie slice. The resulting graph is shown in Output 14.13. When you click on the "Cherry" slice, the browser links you to the table shown in Output 14.14.

```
ODS HTML BODY='c:\temp\PieDrill.htm' GPATH='c:\temp\' (URL=NONE);
goptions device=GIF xpixels=480 ypixels=360;
title 'Pie Chart: Annual Sales by Flavor';
proc gchart data=PieStatsDrill;
   pie PieType / sumvar=sales
      percent=arrow slice=arrow value=none
      HTML=rpt;
run; quit;
ODS HTML CLOSE;
```

**Output 14.13**

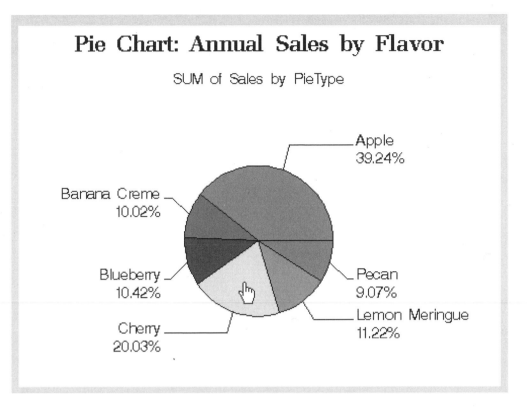

**Output 14.14**

| PieType=Cherry | |
|---|---|
| **Analysis Variable : Sales** | |
| **Year** | **Mean** |
| 2000 | 121512 |
| 2001 | 119245 |
| 2002 | 116924 |

# Part
# 4

*Appendices*

---

# Appendix

# 1

*Sample Programs*

This appendix presents some simple programs that demonstrate ODS output style definitions. These programs are also available for downloading from the SAS Web site, www.sas.com/pubs.

These programs include some advanced ODS techniques not covered in this book. For more information, visit the SAS Web site.

## HTML Style Definitions Display Program

This program creates a linked set of Web pages that display each of the style definitions installed on your system.

```
* CREATE A DATASET WITH THE STYLE NAMES;
ODS OUTPUT Stats(MATCH_ALL=mvar)=Temp1;
proc template;
    list;
run;
ODS OUTPUT CLOSE;

data TemplateListing;
   length type $12 path $255;
   set &mvar;
   if type="Style";
run;

* CREATE MACRO VARIABLES FROM THE STYLE NAMES;
data _null_;
   set TemplateListing end=eof;
   retain Counter 1;
   if eof then call symput('NumStyles',Counter);
   StyleName=Path;
   StyleNum=trim(left(compress("Style"||Counter)));
   call symput(StyleNum,StyleName);
   Counter+1;
run;

* CREATE A SIMPLE DATASET;
Data Test;
        input A B C;
cards;
1 2 3
4 5 6
7 8 9
;
run;

* LOOP THROUGH THE STYLES RUNNING A SIMPLE PROCEDURE;
%Macro DisplayStyles;
ODS LISTING CLOSE;
ODS HTML FRAME="styletestframe.html"
         CONTENTS="styletestcont.html"
         BODY="styletestjunk.html";
%Do C=1 %to &NumStyles;
   ODS HTML BODY="styletest&C..html" style=&&Style&C;
   title 'Available Styles';
   title2 "This Style is &&Style&C";
   ODS PROCLABEL "This Style is &&Style&C";
   proc print data=Test;
   run;
%End;
ODS HTML CLOSE;
%Mend DisplayStyles;
%DisplayStyles;
```

# RTF Style Definitions Display Program

This program creates a series of RTF files, illustrating the various style definitions in the RTF output format.

```
* CREATE A DATASET WITH THE STYLE NAMES;
ODS OUTPUT Stats(MATCH_ALL=mvar)=Temp1;
proc template;
    list;
run;
ODS OUTPUT CLOSE;

data TemplateListing;
   length type $12 path $255;
   set &mvar;
   if type="Style";
run;

* CREATE MACRO VARIABLES FROM THE STYLE NAMES;
data _null_;
   set TemplateListing end=eof;
   retain Counter 1;
   if eof then call symput('NumStyles',Counter);
   StyleName=Path;
   StyleNum=trim(left(compress("Style"||Counter)));
   call symput(StyleNum,StyleName);
   Counter+1;
run;

* CREATE A SIMPLE DATASET;
Data Test;
        input A B C;
cards;
1 2 3
4 5 6
7 8 9
;
run;

* LOOP THROUGH THE STYLES RUNNING A SIMPLE PROCEDURE;
%Macro DisplayStyles;
ODS LISTING CLOSE;
%Do C=1 %to &NumStyles;
   ODS RTF FILE="styletest&C..rtf" style=&&Style&C;
   title 'Available Styles';
   title2 "This Style is &&Style&C";
   ODS PROCLABEL "This Style is &&Style&C";
   proc print data=Test;
   run;
%End;
ODS RTF CLOSE;
%Mend DisplayStyles;
%DisplayStyles;
```

## Printer Style Definitions Display Program

This program creates a series of PDF files, illustrating the various style definitions in the printer output format.

```
* CREATE A DATASET WITH THE STYLE NAMES;
ODS OUTPUT Stats(MATCH_ALL=mvar)=Temp1;
proc template;
    list;
run;
ODS OUTPUT CLOSE;

data TemplateListing;
    length type $12 path $255;
    set &mvar;
    if type="Style";
run;

* CREATE MACRO VARIABLES FROM THE STYLE NAMES;
data _null_;
    set TemplateListing end=eof;
    retain Counter 1;
    if eof then call symput('NumStyles',Counter);
    StyleName=Path;
    StyleNum=trim(left(compress("Style"||Counter)));
    call symput(StyleNum,StyleName);
    Counter+1;
run;

* CREATE A SIMPLE DATASET;
Data Test;
        input A B C;
cards;
1 2 3
4 5 6
7 8 9
;
run;

* LOOP THROUGH THE STYLES RUNNING A SIMPLE PROCEDURE;
%Macro DisplayStyles;
ODS LISTING CLOSE;
%Do C=1 %to &NumStyles;
    ODS PDF FILE="styletest&C..pdf" style=&&Style&C;
    title 'Available Styles';
    title2 "This Style is &&Style&C";
    ODS PROCLABEL "This Style is &&Style&C";
    proc print data=Test;
    run;
%End;
ODS PDF CLOSE;
%Mend DisplayStyles;
%DisplayStyles;
```

# Appendix

# 2

*Operating System Differences*

If you don't use the Windows operating system, don't worry. Most of the code presented in this book works just fine on other systems. ODS is fairly platform independent.

In fact, if you are using the ODS OUTPUT statement, you don't have to change a thing in order to run on any other platform. Just point your LIBNAME statement to the data location on your platform and you're ready to go.

Where the differences occur is with the filenames you specify for your output files in the HTML and RTF destinations, how you identify the printer destination, and a few options needed for transferring files between systems.

This chapter starts with a basic example set up for the Windows operating system. The example is then repeated for every other major operating system, showing the modifications that are needed.

## Setting Up the Example for Windows and OS/2

There's nothing new in the code presented in this example. All of these features have been shown in previous chapters.

The example is a UNIVARIATE procedure that produces some statistics and a graph. The results are sent to HTML, RTF, and a printer. The code for this example in Windows is as follows:

```
ODS HTML FRAME="OSframe.html"
         BODY="OSbody.html"
         CONTENTS="OScontents.html"
         PATH="c:\temp\" (URL=NONE)
         GPATH="c:\temp\" (URL=NONE);

ODS RTF FILE="c:\temp\OSfile.rtf";

ODS PRINTER PRINTER="MyPrinterName";

proc univariate data=CPUtime;
   var CPUmin;
   symbol value=star;
   probplot CPUmin / normal(mu=est sigma=est) pctlminor;
run;

ODS _ALL_ CLOSE;
```

The ODS HTML statement requests that an HTML page be created with a table of contents. It specifies a file location on the local computer using PATH=, and adds the URL=NONE option to keep the path from being embedded in the links between the table of contents and the body page.

Because this code produces a graph, the ODS HTML statement also uses the GPATH= option to send the graphics output to the same location, and the URL=NONE option to keep the graphics path from being embedded in the image tag.

The ODS RTF statement specifies a file location on the local computer. This file can be opened directly from that location using a word processor.

Finally, the ODS PRINTER statement indicates that the printer output will be sent directly to a printer called MyPrinterName. Using the operating system's name for the printer in this way will only work on Windows. On other platforms, you need to first define a printer in order to name it in an ODS PRINTER statement.

## Revising the Example for UNIX (HP-UX, Sun, Solaris, Linux, etc.)

To run the code on the UNIX operating system, you need to make two changes. First, change the pathnames to fit UNIX naming conventions. Second, configure a UNIX printer.

```
ODS HTML FRAME="OSframe.html"
         BODY="OSbody.html"
         CONTENTS="OScontents.html"
         PATH="/tmp" (URL=NONE)
         GPATH="/tmp" (URL=NONE);

ODS RTF FILE="/tmp/OSfile.rtf";

filename local pipe "lpr -d MyPrinterName";
ODS PRINTER FILE=local;

proc univariate data=CPUtime;
   var CPUmin;
   symbol value=star;
   probplot CPUmin /normal(mu=est sigma=est) pctlminor;
run;

ODS _ALL_ CLOSE;
```

The path naming changes are self-explanatory. The printer setup is a bit more complex. You need to set up a filename using the command you normally use to print. The above example is for the HP version of UNIX. It assumes that you have a printer with the name MyPrinterName.

The code varies slightly for other versions of UNIX. If "lpr" doesn't work, try "lp" or "nlp." If the "-d" option doesn't work, try "-P" instead.

If you have problems with your printer accepting PostScript output, try adding PRINTER=PCL5 to your ODS PRINTER statement.

Once you have made these changes, the HTML and RTF files can be generated on your UNIX server, and the printer output can be sent directly to the designated printer.

In order to view the HTML, you will need to use a UNIX browser, or else you must move the files to a Windows system. To load these files to your Web site, simply copy them to your Web server. If you are running a UNIX Web server that is connected to your SAS server, you may be able to output your HTML results directly to your Web site. Check out the URL= option in the ODS HTML statement.

To view or use the RTF results, you will need to use a UNIX word processor, or else you must move the files to a Windows system.

## Revising the Example for CMS

To run the code on the CMS operating system, you need some changes to each of the ODS statements. In addition, the file and path naming conventions are different.

```
ODS HTML FRAME="OSframe html"
         BODY="OSbody html"
         CONTENTS="OScontnt html"
         PATH="A" (URL=NONE)
         GPATH="A" (URL=NONE)
         TRANTAB=ASCII;

ODS RTF FILE="OSfile rtf A" TRANTAB=ASCII;

ODS PRINTER;

proc univariate data=CPUtime;
   var CPUmin;
   symbol value=star;
   probplot CPUmin /normal(mu=est sigma=est) pctlminor;
run;

ODS _ALL_ CLOSE;
```

The filename changes are minor. The path specifications have been changed to use a filemode letter. CMS path specifications must be either a filemode letter or an SFS directory path.

The printer setup simply creates a PostScript file. You have to use a tool other than SAS to print the file. To use the RTF results, you need to copy the file to a system that has a word processor that can read RTF files. The TRANTAB= option allows your HTML files to be copied over to an ASCII-based Web server.

If you are running a Windows or UNIX Web server, use the code above. If you are running your Web site on a CMS server, use the following ODS HTML statement instead. RECORD_SEPARATOR=NONE produces HTML that is appropriate for the operating system it is running on. By default, ODS on the mainframe puts in binary record separators and no line breaks. This can make it difficult to view or edit the HTML code. Setting the RECORD_SEPARATOR= option to NONE ensures that each line of HTML code is written to a separate line of the file, making it possible to view or edit the HTML source code.

```
ODS HTML FRAME="OSframe html"
         BODY="OSbody html"
         CONTENTS="OScontnt html"
         PATH="A" (URL=NONE)
         GPATH="A" (URL=NONE)
         RECORD_SEPARATOR=NONE;
```

## Revising the Example for OS/390

To run the code on the OS/390 host, you just need four changes. First, you need to set up a FILENAME statement for the path. Second, you need to use slightly different file naming conventions. Third, you need to add one option to the ODS HTML statement. Fourth, you need to add a couple of statements to define the printer.

```
filename ODSOUT ".temp.html"
         dsntype=library dsorg=po
         disp=(new, catlg, delete);
ODS HTML FRAME="OSframe"
         BODY="OSbody" (URL="OSbody.html")
         CONTENTS="OSconten" (URL="OSconten.html")
         PATH=ODSOUT (URL=NONE)
         GPATH=ODSOUT (URL=NONE)
         TRANTAB=ASCII;

ODS RTF FILE=".temp.htm(OSfile)" TRANTAB=ASCII;

filename local sysout=a dest=MyPrinterName;
ODS PRINTER PS FILE=LOCAL;

proc univariate data=CPUtime;
   var CPUmin;
   symbol value=star;
   probplot CPUmin /normal(mu=est sigma=est) pctlminor;
run;

ODS _ALL_ CLOSE;
```

The FILENAME statement is used to set up an appropriate location for all of the output files. This FILENAME statement is then used as the PATH and GPATH. The names assigned to the individual output files have been changed to fit OS/390 naming conventions. Two URL= options have been added to the BODY= and CONTENTS= options. These are used to ensure that the links between the frame file, the contents file, and the body file work correctly.

The printer setup also uses a FILENAME statement. The example above assumes that you have a printer with the name MyPrinterName. The printer results will be printed automatically to the designated printer. The PS option for PostScript output is used to ensure that the plots are rendered correctly. To use the RTF results, you need to copy the file to a system that has a word processor that can read RTF files. Be sure to use a binary copy and rename the file with an .rtf extension.

The TRANTAB= option allows your HTML files to be copied over to an ASCII-based Web server. If you are running a Windows or UNIX Web server, use this code. When the files are transferred, you must retain their member names and then add the .html extension in order for these URLs to be correct. Also, be sure to use a binary transfer to move the files to the Web server.

If you want to create EBCDIC HTML output in an OS/390 PDSE, revise the ODS HTML statement as follows:

```
filename pdsehtml '.temp.htm'
                  dsntype=library dsorg=po
                  disp=(new, catlg, delete);
ODS HTML FRAME="OSframe"
         BODY="OSbody" (URL="OSbody.html")
         CONTENTS="OSconten" (URL="OSconten.html")
         PATH=ODSOUT (URL=NONE)
         GPATH=ODSOUT (URL=NONE)
         RECORD_SEPARATOR=NONE;
```

The RECORD_SEPARATOR= option creates HTML that you can work with in an OS/390 editor and use on an EBCDIC Web server. The HTML files are created as PDSE members.

Sending output directly to a printer from a mainframe system may not always work as expected. These examples provide syntax that has been tested on the operating system in question, but because configurations vary, they may not work correctly on your system. Instead, you may find that it is easier to generate a PostScript or PDF file and print it from a Windows system.

## Revising the Example for OpenVMS

To run the code on the OpenVMS operating system, you just need three changes. First, you need to set up a filename for the path. Second, you need to use slightly different file naming conventions. Third, you need to add a couple of statements to define the printer.

```
filename odsout "device:[temp]";
ODS HTML FRAME="OSframe.html"
         BODY="OSbody.html"
         CONTENTS="OScontents.html"
         PATH=ODSOUT (URL=NONE)
         GPATH=ODSOUT (URL=NONE);


ODS RTF FILE="device:[temp]OSfile.rtf";

filename local printer passall=yes queue=MyPrinterName;
ODS PRINTER FILE=local;

proc univariate data=CPUtime;
   var CPUmin;
   symbol value=star;
   probplot CPUmin /normal(mu=est sigma=est) pctlminor;
run;


ODS _ALL_ CLOSE;
```

The FILENAME statement is used to set up an appropriate location for all of the output files. This FILENAME statement is then used as the PATH and GPATH. To use this example, replace the "device" with the name of the device where you want your files to be stored. With this PATH in place, the names assigned to the HTML file are the same as for Windows. The name assigned to the RTF output follows VMS naming conventions and includes the device name.

The printer setup also uses a FILENAME statement. The example above assumes that you have a printer with the name MyPrinterName. The printer results will be sent automatically to the designated printer. To use the RTF results, you need to copy the file to a system that has a word processor that can read RTF files.

## Sources of Additional Information

This appendix has provided a few simple examples of ODS on other operating systems. For more information, you can read the host-specific sections in the "Guide to the Output Delivery System" in SAS OnlineDoc. Another source of assistance is the SAS Web site found at http://www.sas.com/rnd/base. There are a number of ODS examples and papers available online. Try searching this site for references to your operating system and ODS.

If you can't find an answer to your question through these sources, try SAS Technical Support. First go to the technical support area on the SAS Web site and use the search option to see if your answer is there. If not, e-mail or call Technical Support for further assistance.

# ODS Color Output

Note: Due to the differences in the color palette between monitors and the printed page, the colors you see in this appendix may vary from the colors you see on your screen.

**Output 1.4**

For a black and white version of Output 1.4, see page 8 in Chapter 1.

**Output 5.8  COLOR=YES sent to color printer**

## Delivery Failures

## The FREQ Procedure

| Store Location | | |
|---|---|---|
| Location | Frequency | Percent |
| New York | 31 | 32.98 |
| Boston | 44 | 46.81 |
| Washington, D.C. | 19 | 20.21 |

For a black and white version of Output 5.8, see page 77 in Chapter 5.

**Output 9.2**

| Analysis Variable : Sales | | |
| --- | --- | --- |
| Skirt length | N Obs | Sum |
| Mini | 73 | 3975498 |
| Above knees | 194 | 11767742 |
| Below knees | 168 | 10068671 |
| Maxi | 75 | 4777235 |

For a black and white version of Output 9.2, see page 141 in Chapter 9.

**Output 9.3**

| Analysis Variable : Sales | | |
| --- | --- | --- |
| Skirt length | N Obs | Sum |
| Mini | 73 | 3975498 |
| Above knees | 194 | 11767742 |
| Below knees | 168 | 10068671 |
| Maxi | 75 | 4777235 |

For a black and white version of Output 9.3, see page 141 in Chapter 9.

**Output 9.4**

| Analysis Variable : Sales | | |
| --- | --- | --- |
| Skirt length | N Obs | Sum |
| Mini | 73 | 3975498 |
| Above knees | 194 | 11767742 |
| Below knees | 168 | 10068671 |
| Maxi | 75 | 4777235 |

For a black and white version of Output 9.4, see page 141 in Chapter 9.

**Output 12.3**

### Paint Industry Statistics

| Frequency | Table of Base by Type | | | |
| --- | --- | --- | --- | --- |
| | Type(Type of Finish) | | | |
| Base | Paint | Stain | Sealer | Total |
| Latex | 271 | 171 | 78 | 520 |
| Oil | 135 | 68 | 44 | 247 |
| Total | 406 | 239 | 122 | 767 |

For a black and white version of Output 12.3, see page 191 in Chapter 12.

**Output 12.4**

### Paint Industry Statistics

| Frequency | Table of Base by Type | | | |
| --- | --- | --- | --- | --- |
| | Type(Type of Finish) | | | |
| Base | Paint | Stain | Sealer | Total |
| Latex | 271 | 171 | 78 | 520 |
| Oil | 135 | 68 | 44 | 247 |
| Total | 406 | 239 | 122 | 767 |

For a black and white version of Output 12.4, see page 191 in Chapter 12.

**Output 12.5**

### Paint Industry Statistics

| Frequency | Table of Base by Type | | | |
| --- | --- | --- | --- | --- |
| | Type(Type of Finish) | | | |
| Base | Paint | Stain | Sealer | Total |
| Latex | 271 | 171 | 78 | 520 |
| Oil | 135 | 68 | 44 | 247 |
| Total | 406 | 239 | 122 | 767 |

For a black and white version of Output 12.5, see page 191 in Chapter 12.

**Output 12.6**

## Paint Industry Statistics

| Analysis Variable : Warranty Year of Warranty | | | | |
|---|---|---|---|---|
| N | Mean | Std Dev | Minimum | Maximum |
| 767 | 12.1 | 1.4 | 10.0 | 14.0 |

For a black and white version of Output 12.6, see page 193 in Chapter 12.

**Output 12.7**

## Paint Industry Statistics

| Analysis Variable : Warranty Year of Warranty | | | | |
|---|---|---|---|---|
| N | Mean | Std Dev | Minimum | Maximum |
| 767 | 12.1 | 1.4 | 10.0 | 14.0 |

For a black and white version of Output 12.7, see page 193 in Chapter 12.

**Output 12.8**

## ColorPicker

Custom BGCOLOR * : #009966

For a black and white version of Output 12.8, see page 193 in Chapter 12.

**Output 12.9**

## Paint Industry Statistics

| Analysis Variable : Warranty Year of Warranty | | | | | | |
|---|---|---|---|---|---|---|
| Type of Finish | N Obs | N | Mean | Std Dev | Minimum | Maximum |
| Paint | 406 | 406 | 6.7 | 2.8 | 2.0 | 11.0 |
| Stain | 239 | 239 | 6.7 | 2.9 | 2.0 | 11.0 |
| Sealer | 122 | 122 | 6.5 | 3.0 | 2.0 | 11.0 |

For a black and white version of Output 12.9, see page 195 in Chapter 12.

**Output 12.10**

## Paint Industry Statistics

| Analysis Variable : Warranty Year of Warranty | | | | | | |
|---|---|---|---|---|---|---|
| Type of Finish | N Obs | N | Mean | Std Dev | Minimum | Maximum |
| Paint | 406 | 406 | 6.7 | 2.8 | 2.0 | 11.0 |
| Stain | 239 | 239 | 6.7 | 2.9 | 2.0 | 11.0 |
| Sealer | 122 | 122 | 6.5 | 3.0 | 2.0 | 11.0 |

For a black and white version of Output 12.10, see page 195 in Chapter 12.

**Output 12.11**

## Paint Industry Statistics

| Analysis Variable : Warranty Year of Warranty | | | | | | |
|---|---|---|---|---|---|---|
| Type of Finish | N Obs | N | Mean | Std Dev | Minimum | Maximum |
| Paint | 406 | 406 | 6.7 | 2.8 | 2.0 | 11.0 |
| Stain | 239 | 239 | 6.7 | 2.9 | 2.0 | 11.0 |
| Sealer | 122 | 122 | 6.5 | 3.0 | 2.0 | 11.0 |

For a black and white version of Output 12.11, see page 195 in Chapter 12.

**Output 12.12**

## Paint Industry Statistics

| Frequency | Table of Base by Color | | | | |
|---|---|---|---|---|---|
| | | Color | | | |
| Base | Gray | White | Tan | Yellow | Total |
| Latex | 55 | 244 | 118 | 103 | 520 |
| Oil | 21 | 108 | 52 | 66 | 247 |
| Total | 76 | 352 | 170 | 169 | 767 |

For a black and white version of Output 12.12, see page 197 in Chapter 12.

**Output 12.13**

## Paint Industry Statistics

| Frequency | Table of Base by Color | | | | |
|---|---|---|---|---|---|
| | | Color | | | |
| Base | Gray | White | Tan | Yellow | Total |
| Latex | 55 | 244 | 118 | 103 | 520 |
| Oil | 21 | 108 | 52 | 66 | 247 |
| Total | 76 | 352 | 170 | 169 | 767 |

For a black and white version of Output 12.13, see page 197 in Chapter 12.

**Output 12.14**

## Paint Industry Statistics

| Frequency | Table of Base by Color | | | | |
|---|---|---|---|---|---|
| | | Color | | | |
| Base | Gray | White | Tan | Yellow | Total |
| Latex | 55 | 244 | 118 | 103 | 520 |
| Oil | 21 | 108 | 52 | 66 | 247 |
| Total | 76 | 352 | 170 | 169 | 767 |

For a black and white version of Output 12.14, see page 197 in Chapter 12.

**Output 12.15**

## Paint Industry Statistics

*Variable: Price*

| Basic Statistical Measures | | | |
|---|---|---|---|
| **Location** | | **Variability** | |
| **Mean** | 11.07898 | **Std Deviation** | 2.86897 |
| **Median** | 11.01149 | **Variance** | 8.23099 |
| **Mode** | . | **Range** | 9.97714 |
| | | **Interquartile Range** | 5.00348 |

## 6/2000 monthly sales figures

For a black and white version of Output 12.15, see page 199 in Chapter 12.

**Output 12.16**

## Paint Industry Statistics

*Variable: Price*

| Basic Statistical Measures | | | |
|---|---|---|---|
| **Location** | | **Variability** | |
| **Mean** | 11.07898 | **Std Deviation** | 2.86897 |
| **Median** | 11.01149 | **Variance** | 8.23099 |
| **Mode** | . | **Range** | 9.97714 |
| | | **Interquartile Range** | 5.00348 |

## 6/2000 monthly sales figures

For a black and white version of Output 12.16, see page 199 in Chapter 12.

**Output 12.19**

| Pearson Correlation Coefficients, N = 767 Prob > \|r\| under H0: Rho=0 | |
|---|---|
| | **Price** |
| **Warranty** Year of Warranty | 0.01597 0.6588 |

For a black and white version of Output 12.19, see page 201 in Chapter 12.

**Output 12.21**

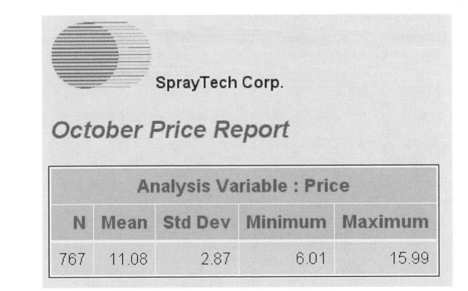

*October Price Report*

| Analysis Variable : Price | | | | |
|---|---|---|---|---|
| N | Mean | Std Dev | Minimum | Maximum |
| 767 | 11.08 | 2.87 | 6.01 | 15.99 |

For a black and white version of Output 12.21, see page 203 in Chapter 12.

**Output 12.22**

SprayTech Corp.

*October Price Report*

| Analysis Variable : Price | | | | |
|---|---|---|---|---|
| N | Mean | Std Dev | Minimum | Maximum |
| 767 | 11.08 | 2.87 | 6.01 | 15.99 |

For a black and white version of Output 12.22, see page 205 in Chapter 12.

**Output 12.23**

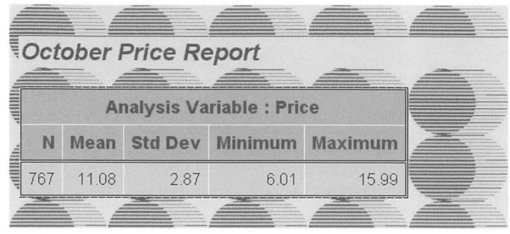

| Analysis Variable : Price | | | | |
|---|---|---|---|---|
| N | Mean | Std Dev | Minimum | Maximum |
| 767 | 11.08 | 2.87 | 6.01 | 15.99 |

For a black and white version of Output 12.23, see page 207 in Chapter 12.

**Output 12.24**

| Analysis Variable : Price | | | | |
|---|---|---|---|---|
| N | Mean | Std Dev | Minimum | Maximum |
| 767 | 11.08 | 2.87 | 6.01 | 15.99 |

For a black and white version of Output 12.24, see page 207 in Chapter 12.

**Output 12.25**

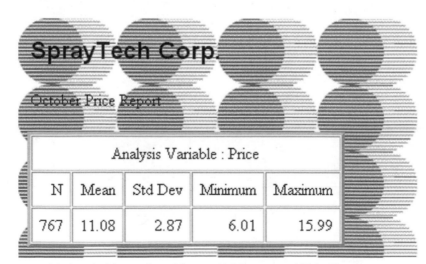

| Analysis Variable : Price | | | | |
|---|---|---|---|---|
| N | Mean | Std Dev | Minimum | Maximum |
| 767 | 11.08 | 2.87 | 6.01 | 15.99 |

For a black and white version of Output 12.25, see page 207 in Chapter 12.

**Output 13.8**

| Table Type | Construction | Average Price |
|---|---|---|
| Coffee | Glass/Metal | $101 |
| | Wood | $61 |
| Dining | Glass/Metal | $400 |
| | Wood | $196 |
| End | Glass/Metal | $104 |
| | Wood | $59 |

For a black and white version of Output 13.8, see page 219 in Chapter 13.

**Output 13.9**

| Table Type | Construction | Average Price |
|---|---|---|
| Coffee | Glass/Metal | $101 |
| | Wood | $61 |
| Dining | Glass/Metal | $400 |
| | Wood | $196 |
| End | Glass/Metal | $104 |
| | Wood | $59 |

For a black and white version of Output 13.9, see page 219 in Chapter 13.

**Output 13.10**

| Totally Tables, Inc. | | |
| --- | --- | --- |
| **Table Type** | **Construction** | **Average Price** |
| Coffee | Glass/Metal | $101 |
| | Wood | $61 |
| Dining | Glass/Metal | $400 |
| | Wood | $196 |
| End | Glass/Metal | $104 |
| | Wood | $59 |

For a black and white version of Output 13.10, see page 221 in Chapter 13.

**Output 13.11**

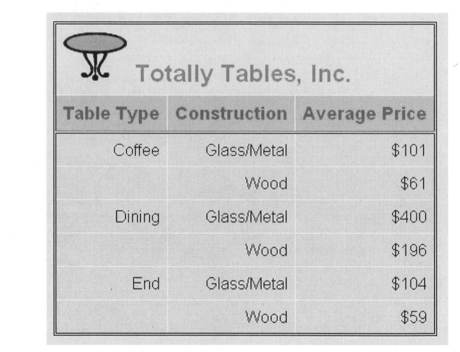

| Totally Tables, Inc. | | |
| --- | --- | --- |
| **Table Type** | **Construction** | **Average Price** |
| Coffee | Glass/Metal | $101 |
| | Wood | $61 |
| Dining | Glass/Metal | $400 |
| | Wood | $196 |
| End | Glass/Metal | $104 |
| | Wood | $59 |

For a black and white version of Output 13.11, see page 221 in Chapter 13.

**Output 13.24**

| | | Average Price |
|---|---|---|
| **Table Type** | **Construction** | |
| **Dining** | **Wood** | $196 |
| | **Glass/Metal** | $400 |
| **Coffee** | **Wood** | $61 |
| | **Glass/Metal** | $101 |
| **End** | **Wood** | $59 |
| | **Glass/Metal** | $104 |

For a black and white version of Output 13.24, see page 235 in Chapter 13.

**Output 13.25**

| | | Average Price |
|---|---|---|
| **Table Type** | **Construction** | |
| **Dining** | **Wood** | $196 |
| | **Glass/Metal** | $400 |
| **Coffee** | **Wood** | $61 |
| | **Glass/Metal** | $101 |
| **End** | **Wood** | $59 |
| | **Glass/Metal** | $104 |

For a black and white version of Output 13.25, see page 235 in Chapter 13.

**Output 13.26**

| Totally Tables, Inc. | | Average Price |
|---|---|---|
| Table Type | Construction | |
| Dining | Wood | $196 |
| | Glass/Metal | $400 |
| Coffee | Wood | $61 |
| | Glass/Metal | $101 |
| End | Wood | $59 |
| | Glass/Metal | $104 |

For a black and white version of Output 13.26, see page 237 in Chapter 13.

**Output 13.27**

| Totally Tables, Inc. | Average Price | |
|---|---|---|
| Table Type | Construction | |
| Dining | Wood | $196 |
| | Glass/Metal | $400 |
| Coffee | Wood | $61 |
| | Glass/Metal | $101 |
| End | Wood | $59 |
| | Glass/Metal | $104 |

For a black and white version of Output 13.27, see page 237 in Chapter 13.

# Index

# Call your local SAS office to order these books from
# Books by Users Press

**support.sas.com/pubs**

A Step-by-Step Approach to Using the SAS® System
for Factor Analysis and Structural Equation Modeling
by **Larry Hatcher**........................Order No. A55129

A Step-by-Step Approach to Using the SAS® System
for Univariate and Multivariate Statistics
by **Larry Hatcher**
and **Edward Stepanski**..............Order No. A55072

Step-by-Step Basic Statistics Using SAS®: Student Guide
and Exercises
(books in this set also sold separately)
by **Larry Hatcher**........................Order No. A57541

Strategic Data Warehousing Principles Using
SAS® Software
by **Peter R. Welbrock**................Order No. A56278

Survival Analysis Using the SAS® System:
A Practical Guide
by **Paul D. Allison** ....................Order No. A55233

Table-Driven Strategies for Rapid SAS® Applications
Development
by **Tanya Kolosova**
and **Samuel Berestizhevsky** ....................Order No. A55198

Tuning SAS® Applications in the OS/390 and z/OS
Environments, Second Edition
by **Michael A. Raithel** ................Order No. A58172

Univariate and Multivariate General Linear Models:
Theory and Applications Using SAS® Software
by **Neil H. Timm**
and **Tammy A. Mieczkowski**....................Order No. A55809

Using SAS® in Financial Research
by **Ekkehart Boehmer, John Paul Broussard**,
and **Juha-Pekka Kallunki** ........................Order No. A57601

Using the SAS® Windowing Environment: A Quick Tutorial
by **Larry Hatcher**........................Order No. A57201

Visualizing Categorical Data
by **Michael Friendly**....................Order No. A56571

Web Development with SAS® by Example
by **Frederick Pratter** ..................Order No. A58694

Working with the SAS® System
by **Erik W. Tilanus**......................Order No. A55190

Your Guide to Survey Research Using the SAS® System
by **Archer Gravely** ......................Order No. A55688

**JMP® Books**

Basic Business Statistics: A Casebook
by **Dean P. Foster, Robert A. Stine**,
and **Richard P. Waterman**........................Order No. A56813

Business Analysis Using Regression: A Casebook
by **Dean P. Foster, Robert A. Stine**,
and **Richard P. Waterman**........................Order No. A56818

JMP® Start Statistics, Second Edition
by **John Sall, Ann Lehman**,
and **Lee Creighton**....................................Order No. A58166

Regression Using JMP®
by **Rudolf J. Freund, Ramon C. Littell**,
and **Lee Creighton**....................................Order No. A58789

**support.sas.com/pubs**